D1609297

PEOPLE OF THE
MOONSHELL
A Western River Journal

Nancy M. Peterson

Illustrations by Asa Battles

RENAISSANCE
HOUSE

A Division of Jende-Hagan, Inc.
541 Oak Street • P.O. Box 177
Frederick, CO 80530

Renaissance House
A Division of JENDE-HAGAN, INC.
541 Oak Street • P.O. Box 177
Frederick, CO 80530

First printing November, 1984
Second printing January, 1985

Library of Congress Cataloging in Publication Data

Peterson, Nancy M., 1934-
 People of the Moonshell.

 Bibliography: p.157
 Includes index.
 1. Platte River Valley (Neb.)--Description and travel.
2. Platte River (Neb.)--Description and travel. 3. Platte River
Valley (Neb.)--History--Sources. 4. Frontier and pioneer life--
Nebraska--Platte River Valley--Sources. I. Title.
F672.P6P48 1984   978.2   84-15919

ISBN: 0-939650-45-2
ISBN: 0-939650-42-8 (pbk.)

For my parents
LUCILLE AND HAROLD MAYBORN
who taught all their daughters
the joy of learning

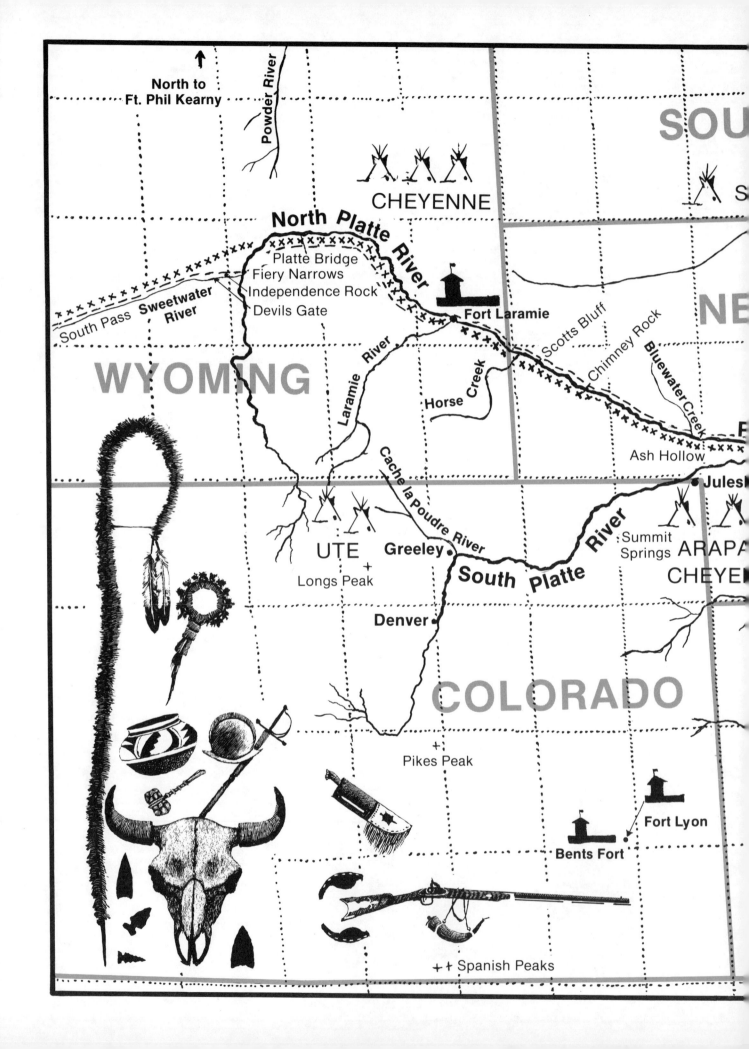

North to
Ft. Phil Kearny

Powder River

CHEYENNE

North Platte River

Platte Bridge
Fiery Narrows
Independence Rock
Devils Gate

South Pass Sweetwater River

Fort Laramie

Scotts Bluff

Chimney Rock

Bluewater Creek

WYOMING

Laramie River

Horse Creek

Ash Hollow

SOU

NE

Jules

Cache la Poudre River

UTE
Longs Peak

Greeley

Summit Springs

South Platte River

ARAPA
CHEYE

Denver

COLORADO

Pikes Peak

Fort Lyon

Bents Fort

Spanish Peaks

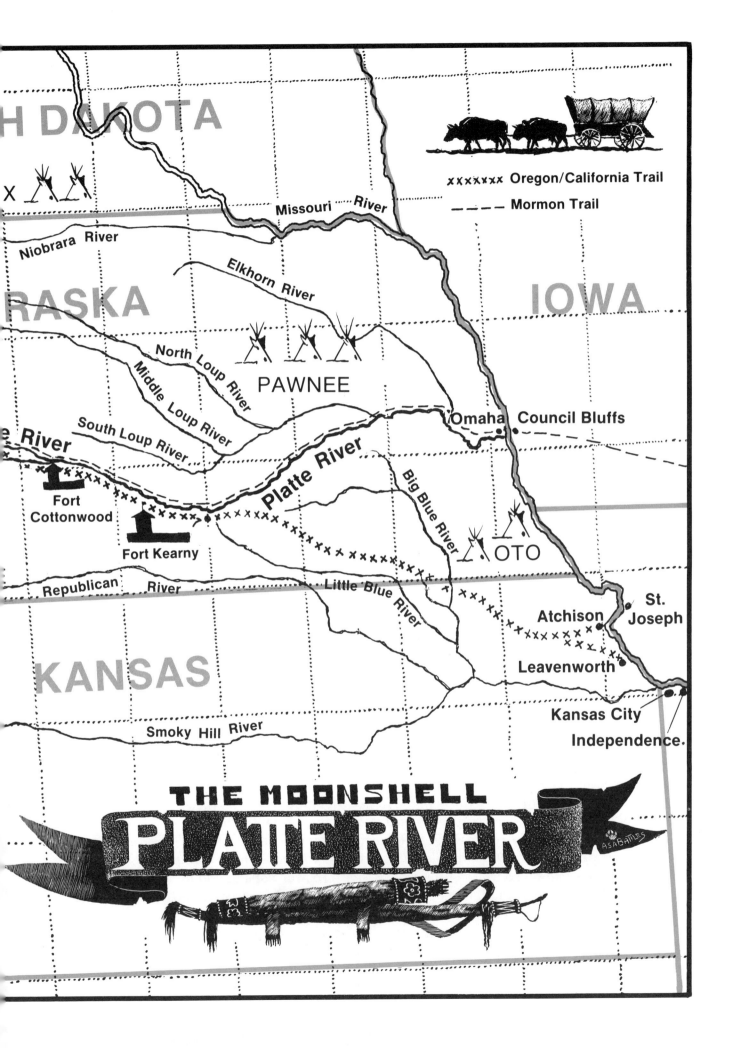

H DAKOTA

Missouri River

Niobrara River

Elkhorn River

RASKA

IOWA

North Loup River

Middle Loup River

PAWNEE

e River

South Loup River

Omaha · Council Bluffs

Platte River

Big Blue River

Fort Cottonwood

OTO

Fort Kearny

Republican River

Little Blue River

Atchison

St. Joseph

KANSAS

Leavenworth

Smoky Hill River

Kansas City

Independence.

xxxxxxx Oregon/California Trail

— — — Mormon Trail

THE MOONSHELL
PLATTE RIVER

ASA BATTLES

Foreword

"Moonshell," a poetic Indian name for the Platte River, makes a fetching title for this book. It musically stirs the imagination, whereas a title like "People of the Platte" (particularly for those unfamiliar with the river) sounds as dull and monotonous as the plains through which it flows. But after "Moonshell" serves its decorative purpose, it is discarded and the author gets on with the epic story of the Platte which, despite its dull sound, may lay fair claim to being the most historically exciting river in western America.

The Missouri River, to which the Platte is tributary, and the Columbia and Colorado rivers, are mightier by far, more majestic in scale, more spectacular in scenery, and certainly of great geographic and historic reputation as well. But if rivers may be measured in terms of the flow of humanity up their valleys, as distinct from the mere volume of their water, the Platte is unique. Because its tributaries, the North Platte and the Sweetwater rivers, led directly to South Pass (gateway through the Rocky Mountain barrier), the Platte became the primary westward migration route of the nineteenth century—America's true highway of Empire.

People going to Oregon called it "the Oregon Trail." Those going to California called it "the California Road." To Mormons bound for their new Zion in Utah, it became "the Mormon Trail," and there are dozens of variant lables, like "Council Bluffs Road," "Fort Laramie Road," and "the Pony Express route." When I researched the overland migrations, I was appalled by the confusion in terminology referring to this grand central migration corridor. I attempted to simplify in my book by calling this route ''The Great Platte River Road.'' This is the route which Nancy M. Peterson describes.

No one migrating to the Far West followed the route of Lewis and Clark up the Missouri River, and the number that went southwest via Arizona and the Gila River was negligible. Unless you went by sea around Cape Horn, or by a combination of sea and land via Central America, the only significant way west was by wagon train up the Platte.

Historians have written comprehensive scholarly histories of the Platte and the westward movement. Ms. Peterson's dynamic narrative of this epic is expressed in terms of its simplest common denominator — individual men and women who effectively symbolize its successive chapters.

Some of these individuals, like Narcissa Whitman, John C. Fremont, William Cody, and Francis Parkman, are historic figures of heroic stature. Others were ordinary people caught up in extraordinary adventures. This is not history by a historian but history by a gifted writer who has studied the past conscientiously and captured its essence in the dramatic personal terms of people pursuing their respective rainbows — knowledge, glory, gold, a homestead in the wilderness, redemption of other people's souls, or the salvation of their own.

The strange, silent, unpredictable, and seemingly endless Platte is the silver thread on which is set the pageant of these actors: the People of the Moonshell.

Merrill J. Mattes
Littleton, Colorado
1984

Table of Contents

Introduction

The river the Indians called the Moonshell is, for the most part, a quiet river, an unobtrusive river. It is not deep, nor fast, nor useful for navigation. It does not transform the countryside through which it flows, but nestles gently into it; a partner with the land rather than a destroyer.

Its dual beginnings run swift and clear where they rise in North and South Parks of the Colorado Rockies. But when the water escapes the high country in two streams, to meander across the plains of northeastern Colorado and southeastern Wyoming and meet again in Nebraska, it relaxes into the land.

In fact, it is so truly a part of the land that it is as much sand as water. Its seldom generous currents are soon divided into separate channels by ubiquitous and ever-changing sandbars. The more resistant patches of soil form numberless islands, whose scrubby growth dots the river with green for most of its length, reiterating the union of land and water.

It is a western river, taking its character from the plains through which it winds. Open to the spreading sky, subtle in color, quiet but pervasive in its influence. Soft, low banks provide only slight hindrance to swollen spring waters, which, before the days of dams and reservoirs, simply spread themselves across the prairie for a mile, or two, or more. Yet in the dry seasons the river could nearly disappear in some sections, shrink to scum-topped pools in others.

White explorers, of more practical than poetic eye, renamed the river the Platte, for flat. In the eyes of these early travelers, it was an inconsequential, undependable, and unuseable river — scarcely worthy of the name. Yet it became the most important water-course in the entire area west of the Mississippi.

This, then, is the irony of the Platte. It had no mighty currents to gouge the land like the Snake and the Colorado, no power to lift barge and steamboat like the Mississippi and the Missouri, no opportunity to shape the edge of nations like the Red and the Rio Grande. Yet the half-formed footprints along its sandy banks attest to an incredible history.

It was the Platte that saw French and Spanish kings in conflict. The Platte that saw the trappers' caravans, the missionaries' lonely campfires, the emigrant wagon ruts, the graves of the Mormon handcart brigades, the telegraph's whining wire and the railroad's shining rails. It saw the Sioux, Cheyennes, and Arapahos first reach a hand in friendship and then raise a closed fist in defense of their existence. It saw the soldiers sent to battle, the scientists sent to explore, the dandies and adventurers who came just for the fun of it. It gave men gold. And women grief.

Platte history, like any history, is in the stories of the people who trudged its banks and settled its valleys. Their experiences, taken individually, tell us what it was to touch the West and be touched by it. Taken collectively, they tell the compelling drama of life that flowed with this enigmatic river.

The Moonshell

Here the plains tribes obtained the glowing pink shells of far-off oceans, so treasured they called the river itself the Moonshell.

rom the earliest times this unpretentious river was important to the people of the plains. As it flowed across the middle of the Great Plains, it served as a middle ground—meeting place—where representatives of tribes from the deep forests of the north, the deserts of the south-west, the inland seas, and even the western coast could meet under truce and trade their handiwork. Here the plains tribes obtained the glowing pink shells of far-off oceans, so treasured they called the river itself the Moonshell.

Here, too, they were able to trade for exotic feathers, shining copper, piñon nuts, medicinal herbs, and the deep blue turquoise. For a month of warm summer nights they feasted and danced, listened to magic tales of distant places, and bartered their goods. Then they fanned out across the plain, carrying furs and caribou antlers south; quillwork west; and—one unmarked year— riding northeast in fear and triumph on the back of the big dog the foreigners called a horse.

Perhaps some among them felt an inkling of the way this strange animal would change their lives. For hereafter, the small stream that flowed into the Moonshell at the trading grounds would be called Horse Creek. But they could not know that the original source of this new creature—the white man—would soon follow his horse into the valley of the Moonshell and into their lives, creating changes beyond the visions of their holiest men. He had been delayed and thwarted by the newness and vastness of their prairies, but he was on his way.

In the 1500s Spanish fingers had stretched up from the south, eager for the feel of gold, but none had quite reached the Indians' Moonshell. The Black slave-explorer Esteban found death rather than riches among the Zunis of the South-west. A discouraged Francisco Coronado, finally disillusioned about the golden cities gleaming always just beyond the horizon, turned his face south at the Arkansas. And Father Juan Padilla, pushing on where Coronado faltered, also met death by the Indians well before he saw the banks of the Moonshell.

It's possible an unauthorized expedition led by Antonio de Humaña squabbled on as far as the Moonshell in 1593. But with dissention and even murder thinning its ranks, it, too, fell under Indian spears. It was a year before the lone survivor made his way back to New Mexico, and another hundred before his countrymen again ventured to the valley of the Moonshell.

While the Spanish probed from the south with clanking columns led by military banners, almost unnoticed another influence filtered down from the north and east. Like drops of water joining a flowing stream, French trappers and traders wedded themselves to both the daughters of the country and the ways of the wilderness. They came alone or in twos or threes, threading their way up the rivers, finding their gold in the warm, brown pelt of the beaver. By 1678 these quiet invaders had visited among the Pawnee villages that lined the river, and by 1700 (while English settlers still clung to the eastern seaboard) French and Spanish forces were already contending for control of the extensive grasslands of mid-America.

Helpless to occupy, or even patrol, so vast an area with their own pitiful numbers, both sides enlisted the local Indian tribes as their allies. Buying allegiance with trade goods and promises of protection, the Spanish sought to buffer their trading territory with tribes hostile to the French. But where the Spanish offered empty promises, the French held out the solid heft of carbines and black powder. They would let the Indians do their own protecting.

Though their methods differed, both France and Spain coveted the same objective, and their opposing forces would meet on the banks of this unpretentious river.

3

A Silver Candlestick

It was the largest single loss that Spanish forces had incurred in 200 years of conquest in the New World.

Lieutenant General Don Pedro de Villasur signaled the trailing column to a halt and stood in his stirrups for a better view down the river valley (the present-day South Platte River). Why his Indian scout Jose Naranjo had given this particular river the name of both the Saviour and the Holy Mother, the young commander could not imagine. Surely some lesser saint would have done as well to designate the sluggish brown currents now working their way among the sandbars toward the flatlands farther east. But Naranjo had chosen Rio de Jesús y María, and the Rio de Jesús y María it was. In spite of its name, it was not blessing his expedition with information.

Behind Villasur the mixed-bloods who made up the King's presidials relaxed in their saddles. Some took the opportunity to shift the heavy leather shields that hung over their backs, hoping that the breeze, though hot, would blow some measure of coolness through their cueras and the sweat-soaked blue jackets beneath. It was a vain hope, for the cueras, long vests four hides thick, offered even better protection from cooling breezes than from Indian arrows.

Others used their flat-brimmed sombreros to bat at mosquitoes settling on the stockinged legs below their breeches. And some merely let the tips of their lances droop and sat quiet, convinced nothing they could do would offer any real relief from the blazing August sun and voracious insects. Farther back, behind the pack animals, their Pueblo Indian allies slipped from their mounts and drank thirstily from the water's edge.

Villasur shaded his eyes and stared across the empty spaces, the features of his broad face dark with frustration. Don Antonio Valverde, Governor of New Mexico, had entrusted him with his first substantial command, and it was important he succeed. He felt sure he had pushed farther north and east than any other Spanish expedition. Yet the objective of his mission eluded him. Where were the French?

With France and Spain at war in Europe, increasing reports of French guns in Spain's American territory had goaded the motley column of 105 soldiers, settlers, and Indians far from the squared adobes of Santa Fe this summer of 1720. They had rafted across the Arkansas and marched north until the shining Sangre de Cristos sank from sight behind. They had reached and passed through the settlement of Apaches at El Cuar-telejo, trading knives and sombreros for information from these allies, who resided on the northern periphery of Spanish influence.

With a half dozen horses per man and pack mules humped with supplies, they left a considerable cloud of dust hanging in the air behind them. But as they continued their tramp up the grass covered plains that spread along the front of the Rockies, even their sizeable column began to feel dwarfed by the lonely distances.

It was as though the soul shrank before the witness of God's greatness. And though the Reverend Father Fray Juan Minquez assured them at nightly devotions that the Holy Mother could watch over them as well in this wilderness as in the chapel at Santa Fe, it was difficult to remain confident. Officers caught themselves speaking with lowered voices, and more and more often the faces of the Indians turned south with longing.

But their mission was reconnaissance, and so far they had gathered no hard facts about the French position. There were tales and rumors aplenty. Tales of a French trader called De Tisne planting a cross for King Louis far up on a prairie river. Tales of Apache allies suffering wounds from French weapons. Tales of an alliance between the Pawnees and the French that threatened invasion of New Spain from the very area where they now stood. Villasur was certain the French had to be near. But where?

He surveyed the shimmering distances and reflected dourly on his choices. He could wait here for days and weeks while a runner returned to Santa Fe for new orders. He could return to Santa Fe with no real information to justify the expense of the expedition. Or he could march even farther east in one final attempt to make contact with the enemy. In his mind only one alternative was acceptable. He swung off his horse and called his officers to a council of war.

After Villasur's manservant had passed a drink of murky water among them, the taste of which was not improved by the fineness of the silver cup, the Spanish gentlemen relaxed in the grass to consider their problem. Several of the officers, carrying more years and experience than their youthful commander, urged a return to Santa Fe.

They had been out 63 days now. They were all worn with the weeks of riding in their hot uniforms. They were tired of dust in their hair, insect bites and the deadly diet of beans and pinole. If there were something to do—someone to fight—

it might be different. But there was nothing in this everlasting grassland except more grass. The column could chase ghosts across the endless plains for years and never come within musket range. There were already 300 leagues to cover between them and home. What was the use of adding to them?

Villasur rose and began to pace as they argued. He knew they were probably right. It did seem a futile expedition. But he also knew the dreary fate of other commanders who had returned empty-handed from their expeditions into the new world. He listened politely while each had his say. Then he suggested a compromise.

A scout reported signs that a troop of Indians had recently passed. They should be Pawnees, in this country. The expedition would cross the river and follow the trail until they found some Pawnees to question—some information to report. Then they would turn homeward. It was agreed.

With the command safely across the Rio Jesús María the next morning, Villasur sent Naranjo to follow the Pawnees' trail. The bulk of the column, moving more slowly, had done only a few leagues when they found themselves on the bank of another stream, much like the Rio Jesús María in character (the present-day North Platte River). Crossing it also, the men decided from the warmth of its waters that it was a branch of the Rio Jesús María. Villasur took time to christen it for the Spanish martyr San Lorenzo, whose feast day was on the morrow, August 10. Though the current rose only to the saddle girth, negotiating half a league of soft sand bottom with loaded animals was not easy, and the Spaniards were glad they had chosen to ford before the two rivers combined.

The scouts had sighted Pawnees several times, but had been unable to approach them. Now they came galloping in to report a substantial village lay ahead on the river's south bank. Villasur lifted his head and grinned with delight. At last he had a chance to make contact. Hurriedly he ordered a Pawnee traveling with them (the servant of a fellow officer) to run ahead and arrange a meeting.

But the Pawnees were not interested in a meeting. The servant came galloping back to camp, pale with fear. He reported the Pawnee village bristled with excitement. The men sang and stomped to the rhythm of the war dance. They had ignored his signs of peace and friendship and threatened him with waving tomahawks.

Villasur was discouraged, but not yet ready to give up. He could not let all those leagues go for nothing. He ordered the column down-river until they were across from the village.

He watched the short, broad-faced Pawnee people who gathered at the river's edge. They seemed excited, but not particularly hostile. He could see no obvious signs of French occupation. Again he sent his greetings, and gifts of tobacco, with the messenger. The messenger was to assure the Pawnees that he came in peace, and to address them as brothers and subjects who served the same king. Villasur breathed a prayer to God and the Holy Virgin for success; then he waited impatiently for an answer.

It came. The messenger called plaintively across the river that the Pawnees would not let him return, and that he had learned nothing.

Frustrated with trying to communicate through savages, Villasur decided to try a note written in French. In flowing script the message asked courteously for information from anyone able to read it.

When the answer came it was illegible. It could have been French, or Spanish, or the scribbling of an illiterate. It could have been a deliberate taunt by a laughing French trader.

Furious, Villasur shouted for another council of war. He was more and more convinced a French voice excited the Pawnees' hostility. He would see for himself just who was speaking for the village. He urged his officers to join him in crossing the river and entering the village.

But the officers were more cautious. They knew Indians better than Villasur, and they were convinced he could learn nothing from a tribe so unwilling to communicate. More than that, they argued, it was dangerous even to camp so close to the volatile village. Their large herd of remounts had to be a temptation for the Pawnees, and their Pueblos showed increasing nervousness.

Then a Pueblo bathing in the river floated too close to the Pawnee shore, and he, too, was taken captive. The issue was settled. They decided to give up the enterprise and retreat to safer ground.

Outvoted, Villasur reluctantly gave the order to break camp, and the Spaniards turned back west. At 4:00 in the afternoon of August 12, after retracing their steps along the river, they recrossed the San Lorenzo and made camp in the river bottom between the two streams. The presidials tramped down grasses and reeds that towered head high to make space for the officers' tents. The Pueblos formed their own camp nearby.

Villasur posted the usual Indian guards and picked at the meager serving of pinole his servant placed on his personal silver platter. He longed for a cup of chocolate to wash the cornmeal gruel down his throat, but the chocolate supply was exhausted. The other men joked and laughed around the fires, glad to be heading home at last, but he sat alone, brooding over his failure. He had nothing at all to report to the governor and to the king. Everyone was convinced the French were here, but he had been unable to find them. There would be no praise for him, and no promotion. In fact, his career might well be at an end.

He lit his candle, dipped his quill into the inkhorn, and started to record the day's happenings in his journal. But his hand was still. He stared at a drop of wax that swelled for a moment on the rim of his elaborate candlestick, then spilled over and streaked down the side. It was too depressing. He pinched out the flame, promising himself he would finish the job tomorrow.

As the camp bedded down and the voices of the men gave way to croaking frogs and singing crickets, another sound caught Villasur's ear. He thought he heard someone or something sloshing in the river. Then a dog barked.

Suddenly alert, Villasur called the campmaster and ordered scouts sent to check the camp perimeter. Hand on sword he waited, almost hoping for a chance to use it. But the scouts reported they could find nothing in the blackness of the summer night. Reassured, everyone settled in to sleep, and eventually even the frogs were quiet.

The sun had barely touched the grassy hilltops that edged the valley on August 13, 1720, the feast day of San Hipolito, when the yawning horse guard gathered the herd and drove it slowly into camp. The Spaniards milled about, finding and roping their mounts, when Pawnee war cries exploded the morning quiet. Unbelieving, the startled Spaniards watched arrows imbed themselves in horses' flanks. Bullets cut through tents and plowed into packs beside them. Heavy fire poured into the camp from all sides.

Some horses fell before the volley; the others stampeded. Officers and presidials alike, caught on foot and without weapons, were mowed down in the withering fire. Villasur yelled for his servant, and raced for his tent and his sword, but there was not time. He fell in front of his tent. His servant fell beside him.

The soldiers not immediately hit drew into a defensive circle to face the attacking Pawnees. Signing themselves against the devil horde, they made a stand. But they felled only a few of the garishly painted enemy before the circle collapsed in carnage.

The few who had managed to catch horses grouped together and charged back into camp, but it was a pathetic gesture. In the dust and smoke of the ruined camp there was no one left to save.

One Alonso Fael de Aguilar, who was wounded in nine places and had already lost one braid to a scalping knife, was snatched from death and carried away in the retreat. But Pedro de Villasur, the Scout Naranjo, and 42 others were left behind, the sands of the river beneath their bodies dark with blood. The Reverend Father Fray Juan Minquez, unable to serve their final earthly need, lay dead beside them.

A dozen Spaniards and 49 Pueblos, having fled without provisions or equipment, managed to limp the long leagues home with news of the disaster.

It was the largest single loss that Spanish forces had incurred in 200 years of conquest in the New World. And it marked an end to their aspirations to the central plains. With one-third of the garrison of Santa Fe lying dead between the Rio San Lorenzo and the Rio Jesús María, they withdrew to the south and watched nervously for signs of a French invasion of their heartland.

Governor Valverde, tried and found guilty of entrusting the expedition to an inexperienced officer, was ordered to pay alms so that masses could be said for the souls of the soldiers who had died in the service of God and the King.

The French, accused in scathing Spanish protests of fomenting the slaughter, shrugged, and disclaimed any part in the disaster.

The Pawnees rounded up the fine horses that would so improve their herd and pondered a use for Pedro de Villasur's silver candlestick.

The Riviére Platte

The prospect of a French invasion sent the villagers of Santa Fe scurrying for new recruits to fill their garrison. The French did come. But not exactly the way nervous Governor Valverde had imagined.

ASA BATTLES

In the winter of 1739, two French brothers huddled closer to a fire that seemed totally unable to ward off the deep cold of a Canadian blizzard. As they fought to keep off the chill, they toyed with the idea of an incredible journey. It would be long, arduous, and unprecedented. It would cover hundreds of leagues of unknown territory. It would be dangerous, and it would be illegal.

But, at the end of the journey, if they lived to reach it, lay Santa Fe. Santa Fe. It had the sound of magic. The sound of silver. They had both heard the stories of carts rolling through the streets on silver tires, and of senoritas clicking the silver heels of their dancing slippers. Surely there was a rich trade there for anyone bold enough to seek it. And, muttered one brother as he poked futilely at the fire—whatever else, it would be warm.

By early spring Pierre and Paul Mallet had recruited six of their frontiersman friends, who weighed risk against possible gain and cheerfully threw their lot in with the Mallets. And as the new green of spring worked its way north in 1739, the eight French-Canadians worked their way south and west through the Great Lakes, down the Illinois and up the Mississippi rivers until they reached the Missouri.

They were a wild-looking group, taking so much of their dress from their Indian friends that they could have been mistaken for them. Long-haired, buckskinned, moccasined, ornamented with trailing furs, claws and beads, only the dark beards on their faces marked them for white men. Even the skin that had been white was bronzed by life in the outdoors—and quite possibly by the addition somewhere along the line of native genes to their bloodlines.

They did not burden themselves with man-servants and silver services, which would have inspired more mirth than awe, but their log pirogues were piled with bales of trade goods. Knives, awls, axes—whatever they knew to be of value to the Indians, and hoped might be of value to the distant Spaniards—was wrapped with care and secured as well as possible from the eager grasp of the Missouri.

For of all the rivers they had floated, the Missouri most taxed their strengths and talents. Bank-full of churning brown water, dotted with angry snags, mined with whole tree trunks that swirled along beneath the surface, the river did its best to carry everything in its path toward the sea.

But the Mallet brothers were heading inland. They sought the headwaters of the Missouri; for there, they had been told, lay Santa Fe. For days the French-Canadians fought to push the double points of their pirogues against the current. It was a wet, cold, and exhausting battle. But worse than that was the uneasy feeling they had to be going in the wrong direction. Each day's struggle took them farther north. Surely, sun-blessed Santa Fe lay south.

At last, at a place where a small river poured swift, clear waters into the Missouri flood (the present-day Niobrara), they made a difficult decision. They must abandon the river course and turn south across the plains.

It went against all their instincts and experience. They never walked if they could avoid it. Most places that could not be reached by water were not worth reaching. The river was like a sister, however difficult its mood. It talked or sang or roared at them in a language they loved and understood. But the grassland? Who could understand its silence? Still, if Santa Fe lay at the other side, perhaps they could endure the crossing between waters.

But to cross the plains they would have to have horses. Finding their way to a Pawnee camp, the Mallet brothers discovered their French tongue brought them a ready welcome. And after an evening of feasting and story telling, some knives and awls from the bales of trade goods bought them horses.

Loaded, mounted, and facing the trackless plain the next morning, Pierre asked for help in setting a course for Santa Fe. The chief pointed to the southwest, and they knew they had been right to leave the Missouri. Pierre kicked his heels into his Indian pony, and the eight voyageurs fell into a line that left the familiarity of the river and angled off across the gentle swells of prairie.

On June 2, 1739, they came upon a shallow river that flowed west to east across their path. Its waters were wide and flat—like the country it crossed. Not given to flights of fancy, nor feeling a need to invoke the goodwill of the Saints, the Mallets named it La Platte—French for flat. For three days they traveled west along its willow-ed banks, grateful for the waterfowl and game they felled with ease for their camp kettle. But again the river failed to serve them as a route. This river was carrying them directly west, and so they struggled over the quicksand bottom of the spreading waters and headed south again.

It was foreign country for men used to the Canadian wilderness, but they adapted. Unable to find wood, they burned buffalo chips for fuel. They overcame the hostility of the tribes along the way with tact and trade goods, and managed to use the Indians' knowledge of the territory to chart a course that was an uncannily accurate route to Santa Fe.

Time and again they struggled across prairie rivers, naming them as they crossed. One they underestimated, and it swept away seven of their horses and most of their supplies. As they lay gasping and sputtering on the far bank, the brothers wondered for the first time if they would really see the riches of Santa Fe.

But the next river to the south held a surprise that spurred them on: stones bearing Spanish inscriptions. They were in Spanish territory. It couldn't be far now. They hired an Indian guide, and on a warm day in early July, the Spanish Peaks rose before them on the western horizon.

On July 15 they stared down into the small square outpost of Taos. Now they faced the question of how the Spanish governor would receive uninvited French traders. The Mallets squatted in the hillside scrub while the Indian guide ran into the settlement with the news of their arrival.

There was an anxious wait before they saw him returning. He carried loaves of fine wheat bread, a delicacy sent as a welcoming gift by the commander. Suddenly the bells of the mission began to peal, and the people of the village surged out to greet them. The Mallet brothers rose to meet the commander and the priest. They were gaunt and worn, in shreds and tatters, but they were welcome in Taos.

A week later, July 22, 1739, they walked the fabled streets of Santa Fe. It was hardly the Santa Fe of their dreams. It was small, and brown instead of silver. The carts squealed by on wooden wheels, and the senoritas were more often barefoot than silver-shod. But the 800 residents of the isolated Spanish settlement were warm and friendly. They were delighted to have the opportunity to trade, and they bought what few goods the brothers had salvaged at 10 times the Canadian price. It could, indeed, be a rich trade area for them. But first they would need a permit from the viceroy at Mexico City.

For nine months the men were treated as royal guests while they waited for the annual caravan to return with the viceroy's answer. One member of the group married, and Pierre and Paul were free to explore the countryside and soak up more sunshine than even they demanded.

But the viceroy's answer was no. The government at Mexico City did not want to open its borders to anyone—and especially not to Frenchmen riding Pawnee ponies. So Paul and Pierre Mallet left Santa Fe and worked their way east to New Orleans, where they reported their experiences to the French governor of Louisiana.

Santa Fe was still a tempting target for trade, and the next year the French governor formed a caravan and hired the Mallets to guide it up the Canadian River toward Santa Fe. But the expedition failed when the river became too shallow for canoes, and the government's commander refused to take to his feet to make further progress. The Mallet brothers, who had themselves answered the challenge of the silent grasslands, could only look on in disgust.

Pierre Mallet was to answer the siren song of Santa Fe one more time. In 1750 he carried goods again to Spanish territory. However, this time he was arrested and sent to Mexico City. From there he disappeared into the Spanish prisons.

But Pierre and Paul Mallet had been the first Europeans to cross the barrier of the plains and tie East and West together. They mapped a new land; made the unknown known. Of the half-dozen rivers they named as they splashed across on their journey down the plains, only one retained the brothers' christening. The Spaniards' saints were deprived of their homage by the Canadians' simple, descriptive Riviére Platte.

A Joust With the Wilderness

As the Rio San Lorenzo and the Rio Jeśus y Maŕia faded from the crude maps of the time to be replaced by the Riviére Platte, so the Spanish influence in the Great Plains waned. As individual French traders took advantage of the vacuum, the Pawnees along the Platte grew accustomed to their presence, and the white man's goods gained importance in their lives. But on the whole the Platte was left to the wandering herds of bison and elk, the spring-legged antelope, and the wolves which followed.

When European politics threw the Great Plains under French control, a French citizen named Napoleon Bonaparte did formulate plans to use the area as a new French Empire in North America. But the plans went awanting when the overextended First Consul had to have some ready cash. United States citizen James Monroe was in the right place at the right time, and United States President Thomas Jefferson was able to rise to the challenge. Fifteen million dollars changed hands, and in 1803 the Riviére Platte flowed through a new American West.

The next year Jefferson's scholarly private secretary set out up the Missouri to see just what the $15,000,000 had bought. Meriwether Lewis and his red-haired army friend William Clark hoped to find the long sought water route to the Pacific. With this in mind, they poked into the mouth of the Platte on a rainy Saturday in July. But a mile or two of scraping bottom with their pirogue convinced them their chances of success lay elsewhere. They poled on up the Missouri, never dreaming the inconsequential river they left behind offered a shorter and infinitely easier route to the Pacific than the one their heroic efforts would map through the mountains to the north.

But when Lewis and Clark's return reports of heavy beaver populations circulated in the taverns and fur markets of the nation, another segment of the citizenry stirred to action. In New York City a German immigrant named John Jacob Astor conceived a plan that would finally result in a real exploration of the Platte. And—strangely—that exploration was to be carried out in the "wrong" direction. This time the wanderers of the Platte would not be reaching from civilization to the wilderness, but from the wilderness to civilization.

hen Robert Stuart left New York harbor on the supply ship *Tonquin* in 1810, his thoughts were for the Columbia River, not the Platte. With his uncle's assistance, the young Scotsman had bought two shares of stock in John Jacob Astor's venture into the western fur regions, and as the *Tonquin* creaked and groaned its way around South America, he longed for the day they would enter the mouth of the Columbia.

For, once there, they could establish a base — Fort Astoria — and begin harvesting furs. Stuart knew that Astor's plan was to gather furs — a large party of trappers was even then marching overland from the Missouri — and to ship the pelts to the rich markets of China. Leaning on the rail as the *Tonquin* inched toward the California coast, Stuart ran a hand through his thick, wavy hair and thought of the money he might make with the Pacific Fur Company. The family croft in Scotland had, of course, fallen to his older brother, so his prospects depended entirely on his own initiative. And on the strength of those prospects rode his chance to marry Elizabeth Emma Sullivan of Brooklyn. Stuart's stern features relaxed when he thought of the fresh-faced Betsy. If only their venture were successful, surely then Mrs. Sullivan would grant her permission for the marriage.

But when the *Tonquin* finally reached the misty shoals of the Columbia, they discovered the river, the weather, the British, and the Indians all seemed equally determined to see them fail. Astor had a good plan on paper, but it took more than paper to subdue the wilderness. Through the summer and fall of 1811 and the winter of 1812, the men hovered on the verge of extinction. The British informed them they were unwelcome interlopers on "British" soil. The *Tonquin* was blown into oblivion during an Indian attack. The overland party straggled in, in starveling twos and threes, having taken nearly a year to cross from the Missouri to the Columbia.

But with spring a new supply ship worked its way through the treacherous mouth of the Columbia, and things suddenly looked brighter. The men split into parties to establish posts in the interior, and Robert Stuart was chosen to carry the necessary dispatches back east to Astor. The partners drew up a report of their losses in men and goods and their need for supplies and reinforcements, and Stuart tucked the papers into a shiny metal box.

Stuart knew the hardships endured by the first overland party, but he was confident his return force would have an easier journey. He thought they could complete the distance before the New Year, and the knowledge that Betsy waited in New York fueled his eagerness to be on the trail. With two Canadian voyageurs, two Kentucky hunters, and a pair of disgruntled Astorians who had had enough of trapping, Stuart set off for the Missouri.

Five months later Stuart and his men sat in a discouraged council. The trees near their small hide cabin, which had hung heavy with buffalo and deer quarters, were nearly bare. They had watched their hard-won provisions disappear, as a war party of Arapahos assuaged their incredible appetites. For a day and a night they had played unwilling hosts to the 12 Indians, and they had kept their hair, but that was about all. The Arapahos had finally ridden off in search of some Crows to battle, but they would undoubtedly be back.

Stuart's shoulders settled in resignation. They would have to move on. Leave the small comfort of their winter camp on the North Platte River (near present-day Casper, Wyoming) and move out again across the frozen countryside.

The men sat in dejected quiet. Stuart did not have to look into their burned and bearded faces to know their thoughts. His were the same. He felt the strain of four months on the trail in every muscle of his body. And in his mind he saw the day they had been forced to drink their own urine to survive in the volcanic wastes beyond the Snake. The day they had been driven to the edge of cannibalism. The day the Kentucky hunter had been driven past the edge of madness.

It had been June when Robert Stuart accepted the dispatches for John Astor and set his steps east. And four months of struggle against the country, the Indians, starvation, sickness, and exhaustion had brought them only halfway on their journey to St. Louis. When they had stumbled onto the North Platte in November they had built their crude cabin, planning to rest and recruit through the worst of the winter storms before pushing on. But it was not to be.

Stuart squared his shoulders and set the men to dressing hides for moccasins. It was only his dogged determination that had kept the group going this far. There had been times they all had wanted to give up. A time when the others would have left the ill Ramsey Crooks to the mercy of the scavenging wolves. A time when only Stuart's cocked rifle prevented suggested cannibalism from becoming ugly fact. A time when even the fiesty Robert McClellan had lain down to die.

But Stuart had not let him die. He had pleaded and insisted, reasoned and badgered, encouraged and threatened them all, through all the miles. For Robert Stuart had learned much in his struggle with the wilderness. For the first time in his life he knew deep, gnawing want and the strength of temptation. For the first time his vision of self-sufficiency was challenged, and he lay awake at night haunted by the phantoms of danger. Gradually he realized that he — and all men — were weak and vulnerable. Out of his new humility came new strength.

Somehow he even kept his sense of humor. In the journal where he kept faithful record of their progress, he referred to their meagre shelter as their "Chateau of Indolence," and to the life-threatening Indians as "rascally neighbors."

On December 13, the men shouldered their packs, took a last look at their chateau, and started again down the river they believed to be the Niobrara. They had long ago lost their horses to the Crows, and all that was left of their scanty provisions was piled on a sorry old pack horse they had bought from the Snakes. Stuart, perhaps feeling a real kinship to Don Quixote, christened the nag Rosinante.

The snow was deep and crusted but it would not support their weight. The sharp-edged crust bit into their feet and legs as they floundered along. Soon the footprints they left behind were edged in red.

In two weeks they estimated they had covered some 300 miles. The country varied from barren to wooded, but gradually the timber disappeared. The bluffs that lined the river receded, and on December 25 they felt themselves lucky to find enough driftwood for a fire.

That night the cold, still air of the Platte Valley (near present-day Minatare, Nebraska) was broken by the crisp accents of Stuart and his fellow Scotsmen, the easy drawl of the frontiersmen, and the colorful expressions of the French-Canadian hunters as the men remembered better Christmases and better times.

It was too cold to sleep, so they were on their way again at first light. Stuart studied the course and the character of the river they followed. It was one and one-half miles wide, cut into innumerable channels, and ran over a bed of sand. He decided that rather than the Niobrara it must be the River Platte.

The plain that faced them December 27 was barren of life. There was no game visible, and wood for fires, if it existed, was buried under 15 inches of snow. How could they live to cross it? Especially when the blizzards howled after them from the west? Reluctantly, Stuart decided they must retrace the tortuous miles to a place suitable for a winter camp and wait there for the spring thaw.

They faced west into an icy wind, and on December 30 they set up camp in a river bottom thick with cottonwood and abundant game (near present-day Torrington, Wyoming). Before dusk December 31 they had raised one wall of their new cabin.

The next day was New Year's, 1813, and although they were far from New York City, they were alive, and that was cause enough for celebration. The men relaxed around the fire as buffalo hump sizzled on the spit and tongue simmered in the kettle. They ate and rested and ate again, juices from the fat meat running down their faces and spotting their already-blackened buckskins. Their tobacco supply was gone, but they still had their pouches. McClellan's pouch was sacrificed and they smoked the pieces, gaining at least a semblance of the fragrance in their pipes. Full and warm and safe, for now, they toasted the New Year.

Back to work on January 2, they soon completed their cabin, killed more buffalo for meat, and settled in for the rest of the winter. When the weather allowed, they hacked away at two hollow trees, shaping them into canoes for use in the spring.

By March 8 the river was running free and full. They broke camp and launched their canoes, but the Platte was not a cooperative partner. Plagued by shallows, sandbars, and channels that led nowhere, they decided the canoes were more work than walking. Once again they set off on foot down the Platte.

The plains that seemed so empty in December now abounded with life. Buffalo shadowed the hillsides and grazed on the rich grass of the bottoms. Swampy areas along the river were raucous with the calls of ducks and geese. Wild horses thundered away as they approached, while the curious antelope edged nearer. But the country was empty of people, and (near present-day North Platte, Nebraska) a piece of wood they found marked by an ax gave them a mystery to puzzle over.

To Stuart the country beyond looked like an ocean, without timber or shaped horizon. The only things that broke the vista of sky were the flocks of cranes that circled their heads and then settled on the river islands. But at last the weather was warming; so warm in fact that their heavy packs pressed uncomfortably on their sweaty backs.

Gradually the antelope gave way to fallow deer and the prickly pear to the beginnings of timber. In April they passed the Grand Isle of the Platte, and the whir of prairie hens disturbed by their passing confirmed Stuart's belief that they must be close to the Missouri. They did not have much success conversing with the Pawnees, but in one camp they found men with whom they could communicate. Two traders, up from St. Louis, rose from the circle of an Oto campfire.

The traders blinked with disbelief when they heard the Astorians had come overland all the way from the Pacific. And the Astorians, only now sure that they would survive their trek, reveled in the surprised respect their achievement elicited. But when they asked eagerly for news of home, they were surprised in turn to learn that the United States was at war with England.

Trading their faithful Rosinante for skins for a canoe, the trappers boated on down the Missouri, reaching St. Louis April 30, 1813, after 10 months of travel.

Only after Stuart had docked his canoe and climbed to the sunset-reddened streets of St. Louis, did he begin to realize the implications of war with England. His overriding concern for most of three years had been simply staying alive. His enemies had been elemental: thirst, hunger, and violent death. Suddenly he was thrust not only into the din and confusion of the city streets, but into the complications of foreign affairs.

The taverns buzzed with speculation. The British were turning the Indians against the Americans. They were already taking over the fur forts of the Great Lakes. St. Louis might be next. Stuart's mind whirled. He could think only of the promising Fort Astoria, an unprotected gem on the distant Pacific. If the British moved against it, as they surely would, Stuart's feat of endurance had been for nothing. Perhaps, like Don Quixote,

he had been fighting to save an illusion.

Stuart's worst fears were realized. He continued on to New York City to deliver his hopeful dispatches to Astor (and to marry his Betsy), but by fall Astoria was in British hands. American enterprise in the Northwest was at an end, for the time.

Stuart continued in the fur business with Astor until 1834, when he settled in Detroit. There he built the city's first brick house for Betsy, was active in business, and became the State Treasurer of Michigan. The religious convictions that had crystalized during his journey from Astoria remained always an important influence on his life.

Though their fur venture in the Northwest had ended in failure, Robert Stuart and his men had pioneered the route that would one day be called the Oregon Trail. As they passed from the Columbia to the Snake to the Green River and on east, they had searched for a southern pass through the Rockies that the Indians knew. And they had found it—a high, wide opening in the chain of mountains at the foot of the Wind River Range. As the *Missouri Gazette* reported in a front page account of their exploits: ''it appears that a journey across the continent of North America might be performed with a waggon....''

And so it might, using the valley of the Platte and the Astorians' South Pass. But in 1813 no one was interested in going to Oregon, and the significance of Stuart's passage down the Platte went unexploited. The route would have to be pioneered again and again.

The Haunt of the Jackal

At 10:00, Tuesday, June 6, saluted by cannon and led by a flag of friendship, the 20 members of the Long expedition set out west for the Platte.

even years later, in the spring of 1820, three horsemen jogged north on the bank of the Missouri River. Two were in their mid-thirties, experienced officers of the United States Army. The third, a lank six-footer with intent black eyes, had only recently become accustomed to being addressed as "Doctor." For Edwin James, 23, was fresh from his medical studies and still slightly surprised to find himself part of a government expedition to explore the Platte River.

James urged his horse along behind Major Stephen Long and Captain John Bell. Long's small group of scientists was all that remained of the ambitious plans for the Yellowstone Expedition — plans which projected five steamboats and 1,000 men pushing up the Missouri as far as the Yellowstone River to establish a military fort. That part of the expedition had foundered on incompetence, scurvy, and the snags of the Missouri. Hoping to salvage something from the fiasco, the War Department gave Major Long orders to take his group of scientists up the Platte, to explore its sources and return by way of the Red River (the newly agreed boundary between the United States and Spain).

Edwin James was a last minute replacement for the group's original physician-botanist, and he and John Bell, replacement journalist, were hurrying with Long to join the rest of the expedition at the Engineer Cantonment (north of present-day Omaha, Nebraska). Plagued by spring rains, they struggled through the muck and the mud and arrived to find the whole encampment in danger of disappearing down the Missouri. James and Bell watched in awe as logs, buffalo carcasses, and whole trees rampaged by in the muddy waters. Troopers rushed to drag supplies to higher ground, as chunks of river bank, undercut by rushing currents, collapsed noisily into the flood.

The river they were to explore was also in flood, but it was not as spectacular as the Missouri. At 10:00, Tuesday, June 6, saluted by cannon and led by a flag of friendship, the 20 members of the Long expedition set out west for the Platte. Resident Otoes shook their heads as they watched the men ride out. They insisted the party was too small and they would be killed by hostile tribes. Edwin James hoped the Otoes were wrong. But 20 men did not throw much of a shadow on the spreading prairie. And before long they met a French trader still nursing a wound he received in a scrape with Indians up the Missouri.

The party James rode with was hardly a re-assurance. The zoologist, geologist, naturalist, two topographers and landscape artist were no better than James at packing horses and mules, and loads were constantly falling or slipping under the belly of a skittish horse. Horses reared and jostled, men sweat and swore, mules balked. It was slow going. Finally Major Long put Captain Bell in the lead and he took the rear himself. There he struggled to keep the column in some kind of order.

The expedition was meagerly financed. Most of the men had to furnish their own horse and tack and they carried only a bare minimum of hardtack and salt pork and little equipment. In fact, at the first opportunity Long bought two brass kettles from Indians they met along the way.

For the first week Long and his men fought the weather and the country. A prairie thunderstorm brought them to a panic halt when lightning blasted into the grass beside the column. Every day brought more rain. The nights brought the misery of mosquitoes. And always, the thick black gumbo clumped on hoof and boot and weighted every step. The zoologist was thrown crossing one creek, and the artist took a dunking in another. Lost horses, inefficiently tethered, caused delays.

Finally, on June 11, proceeding by now in better order, the expedition approached the villages of the Pawnees, above the juncture of the Loup and the Platte. Surrounded by thousands of grazing horses, the domelike earthern lodges of some 6,000 Pawnees clustered along the river for the next several miles. Here and there patches of corn showed green against the dark earth, and Pawnee women and girls bent to its care. White silk banner waving and faces serious, the column rode cere-moniously into the center of the first village.

The few Indians around paid no attention. Squaws tanning hides glanced up and went back to their work. Children looked them over curiously, but no one raised a hand in greeting. Long and Bell exchanged embarrassed glances, and the horses shuffled nervously as the column stood in in-decision.

At last an old chief approached. He explained that the other chiefs were in a medicine feast and could not be disturbed. When Long scolded that they should be there to greet him, the chief replied calmly that they'd be through in an hour or so.

Six hours later a tall, spare Indian strode over to Long's camp. He was Long Hair, chief of the

ASA BATTLES

Grand Pawnee, and his dignified bearing impressed and mollified the impatient Americans. However, he, too, warned them not to continue. "You must have long hearts to undertake such a journey with so weak a force," he remarked, "hearts that would reach from the earth to the heavens."

Edwin James listened to the parley and bided his time. He had a project he desperately wanted to carry out with these Indians. A civilian named Sylvanus Fancher had donated a quantity of smallpox vaccine to the War Department, and James had orders to try to persuade the Indians to undergo vaccination. Smallpox wrought even more terrible havoc among Indian villages than it did in white cities, and the doctors hoped the newly proven vaccine might spare the tribes.

James talked long and hard, trying to explain the disease and the vaccination to the chiefs. He met only stony resistance. They knew the terrors of the disease—19 years before many Pawnees had fallen victim to its ravages—but they wanted nothing to do with white man's medicine. His disease was bad enough.

James persuaded the interpreter to serve as an example. Major Long and the hunter Doughty also bared their arms. But the Indians would not be convinced. Since Dr. James was afraid the vaccine had been ruined by river water when it

was in a keelboat wreck on the Missouri, he decided not to push the matter further. But when he rolled up in his blanket that night, he was kept awake by the howling of dogs and the specter of feverish children with pockmarked faces—children he had been unable to save.

Morning brought another problem. The expedition needed a guide. Major Long sent inquiries to the nearby Pawnee villages, but no volunteer appeared from the rounded huts. Fat and friendly Knife Chief served up boiled corn and buffalo guts and wished them well, but he did not produce a guide.

Perhaps a look at the 20 Americans they were to shepherd up the Platte discouraged likely volunteers. Or perhaps they believed their own dire warnings. Probably the summer buffalo hunt promised surer dividends. At any rate, Long finally had to "volunteer" the French traders Bijou and Ledoux. And they joined the party only when Long threatened to have the government expel them from the village and revoke their trading privileges.

Thus guided, the expedition marched again up a Platte that ran full and brown. Two days later they had sighted, and missed, their first buffalo and were down to a ration of a half-pound of hardtack per man. James and others spent a hungry, miserable night out in the wind trying to keep the tents from flying back to the Missouri. Then June 19 brought more buffalo—and more missed shots.

But soon they were at the forks of the Platte where even they could not miss all the buffalo. Above the junction the men stripped to swim the swollen current of the North Platte, crossed the timberless point between and rode across the lower fork. As they worked their way up the South Platte, they began to see herds of wild horses. James speculated that they must be of Spanish origin. But if somewhere along the way a horse's hoof clanked against a rusted Spanish stirrup, he made no mention.

On the morning of June 30 (near present-day Fort Morgan, Colorado) a bank of white clouds seemed to hug the horizon to the west. Edwin James strained his eyes. Could it be the Rockies? It was too hazy to be sure. Without urging, the men picked up their pace, and by afternoon they were certain. A series of high, white summits rose before them.

Anxious to be done with the hot, barren, fly-infested plains, the men pushed for the mountains, hoping to celebrate the Fourth of July in the cool high country. They did not quite make it, but July 4 turned into a double celebration when Major Long was feared lost and at length returned. They broke open the five-gallon keg of whiskey in celebration. But Edwin James choked and sputtered on his allotment. He had been dry too long.

They set up camp (at the site of present-day Denver, Colorado) and set off to walk to the mountains. When they had covered eight miles and the foothills still lay in the distance, they gave up and returned to camp, victims of an incredibly clear atmosphere that would fool travelers in the West again and again.

As they moved south up the Platte and into the foothills, they fell victim to another traveler's woe. The men discovered bushes covered with currants and gorged themselves on the welcome fruit. But they were quickly struck with stomach cramps, as the currants proved to be an unnecessarily violent physic.

Weak and wobbly from the currants, Dr. James prescribed a cure for another problem—what they thought might be altitude sickness. Many of the men were red-faced, with inflamed eyes and headaches. James proceeded to bleed the men to compensate for the effect of the altitude on blood pressure, and soon they were all feeling better.

All during the trek, James had collected specimens of plant life to take back for identification. Now, in the front range of the Rockies, he was in a paradise. New varieties grew everywhere he looked. He worked feverishly, frustrated that there wouldn't be time to study everything. One flower in particular drew his attention. Its configuration reminded him of the flight of doves, and he called it the columbine.

One objective of the expedition had been to locate and explore the peak Zebulon Pike had noted in 1806. They had been seeing it for days, but when they were ready to climb it, it wasn't there. They had traveled so close to the foot of the mountains that they'd passed it unaware. Embarassed, they backtracked, and on July 13, James and six men set out to reach the summit. Two days later James, trooper Joseph Verplank, and engagé Zachariah Wilson shivered on the wind-swept

height, the first to climb a 14,000 foot peak in the Rockies.

James, heady with exhilaration and altitude, gazed back east over the plains they had labored across, and then west, into the chaos of the Rockies. He could mark the watershed of the South Platte and of the Arkansas, and he took careful note of an ecosystem new to American botany— the treeless tundra.

When James rejoined the expedition, Long christened the peak "James" in honor of his achievement. They left the Platte and traveled south, to follow the wrong river—the Canadian rather than the Red—back to civilization. Once there, they delivered 60 skins of new or rare animals, thousands of insects, 500 plants, shells, fossils, 122 animal sketches, 150 landscapes, and a discouraging assessment of the worth of the plains.

Major Stephen Long went on into railroad engineering and published the country's first manual on the subject. Edwin James served as an army surgeon on the frontier for six years. Later he became Indian Agent at Council Bluffs, and he translated the New Testament and other writings into the Ojibwa language. He settled in Iowa where he continued to write and publish. He saw James Peak revert to Pikes Peak on maps in the 1840s, as honor bowed to popular usage. But his humanitarian instincts remained strong, and soon his farm became a station on the Underground Railroad. During the 1850s he helped many runaway slaves to freedom.

Perhaps, in later years, he would have liked to reconsider. But in 1820 he agreed with Pike and Long in estimation of the plains. "We have little apprehension of giving too unfavorable an account of this portion of the country," he wrote in his journal. "Though the soil in some places is fertile, the want of timber, of navigable streams, and of water for the necessities of life, render it unfit residence for any but a nomad population. The traveler who shall at any time have traversed its desolate sands, will, we think, join us in the wish that this region may forever remain the unmolested haunt of the native hunter, the bison and the jackall."

18

Bullets of Brass

Had it not been for the continued temptation of a large, brown rodent, James' wish for the plains might have been realized. But St. Louis abounded in men who would seek their fortune in furs, and they would willingly pay whatever price the country demanded. They probed up the waters of the Missouri to the Yellowstone, the Big Horn, and the Musselshell, depending, like their quarry, on the rivers for their transportation and their sustenance. As the Platte would not serve them, it ran undisturbed by their poles and paddles.

Then, suddenly, in the summer of 1823, the Missouri and all waters above it were closed to the fur men by the hostility of the Arikara Indians. Stranded below the Arikaras on the banks of the now useless Missouri, William H. Ashley and his men looked west toward the beaver country of the Rockies. If they would have furs, they would have to find another route.

Ashley could see only one alternative. He picked two young men of promise, gave them command of a small band of trappers, and sent them west across the prairie. They would have to make their way to the beaver streams and then find a way to get their harvest home.

ASA BATTLES

As Tom Fitzpatrick rode east through South Pass in late May of 1824, his face glowed with Irish color, spring sun, and a new sense of satisfaction. He had not only survived his first year in the wilderness, he had triumphed. He felt he had made a good beginning of life in his new country.

He led his three men and their fur-laden horses through the sage-dotted incline that was South Pass, reminding himself what it had been like the first time they had passed this way, three months before.

Then it had been weeks of cold; such cold as he had never known; with furious wind that scattered their fires and sapped their strength until they moved only from habit, eyes blurred with tears, breath frozen in their whiskers. Then they had stumbled numbly through this gap in the hills, not even realizing at first that they had found their long sought gateway to the beaver country.

But there, on the west side of the pass, was the Green River, and such beaver country they had only dreamed of. Ashley had been right to send them. It was worth all the trials they had suffered since they left the Missouri the summer past. Finally on the Green, Jedediah Smith and Tom Fitzpatrick had split their forces, Fitzpatrick working the streams north and realizing a rich harvest, while Smith and his men had turned south, promising to meet again in June on the Sweetwater River.

Fitzpatrick thought of Jedidiah Smith as he trotted along toward their agreed rendezvous. "Diah" was an unexpected presence among the wild hellions of the fur trade. Quiet and reserved where they were boisterous, religious where they were profane, serious where they were devil-be-damned. But still respected by one and all. How could you not respect a man who lay quiet on earth splattered with his own blood while he calmly instructed Jim Clyman how to stitch up his grizzly-mangled head?

Tom shook his head at the memory. He hoped what was left of Diah's hair was still in the right place. A man had many a narrow scrape in this country. He knew both of them had learned much in their twenty-fourth year.

They had learned about Indians; who was who and how far you could trust them. (Tom had just recovered his horses from a tribe he had trusted too far.) They learned when to bluff and when to humor. (A loaded gun and stern manner had ransomed his horses from a party four times their size.) They learned to read sign, to bring down buffalo, to predict the weather, to travel with confidence across the great expanses. They had learned they could endure more than they ever imagined. It had been a strenuous year, but a satisfying one. Tom urged his horse ahead, anxious to meet Diah and learn if his hunt had been equally successful.

But Smith was not to be found at the cache on the Sweetwater. Fitzpatrick could see that no one had disturbed the goods they'd buried the previous spring. There was no man and no message. The four men stood in silent disappointment, newly impressed with their vulnerability.

Not knowing if Diah would come in late—or never—Tom knew it was up to him to get the furs to market. He and Jim Clyman rode down the winding, narrow Sweetwater, hoping they could use the river to carry the heavy furs. But it soon became obvious the river was too shallow. Fitzpatrick decided to return with the other men and pack up the furs, while Clyman explored on downstream.

Tom dug up their carefully camouflaged cache and found most of the supplies, wrapped in hides, to be in useable condition. He was spreading their gun powder to dry in the sun when a small group of horsemen appeared on the horizon. Tensely, the three studied the approaching figures. Then Tom let out a whoop that was answered from the distance. It was Jedediah and his men, late but still whole. Laughing and hollering and slapping their backs, the men welcomed them in. The high prairie seemed suddenly less threatening.

As he greeted Fitzpatrick, Smith's scarred face was creased in a smile. His party had also had a fine hunt, and his horses were piled with packs of brown furs. Elated at their success, the two friends decided that Fitzpatrick and two of the men should take the furs on to market and return with supplies, while Smith and the rest remained for the fall hunt. Jim Clyman had not returned from downriver, and when a search revealed Indian sign on his trail, they regretfully decided they would not see him again. A man never knew when his luck would run out.

The Sweetwater, augmented by melting snow, now looked more promising, so Tom and his men loaded their precious furs into a skin boat. Bidding Smith goodbye, they launched themselves into the river and a sea of troubles. The heavy, clumsy tub of a boat was soon worn thin by sandbars and snags, and the men were worn to exhaustion with dragging it downstream. When they barely scraped through Devil's Gate, and more canyons waited beyond, Fitzpatrick decided to give up and cache the furs. Near a smooth gray mound of granite they would come to call Independence Rock, they buried their treasure.

It was lucky they did. A few miles farther the Sweetwater entered the Platte. As the boat boiled through what Robert Stuart had christened the Fiery Narrows, it shuddered against one rock too many. Tom and his men were pitched into the churning water. Suddenly they were swimming for their lives in a current that slammed them against rocks and boulders. They were bruised and battered and spitting water when they finally crawled up on shore.

At first they thought they had lost everything. Then, casting along the shore, they came upon a lone gun. That was all. No food, no bullets, no lead for making more. And 700 miles lay between them and the nearest aid, Fort Atkinson on the Missouri (north of present-day Omaha).

For many men it would have been the end. But Fitzpatrick did not die so easily. He took a rock and began breaking the brass mountings from their only gun. Then he hammered the brass into balls. They pooled and dried the scant powder they could scrape from their wet powder horns. It was enough for a shot or two. With this slender hedge between them and starvation, they set off on foot down the Platte.

At least it was a friendly season on the plains. Grass in the bottoms stood green and lush, although it did nothing to quiet the growling of their empty bellies. Small game appeared, but they did not dare waste their bullets for one day's provisions. Then, in the distance, brown dots moved over the valley. Buffalo. Tom's throat tightened. If he could bring down a cow, they would have a chance.

Carefully he worked upwind and crawled out to a point on a bluff above the valley. The herd grazed quietly, as the month-old yellow calves suckled or napped in the warm sun. Tom picked his target carefully. It had to be a good shot. A wounded animal could run for miles before it fell, and they certainly did not have the stamina for such a pursuit.

He sighted the rifle just behind the shoulder of the nearest cow. She would be poor and stringy meat this time of year, but they couldn't be picky. With a prayer that the rough brass bullet, the twice-dried power, and the battered gun would all work without fault — a tall order indeed — he squeezed the trigger.

Dust puffed from the patchy hide of the cow. She gave a startled bellow which set the herd to sudden motion. In an instant the animals had disappeared over the hills in a flurry of dust and flying clods. But Fitzpatrick's cow remained, sunk to her knees in a small puddle of blood. Tom drew a long breath. Then with a wild shout they ran for the carcass.

It was the last stroke of luck they were to experience for many weeks. Though they carried as much meat with them as possible, and carefully husbanded that, it was still a long way to the Missouri. They passed through the sandstone bluffs that crowded the river, passed the weathered buttes that marked their beginnings, passed down the widening valley into the flatlands. The weather grew hot and dry as they plodded on mile after

mile. Their strength began to fail. They dug for roots. Chewed on bark. Fought wolves for their kill. Or sucked the marrow from their leavings. It was September when — light-headed and shaky-legged — they finally stumbled into Fort Atkinson.

To Fitzpatrick's surprise, Jim Clyman stepped forward to greet him. He had escaped the Indians after all, and a few days ahead of Tom, had spent the summer in his long, and even lonelier journey down the Platte.

Scarcely pausing to recover, Fitzpatrick obtained horses and started back for the valuable furs. This 1,400-mile journey to Independence Rock and back to Fort Atkinson by October 26 didn't even rate a remark from the fort's sutler. ''Fitzpatrick and party have come in and brot beaver,'' is his only comment.

When Fitzpatrick arrived again at Fort Atkinson, his employer William Ashley was already there. The news of the rich harvest and the easy route across the Rockies was a lifesaver for Ashley's struggling fur company, and he could not wait to get into the field with supplies. By November 1, Tom was again on the road up the north side of the Platte, guiding the supply caravan.

It was late in the season for such a journey and the men and animals suffered for their temerity. They pushed through deep drifts of snow, the bitter wind cutting their faces and taking their breath. Horses froze. Game disappeared. The men existed on a cup of flour a day, made into a thin gruel. They huddled around a gloomy campfire at night, too miserable and exhausted even to talk.

Luckily they fell in with the Skidi Pawnees and traveled with them to the forks of the Platte. Goods from these Indians revived the fortunes of the train, and as they started to ascend the South Platte, buffalo appeared.

The buffalo paths through the snow were all that made progress possible. On they struggled through the winter, up the Cache la Poudre and into the Rockies. It was April of 1825 when they finally reached the Green River and their fellow trappers. Fitzpatrick had covered over 3,000 miles since he had left Jedediah Smith on the Sweetwater the summer before.

Tom Fitzpatrick went on to become a leading trapper and head of the Rocky Mountain Fur Company. He came to know the Platte as well as any man ever did, and his name would break the surface of Platte River history for years to come.

The Landmark

In the next few years Ashley's trappers established the Platte Valley route as the way west. In 1825-26 Jedediah Smith led a mounted supply caravan up the south side of the Platte, breaking a trail that would one day lead to Oregon.

Jedediah would continue to break trails all over the West, transversing the country from the Rockies to the Pacific, from the Mojave to the Columbia. But it fell to another to escort the first wheels along the Platte and across the continental divide.

When Ashley's force had battled the Arikaras on the Missouri in 1823, one company of the trappers had been led by a giant of a man. His full, black head of hair topped every crowd at 6 feet 4 inches and he carried 265 pounds on his well-muscled frame. Few of the men he commanded would have guessed he was only 18 years old.

Hiram Scott's bearing and accomplishments belied his age. After only a year in the wilderness, he had been chosen with Jedediah Smith to lead the trappers in battle. And though their efforts to defeat the Arikaras and proceed up the Missouri had been futile, no one involved questioned their methods or their courage.

Most of Ashley's men were young, and many of them were ambitious, but perhaps Hiram Scott felt a special pressure to succeed. Only a year before he had seen his name published as an insolvent debtor. He had brought public shame on the family name. And he had joined Ashley's expedition with the hope of repairing both his fortune and his reputation.

In the next four years Scott made progress on both counts. In the spring of 1827 Ashley appointed him co-leader of the annual supply caravan. Scott, serving as clerk and field commander, spent a busy time combing St. Louis for the horses, mules, traps, powder, lead, blankets, tobacco, coffee, and Indian trade goods the trappers needed to carry them through another year. He also was ordered by Ashley to make an unusual purchase.

By late March the 44-man caravan was on the road. Among the muddy prints of the laden horses and mules, there was a new and different track. For this year Ashley was sending a four-pound cannon to the mountains, and the wheels of its carriage would be the first to roll up the Platte and across the Rockies.

Ashley, taken ill, left his caravan at the frontier, trusting the "entirely efficient" Scott and his agent James B. Bruffee to take the train on to rendezvous. This they accomplished, finding the cannon carriage no major hindrance on the natural road of the Platte Valley.

By July the dust-covered train had topped the gentle hills east of Bear Lake and wound down the grassy slopes to the welcome refreshment of its turquoise waters. Scott greeted his cohorts, Tom Fitzpatrick, Jim Clyman and others, and he listened to their tales of a recent scrape with the Blackfeet. Then he had a special reunion with his brother James, who had also entered the mountain trade. There was one sad note. An old friend was missing. Jedediah Smith had led a force southwest, and neither he nor his men had been heard from for a year.

Scott and Bruffee set up shop and trade began in earnest. The trappers splurged the returns from their furs—grumbling at mountain prices, but spending freely just the same. The camp bustled, as hundreds of Utes and Snakes spread their tepees and horse herds around the lake shore.

Midafternoon of July 3, while the camp lazed in the summer heat, a ragged, emaciated man rode in from the south. It was Jedediah Smith, returned from the dead. The camp went wild with celebration. Searching his mind for a suitable means of recognition, Hiram Scott seized on the cannon. In a moment it was loaded, and the valley echoed as the four-pounder boomed out a welcome to Diah and his two men.

Hiram joined the crowd that gathered around Jedediah as he told of his year's wanderings; an unprecedented journey that had taken him clear to the Spanish settlements of California. There the bulk of his trapping force awaited his return.

Ten days later the rendezvous broke up and Jedediah headed back west for his men and their furs. Hiram Scott and James Bruffee packed up $22,000 worth of beaver pelts and led their caravan east, through the changing colors, reaching Missouri on October 15.

If the men had expected a rest after seven months in the wilderness, they did not get it. In spite of the difficulties suffered in his 1825 journey, Ashley had decided on another fall caravan. He had the goods ready. Trading furs for new supplies, Scott and Bruffee turned doggedly back toward the mountains.

The caravan reached the Wind River Mountains before being stopped by a blizzard. Snows of that incredible winter started in December and continued without surcease until March. The train, unable to move on and deliver its needed supplies, spent the winter battling cold and hunger.

The strain and hardship of such a life began to take its toll. Hiram fell sick. When spring thaws made travel again possible, he struggled on with the train to rendezvous at Bear Lake.

Weak and miserable, he longed for a talk with his brother. But now he learned that James Scott and three others had disappeared into the Snake country in January and never returned. It was bitter news. Grieved, and now almost an invalid, Hiram faced a long and rigorous journey home.

Bruffee left two men to travel with Scott at whatever pace he could manage, while he pushed on with the train. He promised to wait for them once they hit buffalo country, at a place where high bluffs edged the Platte.

Hiram clung to his saddle as long as his strength would permit, as they crept the miles to Green River and over South Pass. But when they reached the Sweetwater, he tumbled limply to the ground, unable to ride farther.

His companions constructed a bull-boat, and the sick young man folded his length into it. For several days they boated down the narrow Sweetwater and into the Platte, while Hiram fell in and out of consciousness, vaguely aware of high blue sky and softly-flowing waters.

But again the Platte proved treacherous. As they tried to run the rapids (above present-day Casper, Wyoming) the boat upset. It was all the men could do to pull Hiram's weight from the water.

Guns, ammunition, food—everything was lost. Their only hope was to reach the caravan at the bluffs. For nine days the men labored on, supporting the weakened Scott. Without food, they scrounged for something to eat at old camp sites, hoping for some tidbit overlooked by the scavengers. Sometimes they found an unbroken bone, from which they hungrily sucked the marrow.

At length the bluffs rose before them. Half-carried by his companions, Hiram forced his feeble body to keep going for the last crucial

miles. Hearts racing, breaths rattling, the three clambered through the badlands at the foot of the bluff.

Their ''Hallow's'' were answered only by echoes. There was no train. No food. No help. Only the scream of an eagle, disturbed by their cries, floated down from the sandstone heights.

Scott had used his last reserve, and now he collapsed. He could go no farther. When his companions had recovered their breath, they held a whispered conference. They had not the strength to carry him farther. If they stayed with him, they would starve. They saw only one choice. Without a word they walked away, hurrying their steps to escape the sound of his cries.

Hiram lay alone in the tall, brown grasses. He was 23 and not ready to die. He made a last effort, crawling after the men—the train—the hope of survival—until even the strength of desperation was gone. Perhaps he wept. Perhaps he cursed. But eventually he lay quiet. He saw the cliffs above him glow rose with sunset; then the cedar-studded slopes blend into the black summer night.

No one knows how long he took to die. But the next summer his bones were found by the fur caravan he might have led. They were gathered and buried beneath the bluff where he died, and the name he thought he had disgraced became a lasting landmark in the valley of the Platte.

Travelers since 1828 have marked their progress by Scotts Bluff, and those who chose to settle there in later years took the name for both a city and a county. In 1919 the bluff which became Hiram Scott's place of death was established as a United States National Monument.

Journey to a Far Country

The wheels of the cannon that Hiram Scott escorted up the Platte in 1828 left no lasting mark upon the land. But they marked men's minds with a new reality: wagon travel to and through the Rockies was indeed possible. In 1830 the fur men sent 10 mule-drawn wagons to rendezvous, with so little trouble they reported to the Secretary of War that a natural wagon road stretched along the Platte.

The report was reprinted widely in newspapers, and once again the Platte beckoned travelers headed west. For the magnet of the Rockies was beginning to pull men with a widening range of interests out into the West. Some sought to share the wealth of beaver, already diminishing; some to share their God with the savages; and some to taste the newness of the land and share their discoveries with the world of science.

ASA BATTLES

On the morning of April 28, 1834, John Kirk Townsend looked back on the double file of 70 men and 250 horses plodding in his wake from Independence, Missouri, toward the Platte. The 25-year-old naturalist was not a man to feel comfortable in the bustle and restraint of cities, but the environment he was entering was strange enough to add an undercurrent of anxiety to his excitement. And not only the land was strange. The people of the land were so different from his Philadelphia neighbors that he felt he was ven-

turing into a far, far country.

Too excited to maintain his place in the slow moving line, John sallied out from the column for a better look. The engagés and trappers who made up most of the caravan were in good spirits. Their songs and laughter echoed along the line. They were mountain men and they looked as wild as the wind on a stormy peak. Though he was dressed in similar fashion — buckskin pants, green-blanket capote, and wide-brimmed, white hat — he knew the clothes were only a costume on him, as they were on his fellow scientist, Harvard botanist Thomas Nuttall.

The gray-haired Nuttall, who rode beside him, was twice his age, and he had been West in 1811 to explore the Missouri River, but he had not hesitated to leave the lecture halls of Harvard when this chance came for further exploration. John owned his presence in the train to Nuttall's friendship and to the sponsorship of Philadelphia's two scientific academies. He was to concentrate on bird study, while Nuttall explored plant life; the two of them being the first to look at the Platte with scientific interest since Long's expedition in 1820.

Surprisingly, the leader of the caravan of trappers, who rode with them, was not a veteran of mountain winters. He was a Massachusetts ice merchant, inventor, and entrepreneur, who was flinging his abundant Yankee energy against the vagaries of the fur trade. This was Nathaniel J. Wyeth's second attempt to establish himself in the fur business, and though the first had ended in debt and disaster, the insistantly optimistic man was giving it another try.

He had cheerfully offered the scientists the protection of his column, and he had invited yet another disparate party to join the train. Toward the rear, on the flank of the pack horses, John could see dust raised by a small herd of cattle — cattle to be driven all the way to Oregon and used to establish a Methodist mission for the Flathead Indians. Among the five men of the missionary party, John had no trouble picking out the tall, powerful form of their leader, Reverend Jason Lee.

John realized the trappers were not entirely delighted with the company of scientific gentlemen and church men. He admired their free and independent spirit, but he was hard put not to show his shock at their rough familiarity. He appreciated Wyeth's skill in handling the mountain men, noting how the respect he granted them was returned in full measure. And when he learned that Wyeth had first approached the West with uniformed "troops," bugles, and strange amphibian wagons, he realized how the New Englander had grown in knowledge and ability in two years' time. This trip Wyeth was the experienced partisan, and John Townsend knew he was the greenhorn.

From the first day, most of John's time was devoted to searching for and collecting specimens of bird life. As they left the heavy woods of the Missouri, the flocks of red and green paroquets

were replaced by yellow-headed blackbirds that swirled around the train, often catching a ride on the horses' pack saddles. And as the lush, tall-grass prairie gave way to short and scattered patches of green, finches and sparrows scattered before the train.

But when they reached the Platte in mid-May, the ornithologist found it a veritable bird sanctuary. The islands of the river offered shelter for new and lovely kinds of birds. Long-billed curlews stalked the edges of the shallow water, their curving spikes of beaks dipping quickly as they fed. The red caps of sandhill cranes moved among the island grasses, and great blue herons glared from snags of cottonwood. Every day he rode out with his shotgun and returned with his game bag full. In the evening John sat before the fire, preserving the skins and making notes of the day's collection.

All members of the train took their turn at camp chores, and John got well-acquainted with the party of missionaries. He learned how two Flathead Indians had journeyed all the way to St. Louis in 1831, seeking knowledge of the white God. When the story of the Indians' quest was reported to the religious world, a wave of Christian concern for the Indians had stirred mission boards to action. Reverend Lee had been chosen by the Methodist Mission Board to answer the Flatheads' needs by establishing a mission in Oregon.

John thought the Methodists had made a good choice in Lee. He not only had a physique equal to frontier life, he had a cheerful, willing courage to see the job through. Neither reserved nor sanctimonious, Lee carried his share of the daily load, whether it was hunting or standing night guard. Townsend found him a welcome companion.

John, too, took his turn at guard duty, a duty they took more seriously now that they were in Pawnee territory. He watched his side of the square camp, answering the cries of "All's well!" every 15 minutes and the call of the hour when it came. He found it a lonely time, and he often took out the single letter he had received from his family before he left the settlements and read and reread the creased pages, wondering when, or if, he would see them all again.

One night when John came in from guard duty, he made a near fatal error. As he stepped through the door of Wyeth's tent and bent to lay his gun by his pallet, he saw a pair of wild eyes gleaming fiercely from a corner. Expecting to feel the sharp fangs of a wolf at his throat any second, he raised his rifle and took aim.

Suddenly there was a loud 'Wah!' and the muzzle of his gun was knocked skyward. An Indian hand grasped his arm. As he struggled to control the gun, another Indian pressed the sharp point of a knife against his throat. He froze, expecting instant death. But the commotion woke Wyeth, and he shouted to the Indian to stop. Then he explained to John that the Indians were Pawnees who were his guests, and—with some difficulty—convinced the Pawnees that John was not after their scalps.

Shaken by the close call, John rolled up in his blanket. But Wyeth silently motioned for his attention, and then pointed to his own rifle, secured between his knees, and the knife and pistol laid ready. John made his own weapons ready, but sleep was a long time coming, and every time he glanced toward the corner, a pair of eyes glittered in the darkness.

When morning sun chased the ghosts from the tent, John and the brave he had nearly killed made friends. Luckily the Pawnee thought it all a huge joke. He and John exchanged knives—a symbol of lasting friendship—and John watched the knife with John Kirk Townsend engraved on its handle slip into the sheath at the Pawnee's side.

Then the tall brave showed John how to shoot arrows. When John expressed curiosity about an arrow with its length coated in blood, the Pawnee showed him how that came about. He pulled back the string on his bow and sent an arrow through the body of an antelope—from chest to hind quarter—and watched it skip across the prairie beyond.

John had been repelled by the Indians in St. Louis, finding them dirty, with appalling habits, such as eating each other's lice. But these Pawnees were straight in their bearing, and he admired their courage. He thought he would never forget this man's expressive face and the fascinating, glittering eyes that had nearly cost him his life.

The buffalo that had covered the valley for 80 square miles a day or two before now disappeared, and the hunters began getting up a party to find some meat. John and Jason Lee eagerly chose to go along. They spent a long, thirsty day in the saddle. When they found a herd in the hill country, John watched with interest as the bulls rolled in

the dusty hollows and carried on sham battles.

He was determined to take one of the huge trophies himself, but when he picked a target and tried to squeeze the trigger, his hands shook so he could not take aim. For several minutes he fought the panic, and finally he was able to shoot. The animals began to gallop, and he thought he had missed. But no. The bull he had selected ran only a little way and stood trembling, blood streaming from his nostrils like gory icicles.

When he fell, John raced to the body and tried to lift the bloody head so he could cut out the tongue. He couldn't raise it. The laughing hunters came to his aid, but they teased him for shooting a tough, old bull when he could have chosen a fat cow.

It had been a long day with no water. John had mimicked the hunters and sucked a bullet to keep his mouth moist, but still he was painfully thirsty. He and Lee were about to ride for the river, several miles away, when the hunter had another suggestion. He sliced open the bull and stuck the paunch with his knife, catching the green juices that flowed out in a tin cup. Politely he offered the gentlemen first drink. John and Jason Lee took a look at the gelatinous ''cider'' and politely declined.

Laughing at their squeamishness, the hunter drank it down and smacked his lips. Then he offered an alternative—blood from the still-warm heart. Frantic with thirst, John resisted no longer. He drank deeply. Then, suddenly ashamed, he gave Lee an embarrassed smile. The missionary took a look at his apologetic, gory countenance and roared with laughter. Back at camp the first swallow of water brought up all the blood. John was never that thirsty again.

The last week in May the company forded the South Platte and found a new misery. Hordes of black gnats attacked men and horses. The whole train rode with heads covered by handkerchiefs, coats, shirts—anything they could lay their hands on. The suffering animals kicked and snorted, unable to shake their tormentors. Nat Wyeth's eyes swelled shut, and he was virtually blind for two days.

The wildlife of the plains continued in abundance. John passed a large cedar with a bald eagle's nest, complete with young. Rattlesnakes crawled away from their path. John often woke early and strolled near the camp before its unaccustomed noises could frighten possible specimens. It was a freshly beautiful world, spiced with the scent of sage and populated with prairie dogs, hares, and field mice, as well as birds. Birds were so common that John threw out his waistcoat, shaving box, soap, and stockings to make room for his many specimens.

As they approached Chimney Rock, the strange spire that reared near the trail, John's hunting urge got the better of him. A curious antelope doe trailed the train, and John rode out and shot it. At once he regretted the impulse, and he was amazed at himself for killing when there was no need for meat. He had thought the pronghorn antelope one of the most beautiful animals, with its delicate ears, coat of tawny brown marked with white, and graceful springing motion. Now he had to dismount and finish off the wounded animal as she writhed on the ground. It was days before he could forget the pain in the doe's large, soft, black eyes, and he vowed he would kill again only from necessity.

But another young antelope that was captured soon became the pet of the train. They named him Zip Coon and fed him milk from the missionary herd. Every morning he would run to the mule that held his traveling cage and wait to be lifted aboard.

The prairie around Scotts Bluff was such a carpet of flowers that even the trappers were heard to say, "Beautiful! Beautiful!" Nuttall worked frantically ahead of the train to save specimens from hoof and boot. And two days later a camp in a cottonwood grove on the Platte gave Townsend a variety of birds such as he had never seen. He worked for an hour taking specimens and with his game bag full was still loathe to leave, afraid he might have missed some.

"It was the El Dorado of my fond anticipations," he later wrote, and he felt keen sorrow at having to move on with the train. He thought excitedly of what could be accomplished by an expedition of scientists—botanists, zoologists, entomologists, mammalologists—with time to really study the inexhaustible field. How it could add to the knowledge of the country's resources!

But he was with a fur train anxious to get to rendezvous, and there was no time. On they went to Independence Rock (where they added their names to others); to the Sandy (where John identified a beautiful new mocking bird); to the rendezvous (where John lost his journal and Nat Wyeth learned he'd lost his chance to supply the trappers).

Still they went on. John marked their progress with Lewis' woodpecker, Clark's nutcracker, the incredible whooping crane, the white pelican, the shoveller, and the canvas-backed duck.

Six months and three days after leaving Philadelphia, John Kirk Townsend arrived at his far country, the Oregon coast. The birds had changed to water ouzels, oyster catchers, and cormorants, and John himself was a changed person. He felt strengthened and invigorated by the exercise of the journey, and with a new confidence he welcomed further adventures. He explored the Columbia basin and sailed twice to the Sandwich Islands before returning home later in 1837.

Bales of specimens he had been sending home for three years revealed he had discovered and named 25 new species of birds. He also identified a new hare, a marmot, a meadow mouse, a ground squirrel, a shrew mole, and a bat. Seventy skins of his bird collection added new and interesting pages to *Birds of America*, recreated there by the brush of John James Audubon.

Townsend planned to publish his own ornithology, but after the first volume in 1840, he had to give up the venture for lack of funds. He did publish one of the most readable and entertaining accounts of the Western experience, *Narrative of a Journey Across the Rocky Mountains to the Columbia River* in 1839. He was planning another exploration, this time around the Cape of Good Hope, when he took ill and died in 1851, at the age of 41. He left one son, along with a warbler, a solitaire, a chipmunk, and a ground squirrel to bear his name.

Nat Wyeth returned from the West in 1836, defeated in business but not in spirit. He turned his talents back to the ice business and received 14 patents in the next 15 years. He died in 1856, a respected and prosperous merchant whose enterprising spirit had touched and changed the West.

The scientists and missionaries he supported were the vanguard of a growing movement. Fourteen of Wyeth's men remained in Oregon as permanent settlers, and the cheerful Reverend Lee by-passed his assigned charges the Flatheads to move on and join the settlers in the Willamette Valley, where, perhaps, the countryside and the souls of the Indians both seemed more tameable. Almost immediately he began a campaign for others to join him. With Lee, the road up the Platte Valley truly became an Oregon Trail.

His Will Be Done

If the Methodists were first on the trail, other denominations were not long in following. In fact an elderly New England parson named Samuel Parker would have journeyed west with the same caravan as Jason Lee had he not reached St. Louis too late to join Wyeth's train. Two men who accompanied him, John Dunbar and Samuel Allis, did set up a mission among the Pawnees of the Platte.

But in 1835 Samuel Parker was there in time to catch the fur train to the Rockies, and with him rode a missionary doctor named Marcus Whitman. So a Congregationalist and a Presbyterian joined the struggle to save savage souls. One would waft through the Indians' country like a true spirit, sincere in his belief that the word of Jesus he carried could leap the chasm of ignorance and bring them to salvation. The other would travel with his feet on the ground, bringing practical medical care—and something more: an unexpected presence that would forever change the concept of the Platte road and the country beyond.

ASA BATTLES

Marcus Whitman knew cholera when he saw it. He knew the hollowed cheeks, the sharpened nose, the blue tinge that spread from lips to sunken eyes. He knew the body's straining with dry heaves long after the stomach had given up all fluid. He knew the writhing response to gripping cramps, and the vacant stare of accelerating dehydration.

For Asiatic cholera had struck in the East in

1832, and Whitman—his medical diploma scarcely hung on the wall—had been totally ignorant of any treatment. He was not alone. Doctors bled their already weakened patients or gave cruelly unnecessary purges of calomel. Two of every three afflicted died, some in a matter of hours. A few lingered two or three days.

Ignorant of bacteria and sanitation, people blamed fresh vegetables and passed laws against their sale. When the plague continued to rage, they fled. As panic emptied cities and business stood paralyzed, doctors had turned to newspapers, which carried the latest theories of treatment—beside the lists of dead and dying.

Now, when fur caravan leader Lucien Fontenelle awakened him in camp on the Missouri at Bellevue, Marcus Whitman stumbled sleepily out to see the dreaded symptoms. He could see panic in the sick trappers' eyes and his own tongue tasted fear. If his skills had been inadequate in cities—among colleagues—what could he do here, alone, on the banks of the Missouri? But he had to try. Already exhausted by the trip from St. Louis to Bellevue, suffering from a chronic pain in his side, Dr. Whitman began a 12-day battle to save the caravan from cholera.

The men he worked to save had not made the missionaries welcome on this journey to the Rockies. There was no Nat Wyeth to soothe the way. Irritated by their ignorance in packing and managing their mules, imposed upon to carry extra baggage, totally out of sympathy with both their genteel ways and their aspirations, the men had not hesitated to let Whitman and Parker feel their displeasure. They had gibed and ridiculed and even rotten-egged the young doctor and his stiff-necked companion.

Nevertheless, Whitman worked to save them. But there was not much he could do. Before long three were dead. More lay prostrate. Fontenelle himself fell sick. But Whitman did know enough to have the camp moved to higher, dryer ground. There he nursed them, fed them, kept them warm, and—removed from contamination—the epidemic waned.

With it went the hostility of the trappers. And that was a fortunate thing, for after the march resumed Whitman himself fell ill with dysentery. Barely able to sit his mule, obliged to stop frequently, he fell behind. Had a clerk of the company not stayed behind to help him on and off his mule, he would have collapsed along the way.

The Reverend Samuel Parker seemed oblivious to Whitman's plight. At 56, he was better suited to the book-lined office of the girls' school he had recently run, than to the rigors of the West. With casual disregard for the realities of trail life, he refused to make or break camp, pack a mule, or even cook a meal for the weakened doctor. He strolled off to dine with Fontenelle, and Marcus was left to the occasional mercies of the mess cooks.

When he had recovered enough so that he could focus on something beyond the ears of his mule, Marcus studied the progress of the six wagons in Fontenelle's company. He knew wagons had made it as far as the rendezvous before. If a wagon could make it all the way to Oregon it would open up all kinds of possibilities. The thought of one particular possibility made him cluck to his mule as he followed Fontenelle's wagons up the north side of the Platte.

With their start slowed by cholera, it was late July before they saw Chimney Rock across the river, and they had just passed Scotts Bluff when a band of Indians boiled out of the west and galloped down on the train. Quickly Fontenelle forted up the wagons. But the whooping crowd shot their guns into the air to signal friendship and trotted peaceably in to visit. They were Indians new to Whitman—and new to the Platte Valley—Oglala Sioux.

They had been drawn south to the Platte country by a new fort the fur men had established a few miles up the Platte. It sat in a meadow where the Laramie River emptied into the Platte, on a natural crossroads of trails. Christened Fort William, it would soon be commonly called Fort Laramie.

As the train jogged on west, it came on the full village of Oglala, 2,000 strong. And so Parker and Whitman rode into Fort Laramie surrounded by the dust, dogs, travois, and horses of a people who would work changes on the Platte no less important than the changes they themselves would bring to Oregon.

The missionaries found the Sioux to be clean and handsome people. But before long the whiskey kegs were tapped, and both red and white men lost their dignity in a gigantic drunk. The Sioux culminated their celebrations in a buffalo dance, while the Reverend Parker fought to counteract the heathen influence by singing hymns of his own. The Sioux could not understand the Reverend's message, but they listened courteously

ASA BATTLES

to his "medicine."

At the fort, a log bastion with the entrance overhung by a lookout tower, the missionaries met the man who would captain the train on to the rendezvous. He was Tom Fitzpatrick, who in 10 years of taking beaver had climbed to the top rank among fur men. He was co-owner of the new fort, and Whitman found him a literate and intelligent man. On an individual scale, he also shared Whitman's compassion for the Indians, for he had adopted an Arapaho Indian boy he found lost in the desert. The boy, named Friday for the day of his finding, was spending the winters in school in St. Louis, and the summers in the mountains with Fitzpatrick, and he seemed to be flourishing under the trapper's care.

But Fitzpatrick did not share Whitman's interest in wagon transport. To the doctor's disappointment Fitzpatrick ordered the company's goods repacked on mules and the wagons left behind.

In 12 days the efficient and unencumbered fur men had the train and the missionaries across to the rendezvous site on the Green River. He saw to it that shelters were set up to display the bolts of calico and flannel, the skeins of ribbon, the hanks

of beads, and the boxes of axes, knives, bells, and vermillion. Then he was ready to trade for skins, and with whiskey kegs spouting, the mountain fair began.

If the missionaries had been shocked by the scenes at Laramie, they were appalled at the two-week carousal that was rendezvous. Trapper and Indian alike sprawled and brawled through the camp, guzzling whiskey, gambling, blaspheming, and fighting over squaws; quiet only when they had drunk themselves to unconsciousness; waking only to begin again.

Yet the missionaries now had some under-standing of the hardships of mountain life, and they had to respect the giants of the trade they were meeting. They watched a small trapper named Kit Carson fight and win a duel for his life, and Fitzpatrick's cohort Jim Bridger showed Marcus a spot in his back where he had carried a Blackfoot arrowhead for three years.

Whitman examined the lump and proposed to operate, which he did — sans anesthetic or steriliza-tion — and with considerable effort he cut out a three-inch iron point that had been overgrown by cartilage. It was a long and bloody operation, and some spectators thought he was doing their friend Bridger more harm than help. But Whitman persevered, and again the results of his medical skills made him welcome. Bridger became his friend for life, and other trappers, and even Indians, crowded around for his ministrations.

But the purpose of their journey was still to be realized. The American Board of Commissioners for Foreign Missions wanted to know if a mission among the Indians of Oregon was feasible. Sun-day, August 16, Parker and Whitman met in their tent with spokesmen of the Flatheads and Nez Perce. The story that the Indians sought know-ledge of the white god was true. Marcus could not understand why Jason Lee had passed by these likeable, intelligent people, and he was anxious to answer their quest as soon as possible.

In order to save time they decided to separate. The Reverend Samuel Parker continued west, alone but for his God and a few Indian guides, to locate mission sites. Marcus, accompanied by two Nez Perce boys (to teach him the language), turned back toward civilization to collect the necessities to equip an Oregon mission.

By late April of 1836 Marcus Whitman had collected his supplies and gathered his party, but it looked as if his mission in Oregon might never be. The steamer which was to have carried them up the Missouri to Bellevue (where the fur caravan was forming) had passed by without stopping. They dared not cross the plains without the caravan's protection; large parties were seldom bothered, but small groups invited attack. If they missed connections with the train they could not go.

Two-hundred-fifty miles lay between them and Bellevue. They threw their belongings together and began a wild dash north. Two weeks of frantic travel had brought them to the south bank of the Platte. But the fur caravan was already on the trail. They would have to cross the river and catch up with the train before they reached Indian country.

Could they do it? Marcus, hardened to the trail, was nevertheless exhausted. What of Henry Spalding—late of the Lane Theological Seminary, and William Gray, a lay assistant—equally green? What of the two boys he had hired as helpers? And most importantly—what of Narcissa and Eliza?

For with him Marcus had his bride of three months, and with Henry Spalding rode his wife, Eliza.

The two women were a study in contrasts. Eliza was dark, slim, and retiring. Narcissa was a vivacious charmer, whose red-gold hair and full figure caught every eye. She had had many suitors—among them Eliza's husband, Henry Spalding. In spite of her popularity she had been well on the way to becoming a spinster school marm. None had moved her, until Marcus Whitman offered her Oregon. It was her dream to serve in a foreign mission, but the mission board did not accept unmarried females. When the chance came to join Marcus in the Oregon mission, she wed him without hesitation.

Eliza's commitment to the mission field was less spectacular, but no less sincere. She was an intelligent, well-educated woman. While she and Henry Spalding awaited the birth of their first child, they had been assigned to serve the Osage Indians in Missouri. When the child was stillborn they remained unencumbered—and Whitman was in a frenetic search for missionaries to accompany him. A last minute arrangement had put Eliza and Henry on the road to Oregon.

The road to Oregon. No white woman had ever attempted it before.

The last two weeks had proved the partnership an uncomfortable one. The fact that Eliza's husband was one of Narcissa's rejected suitors was disconcerting, to say the least, to two women who would have only each other in the wilderness. But the trouble did not develop between the women. Narcissa admired the spunk of the fragile Eliza, who, not yet recovered from the loss of her child, still did not shrink from the journey before her.

But Henry Spalding was a different matter. He could not forgive past slights. Narcissa's every action was a target for his criticism, and the strong-willed woman did not suffer his gibes in silence. The fact that assistant William Gray was not bashful about admitting that no one in the party could match him for piety, dedication, and godliness (to say nothing of humility), did little to increase the harmony of the travelers.

Still, with a nightmare of forced marches behind them, and only uncertainty before them, the missionaries determined to cross the Platte and take their chances on catching the train. If they knew the chances of a tenderfoot party with wagons, women, and cattle overtaking an expertly

ASA BATTLES

driven supply train, they were not deterred. They put their faith in their Lord and splashed into the swollen river.

It was a two-day labor. With Spalding ill and the hired boys basically useless, Marcus Whitman carried the load. Time and again he swam the river, transferring baggage, driving their small herd of cattle, assisting the women and struggling with the wagons. As he crossed with the last load, his strength failed, and Narcissa and the others had to pull him from the water.

It was obvious now that they had brought too much with them. Eliza and Narcissa sorted through their belongings in an act they would repeat many times, and a pile of expendables, topped with Henry Spalding's theological tomes, was left for the Pawnee mission. They repacked the heavy farm wagon and the Spaldings' fashionable Deerhorn with its blue and gold wheels. Then the vehicles that were to become Marcus Whitman's obsession started up the north side of the Platte.

With the caravan four days ahead, they traveled guiltily through the Sabbath, crossed the Elkhorn on Monday and drove a dogged 60 miles Tuesday, some of the party reaching the Loup at 11:00 p.m. But the cattle couldn't keep up the pace, and Narcissa and Marcus stayed behind with their Nez Perce Indian boys and the herd. After a supper of milk and a night in the open, they drove the herd in the next morning and praised God to see the fur train camped across the Loup. Another day of superhuman effort put them across the river and down the trail. It was 1:00 a.m. Thursday when the exhausted party crept into the fur company camp.

None too soon. The next day they would pass the Pawnee villages.

Narcissa awoke to the braying of mules and the din of 70 men breaking camp. By 6:00 the call came to "Catch up!" and the train took the trail; Tom Fitzpatrick, familiar to Marcus from the summer before, at the head with the pilot, some 400 animals and a cart and wagons raising dust behind. The missionaries pulled their wagons in at the end of the line, and for the first time in three weeks, Narcissa could relax and begin to enjoy her adventure.

Narcissa had a great capacity for enjoying life. And now, as she honeymooned up the Platte, the hardships of life in the open seemed only a welcome challenge. She cheerfully sat on the ground, or Marcus' knee, ate from a tin plate with a knife and a sharpened stick, proudly learned to bake bread in the coals (though baking enough for 10 people to eat three times a day was rather a trial). At noon rest she wrote to her family, "I was never so contented and happy before. Neither have I enjoyed such health."

Carrying civilization in her wagon, Narcissa invited Fitzpatrick and the company men to tea. Her tea table was the ground and the cloth a sheet of India rubber, but the gentlemen knew they were being entertained by a lady. Tom Fitzpatrick, who had crept starving along this Platte 12 years before; Black Harris, an old hand with a trap and with a trapper's yarn; Milton Sublette, a mountain man going home to his mountains despite an amputated leg; and a Scottish sportsman named Stewart gathered round to bow their heads over Narcissa's table and warm themselves by Narcissa's fire.

As they reached the forks of the Platte, the first buffalo appeared. Narcissa and Eliza scrambled up a sand bluff along the trail to get a closer look at a huge bull. Marcus was indulgent but also practical. He shot a cow for meat. Then he showed Narcissa what to use for fuel when wood disappeared. She gladly let him display his talents for roasting the meat. Gratefully she wrote her sister, "If I had looked the world over I could not have found one more careful and better qualified to transport a female such a distance."

But it was such a distance. Riding sidesaddle in their voluminous skirts, bouncing about in the springless wagon, walking at times to lighten the load, they covered the miles.

It was too much for Eliza's constitution. With alkali water to drink, and nothing but meat and tea for meals, she became ill. More and more often she rode in the wagon. From her seat on a trunk, she gazed across the June prairie and admired the great bluffs and the slopes pink with wild roses, but the most pleasant sight of all came on June 13, 1836, when the tan walls of Fort Laramie shimmered like a mirage on the horizon.

The women reveled in a week's rest. A chance to wash clothes (their first in six weeks), to sit in a chair (even one of buffalo skin), to observe the Sabbath with rest and quiet. Henry Spalding stood in the small, dusty courtyard and delivered a sermon on the Prodigal Son, and Eliza gave a Bible to a trapper who had been touched by the message.

Here the fur company again transferred its goods from wagon to muleback, and Fitzpatrick advised Marcus Whitman to do the same. But Marcus was determined that a wagon should go all the way to Oregon. He was finally persuaded to leave the heavy wagon, and again the women eliminated possessions. Marcus and Narcissa had a domestic discussion about the importance of Marcus' dress clothes, but Narcissa prevailed, and he kept the black suit and overcoat. He also kept the light wagon.

Fitzpatrick, seeing Whitman was determined, assigned a man to help them along, for past Fort Laramie the going was much rougher. Even with help, the labor of getting the wagon over rocks, around gullies and up and down hillsides kept Marcus working from dawn to long after dark. He grew thin and hard, but he did not consider giving up the wagon.

The strain was also telling on Eliza. Weak and weary, bounced and jolted through the desolate, never-ending landscape, she knew she might not live to reach the mission. "He who knows all things, knows whether this debilitated frame will survive," she wrote in her diary. "His will, not mine, be done."

But each step was bringing them closer to their charges. Narcissa and Eliza both worked with the Nez Perce boys, knowing every word of Indian language they could master would soon be needed.

And it was. As they crossed South Pass and turned up the Green toward rendezvous, a mad horde galloped down on the train. With shrieks and howls and bursts of gunfire they rode down one side and up the other. Then they threw themselves from their horses—and now the shaken women could see they were both white and Indian—and rushed to welcome their fellow trappers on the train.

When they caught a glimpse of golden hair, and saw that the men of the train included two unusual figures—skirted, white, and riding sidesaddle—they stopped in shock. Never before had white women come to the mountains.

Narcissa and Eliza had been startled by their greeting party on the trail, but they were overwhelmed at rendezvous. The moment they alighted from their horses they were engulfed by a crowd of chattering Indians. The curious squaws shook their hands and planted hearty kisses on their white sisters. Children crowded closer, fingering their flowing skirts, touching the white skin and the shining hair. It was a warm welcome, and it touched the hearts of Eliza and Narcissa. Here began the mission they had come so far to fulfill.

From rendezvous the party plunged into another two months of rugged travel. The wagon was cut down to a two-wheeled cart before they reached Nat Wyeth's Fort Hall, and finally even that was abandoned on the shores of the Snake River. With it went Narcissa's last precious trunk of possessions. But by September 12 they were safely and thankfully in Fort Vancouver. Two women had survived the journey across the Great American Desert. More would follow.

Whitman and Spalding scouted the country for mission sites, and once again the Flatheads saw the missionaries go to other tribes. The two couples built separate missions (the months of travel had not lessened the strain between them) and began a herculean labor to civilize the Indians and bring them to salvation. Narcissa gave birth to a daughter in March of 1837, and Eliza had a successful pregnancy in the fall.

The following years were filled with hardship and disappointment. The baby Narcissa had conceived along the Platte was drowned in her second year, and Narcissa bore no more children. She worked to teach the Indian children and later adopted a family of seven who had been orphaned on the Oregon Trail. Marcus ministered, doctored, farmed, and enlisted and aided settlers for Oregon for 11 years.

In November of 1847, the Whitman's Cayuse charges rose in superstitious response to an epidemic of measles that was decimating their people. To stop the white man's disease they killed the white man. Narcissa had a frantic hour to nurse her dying husband and pray for her adopted children before she, too, was dragged out into the mud and slaughtered.

Eliza and Henry Spalding had greater success with the amiable Nez Perce, although what the Indians learned of the white God was not exactly what they had expected. Still, it was a life of unceasing labor. Finally worn down past recovery, Eliza died four years after Narcissa. Henry Spalding, who had missed being caught in the Whitman massacre by minutes, in the end proved to be a capable, effective servant of God.

The efforts of all of them, taken together, were instrumental in giving the United States a toe hold on the Pacific coast.

From Mountain Slope to Birnam Wood

*The striking, dark-haired Scottish sportsman who had taken tea
with Narcissa Whitman on the banks of the Platte was not seeking
salvation, riches, or scientific knowledge. What interested Sir
William Drummond Stewart was adventure.*

ASA BATTLES

At 37, with looks and a soul that seemed more French than Scottish, William Drummond Stewart came to the Rockies to hunt buffalo. His itching feet had already carried him to Turkey and Russia in a protracted wandering that sought to recreate the excitement he first felt on the field of Waterloo. Now he was drawn to the American West. The retired army captain gladly left the family castle where he was only a powerless second son, a family scandalized by his unthinkable marriage to a neighbor's serving maid, and the son his marriage had legitimatized.

When he sipped Narcissa's tea in the summer of 1836, he had already spent three years in the mountains, and he had taken them for his own. For the hardships of mountain life provided Stewart with the challenges he sought, and his ability to meet those challenges had made the mountain men grant him equal status—an honor seldom, if ever, granted to European dandies.

He could drink and gamble with the simplest trapper, bait a trap, and face a grizzly, but around the campfire in the evening he might break out with a stanza of poetry, or transfix the trappers with word pictures of ancient cities and strange customs in foreign lands he had traveled. His penchant to romanticize made him see his trapper friends in heroic colors, and he felt no need to patronize. He welcomed the democracy of the frontier, and the trappers responded to his open acceptance.

The year after Narcissa passed up the Platte road, Captain Stewart was again on the trail. But he did not travel with the sparse provisions of the missionaries. He brought wagons loaded with treats for his gourmand appetite: tins of ham, sardines, dried fruits, marmalades, flasks of brandies and fine wines. And, wedged in one corner, an unexplained wooden crate. His outfit also included a heavy Monton rifle, a beautifully formed tomahawk-pipe, and a painter of pictures. For, knowing his time to enjoy the mountains was near an end, Stewart had brought with him a young landscape artist. His commission was to preserve Stewart's beloved West on canvas.

The sad-eyed young artist who found himself whisked from his portrait studio in New Orleans to the wilds of the Platte was named Alfred Jacob Miller. He had learned what it was to scratch for a living as an unestablished artist, but nothing in his 26 years of life in Baltimore and European art schools had prepared him for a painting safari. When he found he was expected to catch and saddle his own horse every morning, unsaddle and picket it every night, plus stand his turn of guard duty, he marched indignantly to Stewart to protest.

Stewart, so trusted by the fur men that he had been placed second in command by brigade leader Tom Fitzpatrick, was organizing the caravan with military precision. He fixed Miller with a haughty glare and assured him each man carried his own weight on the plains—artist or no. He did bend far enough to allow Miller to hire a man to take his guard duty, but the money was to come out of Miller's own pocket. And he must learn to manage his own horses and gear.

Miller had the usual greenhorn's struggle to learn the ways of the trail, but soon the novelty and variety of the new country had him busy at his sketchbook. He pictured the caravan crossing the Kansas River and painted the portrait of a proud Kansas chief, complete with the peace medal he had received from President John Quincy Adams. When a delegation of Oglala Sioux visited farther up the trail, Miller was enthralled, admiring their deerskin clothing, painted shields and magnificent war bonnets. His artist's eye studied their tall, straight bodies. ''Nothing in Greek art can surpass them,'' he wrote in his journal. He longed for sculptors who would come West and duplicate their form and grace in marble.

As they crossed the South Platte and angled northwest, Miller painted the landmarks so familiar to the traders' eyes. He caught the shaft of Chimney Rock against an orange sky, and farther on he interpreted the lonely mass of Scotts Bluff as it loomed dark above the plain. His brush would be the first of many.

Buffalo had been slow to appear this march, and when they finally did, Miller gratefully switched from sage hen to ribs of fat cow. However, Captain Stewart had different plans for some of the calves. He and his half-breed hunter Antoine rode out one morning and returned driving three half-grown calves. The squalling, struggling animals were roped to the back of a wagon until they grew used to being handled. Then Stewart sent them back toward Bellevue, to travel the Missouri, the Mississippi, and the Atlantic, and finally decorate the game enclosures of the Scottish castle.

The nearest thing to any kind of a castle on the plains was Fort Laramie, and the cavalcade reached its shelter in mid-June. Miller was surprised to see framed engravings on Lucien Fontenelle's log walls and to find a small library of classics. While the train refitted he did a watercolor of the shaved-log stockade, the crowded quadrangle, and the Oglala village camped there to trade. Fontenelle wined and dined them in the best mountain tradition, but what tasted best to Miller was the fresh butter and the foaming milk that was dipped up from large crocks.

As they journeyed on west the days were made longer by wind and cold rain. Miller's mood sunk with the weather, and he rode head down, feeling rhuematism in his joints and gloom in his heart. He jumped when Stewart reined in at his side and proceeded to chastise him for his moodiness. "On days of rain I am more exhilarated, if possible, than when the day is clear," scolded the Captain. "There is something to contend against!" With that he galloped off down the column to contend, leaving Miller to wonder if cold feet and soggy blankets were really a cause for celebration.

When they neared Independence Rock, Miller strolled happily off to sketch the strange formation. Out of sight and sound of the train, he sat engrossed in his work. Suddenly a heavy hand forced his head down on his knees. Indians!

Helpless, he waited for the stroke of the tomahawk. It didn't come. At last the pressure was released and he looked up into the stern face of Captain Stewart, who gave him a now unneeded lecture on his carelessness. The hand could just as well have been Indian, and one could not expect special dispensation just because he was an artist.

While Stewart hunted mountain sheep and rounded up more buffalo, this time full grown, to ship to Scotland, Miller added scene on scene to his portfolio. During the day he sketched in pencil or ink, adding color when the train stopped for the night and he could work with greater leisure.

But his greatest inspiration was to come at rendezvous. Here, spread out along the Green River, were the fascinating components of an ever-changing composition. Smoke of campfires softened the green of the river grass and blurred the poles of the distant lodges, before losing itself among the grazing horse herds. Movement was everywhere.

Miller saw trappers of every size, shape and nationality, Indian maidens, bronzed warriors, tepees and travois, papooses and patriarchs of the tribes. He saw card games and wrestling matches, marksmanship contests, horse races, and the consuming struggle to empty all the whiskey kegs. The missionary eyes of the year before had

ASA BATTLES

seen rendezvous as a bacchanal, but Miller's eyes judged color tones rather than morals. He was enthralled.

The next day the Snake contingent arrived and saluted Stewart with a great parade. Miller sketched frantically to catch the galloping horses, the magnificent braves, the feathered lances, the grotesque medicine men, and the following crowd of squaws, children, dogs, and travois. He could not have dreamed of a more colorful spectacle for his canvas.

After the excitement calmed, Captain Stewart summoned his trapper friends to meet before his tent. As they gathered—Kit Carson, Joe Walker, Black Harris, Jim Bridger, Fitzpatrick, Fontenelle and others—Stewart's men unloaded the heavy wooden crate that had remained in the corner of the wagon since Independence. It had raised several bumps of curiosity, but it had not been opened or explained.

With a flourish, Stewart pried open the lid and lifted out the shirt of armor and helmet that were the uniform of the British Life Guards. Then he presented the shining metal cuirass and the plumed helmet to an astonished Jim Bridger.

Whatever the joke that had prompted Stewart to transport a suit of armor from Scotland to the Rocky Mountains, it proved he had the true spirit of a mountain man. Anyone who could make Jim Bridger even temporarily speechless had scored a real coup. Gamely Bridger buckled on the heavy cuirass, put on the plumed helmet, and struck a noble attitude for Miller's brush.

The Indians often crowded around to watch Miller work, and most admired his paintings, but one chief wanted to try his own skill. He asked to borrow Miller's paints and a brush. With the stick end of the brush (Miller did not presume to correct him), he illustrated one of his coups— representing his enemies as midgets before his strength, with 15 arrows to show how many he had bested. Then he presented the painting to Miller, and the Romantic treasured a true primitive.

When rendezvous had run its course, Stewart took Miller on a hunting sojourn in the Wind River Mountains. There the painter survived fording streams (he could not swim) and painting buffalo stunned for his use by the hunter (he learned to make a fast retreat when the beast revived). Then the party returned to the States, bearing with them what would be the only illus-

trations ever made on location of the short-lived fur trade.

In 1839 Stewart's brother died and he learned he was now Lord of Murthly and Grandtully Castles. He had to return to Scotland, but he did his best to take the mountains with him. He gathered red birds, cranes, a grizzly, and buffalo; grass seed, plants, blue spruce, and hemlock; gourds, wild currants, gooseberries, and two Indians. He took his hunter Antoine with him and made arrangements for Miller to follow. Miller did, and he spent a year in the lordly grandeur of the gloomy castle, reproducing his sensitive watercolors in heavy oils.

In the next few years, with Miller's oils decorating the walls, with buffalo robes and buffalo chairs, with a velvet-clad Antoine to serve his wants, Stewart tried to transform Murthly Castle into the American West. The saplings were given ground beside a giant oak and sycamore, and so trees from the Rockies gave new growth to the ancient Birnam Wood.

Stewart made a last, incredibly sumptuous trip to the Rockies in 1843, and then returned to Scotland forever. He tried to recreate his mountain days in two novels, but he was a sportsman, not a writer; he could not transmit the richness of his experiences to paper. Ten years after his death in 1871, the last buffalo in his reserve broke loose and charged a mail coach. One of the passengers fired his rifle, and the final link between the Lord of Murthly Castle and the reaches of the American wilderness fell heavily in the road.

Alfred Jacob Miller's Western paintings gained him a highly praised one-man show and an invitation to the White House. With a reputation as a painter of Indians, he spent his life as a reasonably successful artist. He kept his watercolor sketches of the West in drawers in his Baltimore studio, referring to them now and then for detail when someone wanted him to paint an Indian.

After Miller's death in 1874, his notes and sketches passed to his descendants. They were rediscovered in a Baltimore museum in 1935 and recognized as a unique and valuable record of the trapping life of 100 years before. It was a romantic period of American history, and Miller was the only illustrator who viewed it first-hand. His collection, from pencil sketch to luminescent watercolor, lets us experience life along the Platte when it was still wild and free.

The Sinners

ASA BATTLES

When William Stewart wended his way up the Platte with his artist
in residence in 1837, he had trod a charmed path. For to the north
another presence was making itself felt. A terrible presence that had
traveled up the Missouri in a steamboat, making fateful stops along
the river bank, and then washed out across the plains. It would
change the valley of the Platte and the whole northern plains as no
white man had been able. It killed without bullets, demoralized
without whiskey, wiped out traditions and bloodlines without blue
beads and empty promises. It would destroy the Arikara, decimate
the Mandans, humble the Blackfeet, and quiet the Sioux. It was
smallpox.

The Skidi Pawnee set off on their winter buffalo hunt in 1837 with high spirits. Though they counted the villages along the Loup as home, they spent only spring and fall months there—just long enough to plant and tend their crops in spring, to enjoy the harvest in the fall. Between they roamed the plains, hunting buffalo, indulging in their favorite sports and stealing horses from the southern tribes.

In early years the Pawnee had had the Platte largely to themselves, but now the Sioux had moved in, frequenting the new Fort Laramie and contesting with the Pawnees for buffalo at the forks of the Platte. The horses the Pawnees stole in the south were regularly lost to Sioux raiders— as were numerous Pawnee scalps. The Pawnees had learned to fear their lightning raids on their villages and hunting camps, but, heedless of this, the column marched enveloped in its usual bedlam.

There were horses by the hundreds, whinnying, kicking, and raising dust; mules braying; dogs yelping and howling; children crying, screaming and yelling; braves shouting, laughing, and chanting songs of the hunt; and over it all the women shrilling orders. The roar of their coming could be heard for miles across the brown prairie.

In spite of their racket they eventually found buffalo. They set up camp and turned to the priests, who had to confirm that the omens were right for a good hunt. Sometimes they waited for days, until the priests were able to declare the gods were in the proper humor. Then the chiefs and priests led out a column of hunters and the chase was on.

They had only begun the hunt on a frosty February morning, when a party of Pawnees discovered different game. They stumbled on the small camp of an Oglala Sioux chief. Delighted to find their enemy in a vulnerable position, they charged through the lodges, killing the chief and most of the men. Then they rounded up the women and children and triumphantly marched their prisoners back to camp.

They were not greeted with the celebration they expected. Though victories over the Sioux were hard to come by, the chiefs were alarmed rather than gratified. They knew the Sioux would strike back. Quickly they broke camp, abandoned the hunt with the meat sacks still empty, and returned to their village on the Loup. There they faced a hungry winter, watching fearfully for the expected revenge of the Sioux.

But it was their helpless prisoners who did the damage. One by one the Oglala women and children broke out with smallpox. Soon there were only three or four alive out of 20. Then the Pawnees began to go down, and the virulent strain that had depopulated the Missouri banks worked its way along the Platte.

As two earlier epidemics had partially immunized the older people, most of this year's victims were children. Their small bodies swelled. They burned with fever. Their skin erupted in ugly pustules. They ached, vomited, babbled in delirium, turned black and died, one after another, until there was wailing in every lodge and the village stank with death.

The priests did what they could. They fasted. They sang. They danced. They invoked the spirits with their medicine bundles. But still the death song rose over the village until nearly every child was dead.

When the other Pawnee tribes returned from their hunt in the south, they, too, fell victim. News of the scourge reached Bellevue and missionary Samuel Allis. After coming out with Samuel Parker in 1834, Allis had spent three years trying to minister to the Pawnees, and he hurried out to help. He worked through the stinking lodges with vaccine, succeeding where Edwin James had failed, persuading them to undergo vaccination. Gradually the epidemic waned, and Allis returned to Bellevue.

The Pawnees were left to accept their loss. Some 2,000 of their people were dead, and the lodges were empty of children under 13.

The Skidis—always the most religious of the tribes—stunned and heartsick over the loss of their children, decided they must have sinned terribly to have brought on such a terrible punishment. It had been many years since they had placated their god, the Morning Star, in the ancient way, and they had paid the penalty. The priests called a council of 80 of the wisest men, and after consultation with the spirits, they determined to perform the ceremony of propitiation of the Morning Star.

Among their prisoners was a 14-year-old Oglala girl named Haxti. As the spring sun began to warm the prairie, Haxti was given special privileges. She was separated from the prisoners who had to work. She was no longer beaten and abused. She

was provided with ample food and given to understand she could look forward to a feast day soon.

Then the priests entered on a week of prescribed ceremonies, each detailed and intricate and done with painful exactness. Every fast, every dance, every chant had to be done on a level of perfection that would please the gods. Buffalo heads were dissected for augury. The sacred pipe was smoked. The spirits of the feathers, skins, and bones in the medicine bundle were glorified and supplicated. At last, on April 22, everything was in readiness.

Haxti was sent around the village to collect wood from each lodge. Then, at dusk, she was adorned with an eagle headdress and led to the site of the ceremony.

Only when she saw the wooden scaffold and the fire below did she realize her fate. Quickly she was tied to the two upright posts and stripped of her finery. Her body was painted half red and half black, and as the stars began to shine in the night sky the ceremonies of sacrifice began.

Led by the priests, chanting and dancing, boys shot joint grass into her body, until hundreds of small spikes stabbed, stuck, and began to burn. The fire below flared higher, the dancers' frenzy mounted, and the chants became wild yelling that almost drowned out the screams of the victim. At last the gods were served, and the chief of sacrifice put an arrow through Haxti's heart.

He cut out the heart and burned it, so that the tribe's tools of war, hunting, and farming might be passed through its magic smoke. Her body was cut into chunks that fed the village dogs, but her skeleton was left hanging, so that the Morning Star would have a lasting reminder of their veneration.

So did the Skidi Pawnee atone for the sins that had cost them the lives of their children. The expressions of grief of the other Pawnee tribes were not so dramatic, but the whole Pawnee people had lost most of a generation, and such a loss could never be recovered.

A Robe of Black

Frightened at the diminution of their people, the Pawnee chiefs went to Belle-vue in 1839 and asked for the help that had been promised them in an 1833 treaty. They said they were ready to settle down and farm, if the government would provide teachers and protection from the Sioux. Samuel Allis and the Reverend Dunbar went out to choose a site for the mission. While the Pawnees preferred a site south of the Platte as protection against the Sioux, the government preferred a site north of the Platte well away from the Platte River road. The site chosen was north of the Platte.

Samuel Allis plowed up some land and invited the Pawnees to join him in farming. But it was time for the summer hunt, and while the Pawnees liked and admired Samuel Allis, they had more important things to do.

While Allis sat in disappointment in an an empty village, a man with a different philosophy toward Indians turned his footsteps up the Platte.

n his younger days he had been known as Samson, and he still retained the strength the nickname implied, though his agility was somewhat restricted by the 200 pounds he carried on his 5-foot 7-inch frame. The long black robe that whipped around his ankles only accented the rotundness of his figure, and his cheerful, open face topped the roundness of his presence with yet another circle. He was Belgian by birth, a Jesuit by conviction, and a missionary to the American Indians by personal desire.

Father Pierre-Jean DeSmet had spent the 1820s and '30s in St. Louis, teaching languages, history and philosophy at the Jesuit St. Louis University. But he had longed from the beginning to be out in the field working with the natives. The year after the plague of smallpox, he was finally allowed to establish a mission for the Potawatomies near the mouth of the Platte, and he settled in to work among these Indians, learning their natures and their problems.

In the fall of 1839, two emissaries from the Flatheads appeared at his mission door. They were still seeking a teacher who would help them learn about the white man's God. They had been disappointed several times. Was there a Black Robe who would go over the mountains and minister to their people?

There was indeed. Father DeSmet immediately volunteered. He convinced the hierarchy of the church that this mission field should be investigated and that he was the one who should do it. On April 30, 1840 the energetic priest joined the annual caravan of the American Fur Company — still the best and only way to go West — and took the road toward the Platte.

Delighted to have finally begun the work he had sought so long, Father DeSmet jogged happily along, admiring the richness of the spring prairie. If the trappers were at first a little put off by another holy man, they soon responded to Father DeSmet's congenial nature. He loved a joke and they learned to recognize the robust laugh that carried back along the column. His joy in life was contagious.

But they were only six days out when he was struck with a malarial fever. The company men, sincerely concerned for his welfare, urged him to return to the settlements.

He refused. The Flatheads would be expecting to meet him at rendezvous. He would not disappoint them. And he had waited too long for his mission. If he turned back now there might never be another chance.

Alternately shaking with chills and burning with fever, he followed the caravan, sitting his horse when he could, lying in a cart when he was too weak to ride. There he jolted about on the wooden crates, sliding from one end to the other, as the wagon tipped down one side of the ravines and tilted up the other. Sweating, shivering, with nothing to drink but warm, stagnant, dirty water, Father DeSmet began his mission to the Flatheads.

But even illness couldn't keep his bouyant spirits down for long. The fevers continued to strike intermittently, but Father DeSmet took advantage of his good days to record his impressions of the country. He was charmed by the Platte and its wooded islands, which reminded him of the ponds of European estates. He likened the islands to fleets under sail, draped with green and studded with flowers. The valley of waving grass, cut by the winding river, and shadowed here and there by clouds, struck him as a scene ''fresh from the hands of the Creator.''

But the practical side of Father DeSmet was never long buried, and he also noted that, as the river was 6,000 feet wide but only three to five feet deep, ''This want of proportion destroys its utility.''

Other sights along the Platte drew his interest. In one place the whole plain was covered with circles of buffalo skulls and painted bones—a sign both Pawnees and buffalo must be near. Soon they were passing the burial huts of Pawnee warriors, where each fallen brave sat amid the dried meat, tobacco, lead, powder, gun, bow, and arrows that would provide for him on his journey to the land of souls.

One morning Father DeSmet rose early and left camp alone. He worked his way cautiously through a ravine and then began climbing a high bluff. Panting, he pulled himself carefully to the top. There, spread below him, was what he had come to see. For perhaps 12 miles around the plain was covered with buffalo.

Some moved majestically in single-file, others cropped the dew-covered grasses. Still others, whole bands, lay quietly, not yet ready to start the day. It was a scene of peace and contentment that moved the heart of Father DeSmet, and for an hour or more he sat watching the shifting patterns as shaggy brown forms drifted over the green valley.

ASA BATTLES

Suddenly a wave of excitement swept the herd. Heads lifted. Animals clambered to their feet. To the east one cow started to run, and the whole herd was in instant motion. In the dust and din of the running herd, Father DeSmet could pick out the hunters of his train. Smoke from their guns puffed to the right and left as they rode with the herd, until the mass of animals disappeared in the distance, and only the dark forms of the fallen few dotted the prairie.

Dejected, Father DeSmet scrambled down from his perch and accompanied the hunters back to camp. He was as tired as anyone of their salt pork rations, but he winced when he thought of his peaceful prairie, now blemished with the butchered carcasses. That night he woke to a cacophony of howls and barks, raised by the wolves as they feasted on the remains of the slaughter.

As they continued up the Platte, Father DeSmet pondered the future of the desert. There were some places, he thought, along the rivers, where farming could succeed, and some areas where herds could graze, but most of it would be merely a barrier between civilization and barbarism. He feared a new race of people might arise, a blend of savages and adventurers who would use the vastness of the desert as a theater for robbery and pillage.

After they crossed the South Platte, the buttes and bluffs that lined the trail up the North Platte were a source of fascination. Father DeSmet compared them to towers, castles, and fortified cities. He was drawn to the Chimney—though he deplored the lack of romance in the name and thought it more nearly resembled an inverted funnel. Noting a large crack near the top, he expected it would weather away and in a few years be nothing but a little heap on the plain.

At Fort Laramie a village of Cheyennes was camped for trade, and Father DeSmet joined them in a feast. Then it was on to the rendezvous and the scheduled meeting with the Flathead delegation.

The Flatheads could scarcely believe their quest was to be answered at last, and they took Father DeSmet to their hearts. He wept with joy at his reception. Then, still suffering attacks of fever, he journeyed north to spend the summer with the main tribe.

Finding their desire for missionaries deep and sincere, and still unanswered by the Protestants, he set out for the States, promising to bring out a larger party the next year. With only a single companion much of the way, he reached the Missouri, descended it, and arrived back in St. Louis the last day of 1840. He had less than four months if he were to finance and recruit a party for the Flathead mission in time to join the spring caravan of the American Fur Company.

Wagons Roll From Sapling Grove

    The trouble was, there would be no spring caravan of the American Fur Company. The past five years had seen a steady diminishing of returns from the mountain trade, as beaver were driven toward extinction, and pelts demanded less cash on the open market. The enterprise which had opened and mapped the West, and incidentally provided convenient transport for so many of a westering society, would move out no more for rendezvous by a mountain stream. If men wanted to go West, they would have to find another way.

There were those who would go. In the spring of 1841 a group of 69 men, women and children perched in indecision at Sapling Grove, Missouri, just west of Independence. They knew only that California lay to the west. Not one in the group had ever been beyond the settlements. Not one knew even an approximate route. Not one knew just where it was he wanted to go. Not one had had the foresight to engage a guide.

John Bidwell, a 22-year-old teacher, was the sole representative of the 500 member Western Emigration Society that had ballooned during the winter, when it was easy to take the road to California and still remain beside a cozy fire in Missouri. But by spring rumors of Indian raids, the hostility of California's Spanish government, and the reality of actually pulling up roots had caused more than a few second thoughts.

Only John Bidwell had persevered. Scraping together all he had saved from his various teaching assignments, he bought a wagon, an old flintlock, and provisions. He had nothing left for horses.

John was stymied until a semi-invalid from Illinois appeared with a horse, $15, and a desire to go West for his health. John persuaded him to trade the horse for a yoke of steers and a one-eyed mule. Together they set out for the established meeting place at Sapling Grove.

One wagon awaited them. Another trickled in from Arkansas. Then the Kelsey clan arrived from Kentucky: Benjamin and Sam with their wives, children, two bachelor brothers, and their sister-in-law, the Widow Gray. John Bartleson came in with another young teacher named Nicholas Dawson, and seven more Missourians. A cultured gentlemen calling himself Talbot Green arrived hurriedly from Pennsylvania—a pleasant-enough man, but one who seemed unduly concerned for the safety of a box of lead he carried with him. Each day added one or two more until their numbers totaled 69.

Their assets totaled scarcely more. The whole group could not put together $100 cash. Nicholas Dawson jingled seventy-five cents in his pocket after he purchased an old mule and a share in Bartleson's wagon. They had assorted wagons, 14 covered; some carts, oxen, horses, and their determination to go West. If only they knew the way.

As they teetered on the edge of the wilderness one morning, about to begin their journey—guide or no—word came that a missionary party was on its way. And with the party was a mountain man named Broken Hand Fitzpatrick, who was serving as a guide.

Immediately the train was embroiled in argument. Should they leave as planned, or wait for the missionary party? Some scorned waiting, sure the missionaries would only slow their travel. But some had to admit a guide might come in handy. After a flurry of independent speeches, they sobered down and waited. The next day a portly Jesuit priest and the dozen men of his party pulled into the grove.

Father DeSmet had had his own problems putting together the two priests, three laymen and assorted engagés who would carry his mission to the Flatheads. He had personally raised the funds that made the mission possible, and then seen most of their supplies burned in a steamboat fire. Next he discovered the fur train wasn't going out, and the priests had spent three days in the abandoned cabin of a dead Indian at Westport—their whole mission in the balance—before he was able to engage Fitzpatrick.

Tom Fitzpatrick must have been reluctant to escort so small a party, but times were thin in the fur business and a man had to take what came along. Now 42, Tom was old in experience on the plains, and his crippled hand, damaged by an exploding gun, gave him the colorful name of Broken Hand, which only enhanced his standing as a mountain man.

In a short time Fitzpatrick had the train organized and ready for the road. The emigrants had elected the pleasant Talbot Green president, and the unpleasant John Bartleson captain—when he threatened to take his wagons and go home if not so honored. But even that quarrelsome Missourian hesitated to argue with Broken Hand Fitzpatrick. Soon they were on the road, with the missionaries in the lead and the would-be settlers stretched out behind.

John Bidwell was immediately charmed by Father DeSmet. He thought him a genial and saintly man and was amazed that nothing seemed to disturb his temper. No matter that his carts overturned in river crossings, that their fireless camps meant cold suppers, that the May days meant chilling rains and muddy trail, Father DeSmet remained optimistic and cheerful.

But Bidwell didn't quite know what to make of another optimistic man of God who overtook the train four days beyond the Kansas River crossing. He was the Reverend Joseph Williams, a Methodist preacher, and in the tradition of Samuel Parker, he had ridden out alone and unarmed, trusting his life to Providence until he caught up with the train. A white-haired 64, he wanted to preach to the Indians and see the country, and he intended to do both.

Father DeSmet gave him a warm welcome, but Tom Fitzpatrick must have expressed his impatience with people who wandered the desert unprotected, for Reverend Williams put him down as a "wicked, wordly man, opposed to missionaries."

As the train moved toward the Platte, its members shook down to life on the trail as a moving society. John Bidwell and the other young teacher, Nicholas Dawson, did not see much of each other because Dawson was a Bartleson man and thus of a different faction. Father DeSmet and his fellow priests enjoyed the company of Tom Fitzpatrick and spent much time in philosophical arguments with the Reverend Williams. Williams traveled in a state of shock at the wickedness of the company and freely prophesied the sinners would receive their just reward.

Benjamin Kelsey's wife, 17-year-old Nancy Kelsey, was kept busy watching her two-year-old daughter Ann. But Benjamin's brother Isaiah turned his attentions to the daughter of the Richard Williams family. By the time they reached the Platte, he had proposed and been accepted. On June 1 the Reverend Joseph Williams performed the ceremony, and the banks of the Platte saw their first June bride.

One afternoon as the wagons creaked slowly up the road, the figure of a man appeared from the hills to the south. He was on foot, running for his life, arms waving wildly, shouting something no one could quite make out. As he came closer the train could see it was Nicholas Dawson, without gun and in his underwear. Suddenly they could all understand his cries. "Indians! Indians!"

The word spread like fire through the train and in an instant every man was whipping his animals to a gallop. Gasping with exhaustion Dawson barely managed to swing aboard a wagon before the whole train was off on a wild race down the valley. Thrown from one side to the other in the careening wagon, Nancy Kelsey clung to her baby, sure the long-dreaded Indian attack had come.

Vainly Tom Fitzpatrick tried to stop the panic.

ASA BATTLES

He could not be heard, let alone heeded, in the mad scramble. He spurred his horse ahead of the dashing train, and as each wagon reached a bend in the Platte, he pulled it into a protective square. Then, while horses blew and shaky-legged men stared behind them at an empty prairie, Fitzpatrick had a talk with Nicholas Dawson.

It seemed he had been off chasing antelope when he was startled by a yell, and Indians rose from the very grass around him. He had tried to run, but they caught him easily, took his gun, his mule, and most of his clothing. Then he had managed to break away and run for the train. There were hundreds—even thousands—of Indians out there, and the train was sure to be slaughtered.

Fitzpatrick tried to quiet his hysteria and reassure the members of the train. They herded the animals inside the square and prepared to defend themselves.

Presently Indians did appear. About 40 Cheyennes rode up and pitched their tepees nearby. Fitzpatrick went out to parley. The Cheyennes told him they didn't mean to hurt Dawson, but he became so terrified on seeing them that they had had to take his gun to keep from being shot. Why his mule and his clothes were threatening they didn't explain.

Fitzpatrick didn't ask. He was well aware of the Indian sense of humor, and also aware that Dawson would now be dead if they meant any serious

47

harm. He bargained for the return of the mule and gun, and returned with them toward the train.

Dawson, recovered from fear and now burning with anger, met him. He snatched his gun and vowed to shoot the Indians who had caused his humiliation. Fitzpatrick grabbed his arm and forced him back to the wagons. Then he told him, in his more than adequate Irish vocabulary, that he was lucky to get off alive.

Dawson cooled down. But he was not allowed to forget the incident. From then on he was known as Cheyenne Dawson.

The excitement of the Indian scare had barely subsided when a larger danger threatened. For two or three days the heat had been building, wave on shimmering wave, as the sun beat down on the valley floor. When clouds began to gather on the horizon, the train looked forward to a cooling shower. But these were not gentle rain clouds. They roiled and billowed, piling white towers above the plain. The air grew still and heavy, and the sky took on a sickly greenish cast. Then a wind swept across the prairie, fresh and strong and incredibly cold.

The first drops were huge, splatting down on the wagon tops, kicking up dust along the trail, sending Nancy Kelsey and her sister-in-law on the run for the wagon. Then the storm began. Rain poured down in sheets, quickly flooding the rutted trail, blinding both horses and riders. A few white balls rippled the puddles, and then there was a roar as the air was filled with hailstones. They pelted the mules, beat noisily on the open wagons, drove through the canvas tops of the others. The train milled in confusion as men fought to control their animals. Hailstones as big as turkey eggs rained down until hail was piled four inches deep.

Just as the hail was abating, the pummeled party heard an incredible roar. Behind them the clouds swirled and gyrated, and suddenly dipped into a funnel.

Transfixed they watched it approach the Platte. Trees were uprooted, splintered and scattered before their eyes. Wind tore at the wagons, and they rushed to brace them against its force, though whether they were holding the wagons or the wagons them, they couldn't have said.

Scarcely a quarter mile behind them, the funnel moved north across the Platte, sucking its waters into the vortex until it was a giant waterspout. Once across the river the tornado skipped and jumped to the north, dropped its burden of river water, and disappeared back into the sky.

The dazed travelers nursed their bruises, wrung out their sodden clothing, and limped on their way. Father DeSmet had seen his idyllic Platte in a different mood, and the Reverend Williams was quietly thankful that God had seen fit to withhold his just punishment of the wicked. The emigrants walked quietly, with a new sense of awe for the task they had undertaken, the country they had set out to conquer.

Now they came to the sea of buffalo that surrounded the forks of the Platte. John Bidwell and all the men had their fill of hunting, and left unused meat rotting on the ground. But they were not the first to slaughter buffalo here, and Bidwell noted that the valley was so full of bones that ''if they continue to decrease in the same ratio they will be extinct before long.''

That time had not yet come. By day they wound through endless herds, and one night a stampede threatened to pound them all into the ground. They were saved when Fitzpatrick led out riflemen who kept up a fire that turned the vast river of animals aside. Their pounding hooves shook the ground until the wagons trembled, and little Ann Kelsey screamed with fright in her mother's arms. It was nearly dawn before the last of the herd charged by and quiet returned to the plain.

On June 9 they crossed the South Platte (near present-day Brule, Nebraska). Tight-lipped men drove their wagons into a swift current that pushed them relentlessly downstream. But the mules and oxen were able to keep their feet and all crossed safely. Father DeSmet felt sorry for the various dogs of the train, left sitting forlornly on the far shore. They whined and howled their misery until, one by one, they found the courage to swim across and join the train.

Four days later tragedy struck. As young George Shotwell pulled his rifle from a wagon, it discharged. The shot struck him full in the chest, and there was nothing anyone could do but try to comfort him until he died. They buried him beside the trail west of Ash Hollow, and Reverend Williams read the words over his grave. As Nancy Kelsey watched the grave fill with foreign-looking yellow clay, she thought of George's mother in Kentucky, who had begged her son not to go West. Depressed and upset, the emigrants pushed on, only to spend the next day huddled in their wagons, as it was too wet and muddy to travel.

On June 22 they rolled into Fort Laramie. It was still cold and a brisk wind raked the meadow grass. Joseph Williams tried to preach, but no one would listen. George Shotwell's belongings were sold at auction. One emigrant looked down the rocky road that led on west and decided he had had enough. The wagons moved out June 24 without him.

As they followed the course of the Platte north to skirt the blue-shadowed hills west of Laramie, Nancy Kelsey began to realize the first six weeks had been the easiest. Now the trail was cut by gullies and blocked by bluffs. The river disappeared in a brown-walled canyon, and they had to work their way over the highlands. The gray-toned sage bushes increased in size and numbers, scraping against the wagons as they passed, tearing at the women's skirts and the men's already-worn breeches.

When they reached the North Platte crossing, even Father DeSmet blanched at the current they had to enter. Snow-melt from the Rockies swelled the river to a nearly impassable barrier. Tom Fitzpatrick needed all his skills to prevent the crossing from turning into disaster. Wagon teams had to be forced into the torrent, and once in, driven mercilessly for the far shore.

The largest wagon was too much for the animals' strength, and it washed downstream for several

heart-stopping minutes before the animals' hooves found bottom. Scrambling mightily, they were able to pull it ashore. Another overturned, mules and harness in a gigantic tangle that threatened to drown both the animals and the men who struggled to help. John Bartleson stood on the bank, arms raised, crying for help, while others dove in to save the team.

Father DeSmet hung back in fear until he saw a hunter lead a horse carrying his one-year-old daughter into the river. Then, shamed at his lack of courage, he forced his horse into the water. He arrived, dripping but safe, on the far side, and he laughed to see a brother priest also emerge, plastered to the neck of his mount as if the two would never again be separate entities.

When it was all over the train had lost only one mule to the waters of the North Platte.

With July heat baking the desert it did not take long for everyone to dry out. They angled briefly southwest along the Platte until the main channel turned south toward the mountains, then crossed an alkali flat to reach the tributory Sweetwater which would lead them west. Near its mouth they stopped to examine Independence Rock and spent the morning of July 6 adding their names to those of the trappers, explorers and missionaries who had gone before.

Two days later John Bidwell saw the white peaks of the Wind River Mountains rise to the north. He had never before seen snow in the summer, and as he slogged through the alkali dust, the thought of the cool snowfields played on his mind. He also was startled to see unmistakable wagon tracks through South Pass, and he credited them to trapper Bill Sublette, unmindful that wheels of Hiram Scott, Jedediah Smith, Marcus Whitman, William Stewart, and others had helped to mark the trail.

As July drew to a close they reached the Green River, participated in a miniature rendezvous (Bartleson provided the whiskey, for a price), and saw the Widow Gray married to a trapper from Fort Laramie. Three more men turned back for the States. And on August 1 Nancy Kelsey celebrated her eighteenth birthday.

But the train was near a parting of the ways. Who was for Oregon? Who was for California? Even the Kelsey family was split as to which was the better destination. But the decision could be put off no longer. At Soda Springs, a lovely and final oasis, the train divided.

Tom Fitzpatrick was leading Father DeSmet north to Flathead country and thus toward Oregon. Thirty-two chose this relative safety. Bidwell and Bartleson were both for California, and 30 others would join them—28 men, Nancy Kelsey, and little Ann.

The Oregon group reached its destination safely, but the Bidwell-Bartleson party was to suffer a harrowing ordeal. With no map and no guide they struggled west from the Great Salt Lake. Driving wagons through the sand was impossible, and the exhausted party abandoned them, packing what they could on their starving animals.

For weeks they wandered, eating first coyotes and then their own mules. They argued, separated, came together again. Finally they reached the base of the Sierras and the Walker River, which might or might not take them through. It was mid-October. Should they risk freezing in the mountains or turn back and face starvation? They decided to move on up the narrow, twisting canyon by a margin of one vote.

For two weeks they drove themselves on through the rugged mountains. Cheyenne Dawson was ready to sit down and freeze to death when he looked back and saw the barefoot Nancy Kelsey carrying her daughter through the snow. He kept going. Somehow they all kept going. On October 18 they crossed the summit of the Sierras, and on November 4, 1841 the San Joaquin Valley lay before them. The road they had taken in May up the Platte was now a California Trail.

John Bidwell stayed in California and became a substantial citizen, serving in the 39th Congress and running for President on the Prohibition ticket in 1892. Nicholas "Cheyenne" Dawson spent three years in California before leaving for Mexico, New Orleans, and finally settling in Texas. Talbot Green—the gentleman who had carefully guarded the box of "lead"—set himself up with the money he had embezzled from a bank back in Pennsylvania.

The Reverend Joseph Williams completed his tour of the wilderness, preaching where he was welcome and where he was not. He returned safely to the settlements the following year, having "tried to bear testimony to the name of Jesus in the mountains, on the plains, on the hills and in the valleys, wherever sinners were to be found."

Father DeSmet spent much of the next five years in the northwest establishing missions. He cultivated the Indians' souls, but he did not force them to cultivate the land. The Flatheads had found their teacher, and in the years to come Father DeSmet's black robe was loved and honored by all the Plains tribes.

Nancy Kelsey continued to follow her wandering husband; to Oregon, to Mexico, and to Texas, where one of her daughters was scalped by Indians but survived. Eventually they returned to California. When interviewed in her later years, she remarked, "I always thought it easier to go along than to have to stay home and worry about him." Thus the first white woman crossed the Sierras to enter California.

A Strange Creature

He brought back the most accurate and complete knowledge of the Oregon Trail the country had ever known. And, with his literary flair and Jessie's assistance, he produced a report of his journey that flowed with his enthusiasm for the West. It was widely read and did much to counteract the stigma of the Great American Desert.

ASA BATTLES

The day after Nancy Kelsey limped over the summit of the Sierras, a secret wedding took place in a Washington, D.C. hotel. The groom was only moderate in height, with dark, curling hair and a prominent nose, but there was an energy in his bearing that demanded attention. At 28, nothing about him suggested that he was the illegitimate product of an affair that had scandalized southern society and forced his mother to raise him in conditions of poverty.

The 17-year-old bride was also poised. Poise came naturally to the beautiful daughter of an important United States Senator. But here, too, there was something more. There was a bright intelligence, and a will that would defy her father's wishes and make her the bride of Lt. John C. Fremont. For Jessie Benton's father had expressly forbidden this marriage, and it would be some weeks before the young couple faced the Senator with their news.

When they did Senator Benton raged and blustered, but there was nothing more he could do. Jessie brought her husband home, and by the New Year the two men had discovered they shared a common ambition.

Senator Thomas Hart Benton had long pushed for western expansion, and he felt the time was ripe for an accurate, scientific report on the natural route up the Platte to Oregon. John C. Fremont, a second lieutenant in the Topographical Corps, had spent several years in study and exploration with the noted Joseph Nicolas Nicollet, and he was ready for a challenging assignment. Exploration suited his active nature as nothing else could, and he quickly caught Benton's enthusiasm for opening the West. Jessie Fremont had supreme confidence in her new husband's abilities, and she cheerfully prepared to send him off to make his mark in the wilderness.

But before Fremont left Washington, an inventor appeared at the door of the Benton home with a large crate. An excited Fremont helped him carry it into the gallery adjoining the dining room, where they unpacked the contents — what appeared to be yards and yards of Indian rubber, shaped into an oblong form.

It was a boat, or would be when its air-tight compartments were inflated. John Fremont had conceived the idea and ordered it made. He intended to use it to cross and explore the western rivers.

Jessie admired his inventiveness, but as the stench of the rubber's chemicals filled the house, she quickly banished the boat to the stables to await the day of departure. On May 2, 1842, John Fremont, Jessie's 12-year-old brother Randolph, and the rubber boat left on their journey to the West.

When they pushed off from the Missouri River six weeks later, Fremont felt his expedition was "like a ship leaving the shore." With him in addition to Randolph were the frizzle-haired Charles Preuss, a German topographer; Henry Brant, 19, a family friend; 21 Canadian voyageurs; and mountain man and guide Kit Carson.

John Fremont took naturally to the open prairie and life on the trail, but topographer Charles Preuss had a different reaction. He was 10 years older than Fremont and he felt every year. He found the food bad, the bed "damned hard," the camp disordered, the cook dirty and the eternal prairie grasses as interesting "as a book

with blank pages." He couldn't stomach the fresh meat he was expected to eat, and he was kept awake at night by owls with their "disgusting hooting." Horseback riding made him stiff and sore. He thought Fremont a fool for his persistent optimism, and he wished fervently that he were back in Washington with his wife and small daughter.

But they were a long way from Washington. In four days they reached the ford of the Kansas River, and Fremont had a chance to try his invention. He had his eight carts unloaded and dismantled, and placed wheels, body and load of one cart and three men with paddles into the 20 x 5-foot boat. They shoved off into the current. At first they made no progress with the unmanageable load, but after one man took a line in his teeth and swam across they were able to draw six loads over without incident.

The passage had used up the afternoon, however, and it was getting dark. Anxious to have everything across before nightfall, Fremont impulsively ordered both remaining carts put on the boat for a final crossing. For a moment the heavy load lunged in the current. Then the boat was bottom up, and barrels, boxes, carts, and bales were sailing down the river. From both shores men jumped in to save their provisions. They lost part of their sugar, most of their coffee, and two non-swimmers nearly lost their lives.

As they neared the Platte, Fremont noted elk, antelope, deer, and turkey. Charles Preuss noted mosquitoes, mosquitoes, and more mosquitoes. He longed for some congenial companions, "Germans, of course," and would have sold his soul for a good bottle of wine to ease his miseries.

Fremont seemed to have no miseries. He took pleasure in his exacting scientific studies, often spending half the night in the astronomical observations necessary to determine place, distance, and direction. But he was always up and eager to get on the way the next morning, and he managed the voyageurs, the route, and the whole responsibility of the train with such cheerful energy that Preuss became tired and depressed just from watching.

Shortly after they reached the coast of the Platte, three Indians approached their camp. They were Cheyennes, returning home from a fruitless raid on the Pawnees, and one boy was about Randolph's age. The braves asked if they could travel with the whites for protection. John

Fremont quickly agreed, and before long Randolph and the Cheyenne youth were squatting side by side for their salt pork supper. While Randolph chewed with resignation, the Indian boy choked and spit his pork into the dirt. He liked the bread, coffee, and sugar, but he didn't think much of the white man's meat.

When they woke the next morning there was a dull murmuring sound on the cool air. The Cheyennes perked up immediately. No more salt pork. Tonight there would be buffalo. Their excitement spread to the voyageurs and song lifted along the line of march. That night camp was one long feast, with the fires left burning and the men waking to eat again and again. "Indians and buffalo make the poetry and life of the prairie," Fremont wrote later, and even Charles Preuss had to admit the buffalo could have been better than beef—had it been properly prepared.

A little farther west they came on a strange sight. Trunks, dressers, rockers, and other household goods sat abandoned on the prairie. The second annual migration was on the road to Oregon ahead of them. Already they had had to lighten their loads. Fremont could see an accurate accounting of trail conditions might save much difficulty and heartache.

Dividing the company at the forks of the Platte, Fremont picked three men to explore up the South Fork with him, while the rest were to continue up the North Fork to Laramie. The three Cheyennes bid Randolph goodbye and traveled with Fremont to join their people on the South Platte. After a disappointing attempt to obtain provisions at Fort St. Vrain (near present-day Evans, Colorado), Fremont joined the rest of the force at Laramie on July 15.

Here was disquieting news. Indians to the west were in a hostile mood. The emigrant train they were following had hired Tom Fitzpatrick to see them safely to Fort Hall, and chiefs at the fort warned that the road was to be closed. Fremont was urged to go no farther.

Charles Preuss couldn't have been more delighted. Here was a perfect excuse to turn around and go home—his heart-felt wish. He saw absolutely "no honor in being murdered by rabble just to determine a few longitudes and latitudes." The voyageurs were also reluctant to go on, and when word got out that Kit Carson had made his will, the men began to panic.

Fremont called them together and told them he

ASA BATTLES

intended to go on. They were well-armed and he had hired an interpreter to go with them to stave off trouble. Any who were too cowardly to go with him would be paid off and left behind.

Only one man stepped forward. Charles Preuss was sorely tempted, but he could not quite bear the dishonor. Tents were struck, carts loaded, and the men mounted. Fremont felt there was no great danger, but he left a disappointed Randolph and Henry Brant at the fort, just in case there should be trouble.

They moved through a blizzard of grasshoppers up a Platte that was shrunken by drought. The soil took on a burned appearance, and what grass the insects left was yellow and crisp. They did meet Indians—returning from harassing the emigrant train—but Fremont presented a strong

53

defense, and they had no trouble. However, reports of continued drought and lack of grass and buffalo made him decide to cache the carts and continue with only pack animals. Preuss, who had had the high pleasure of riding in a cart since Laramie, was forced back on his hated horse.

At Independence Rock, Fremont stopped to try another innovation he had included in his equipment. The daguerreotype camera was only three years old and still largely experimental, but he wanted to try to photograph the famous landmark. He exposed five plates, but none of them was successful.

Along the Sweetwater in August the drought was broken with a vengeance. For days they were pelted with cold rains, and the peaks of the Wind River range shone white with fresh snow. Spattered by rain drops, they rode through South Pass, trying with difficulty to decide on its highest point. In spite of what he had been told, Fremont had expected something more of this fabled gateway he had come so far to see. But he could only compare the ascent to that of Washington's Capitol Hill. Charles Preuss was characteristically scornful. The Rockies couldn't compare to his beloved Alps.

Once through the pass—the road well-noted and his mission accomplished—Fremont turned north to explore the Wind River Mountains. His greatest joy was "the drinking first at nature's springs," and he wanted to be first to climb what he thought was the highest peak in the Rocky Mountain chain. The beauty of the mountain country stirred him to rapturous descriptions—the dark pines, the rushing waters, the masses of rock piled ever higher—expanded his mind and woke poetry in his soul. Even Charles Preuss was forced into reluctant admiration as they worked their way into the Wind River chain.

Just as they prepared for ascent, a mule slipped in a rocky stream and their last barometer lay broken. Fremont was devastated. Now there was no way to measure the mountain—no real reason for ascending it. He struggled for two days trying various means to repair it, and finally succeeded by attaching a translucent powder horn. It was a small feat of genius, but Preuss could only call it lucky.

On August 12 Fremont, Preuss and 15 men left camp for an ascent and return they expected to take two days. It was noon of the fifteenth before they stood on top of the mountain, but Fremont was exultant, sure he stood "where never human foot had stood before." They took turns teetering on the small rock that was the very peak, and Fremont unfurled a small flag. When the barometer was broken past repair on the way down, he thought it fitting that, like a glass shattered after a toast, it would never be put to less noble use.

Flushed with success, Fremont had only to retrace his steps to the States and report his findings. But he had his mind set on one further adventure. When they again reached the Platte, he ordered the rubber raft inflated. On it he loaded all of his journals, registers, telescope, sextant, and other instruments, and the best of the party's provisions. Then, with Preuss and five men he pushed out into the stream, ordering the rest of the force to meet them at an island 12 miles downstream. If all went well and the boat reached the island first, they would leave a note and continue downstream for a later meeting.

For an hour they floated serenely and Preuss was almost cheerful at the thought of the miles he wouldn't have to cover on horseback. Then there was a roar of rapids ahead.

Fremont reconnoitered and, reluctant to unload and portage, he decided they would run the rapids. They tied down all equipment and stripped off most of their clothes. Then Fremont tied a 50-foot line to the boat and ordered three of the men to follow along the cliffs, holding back the boat to keep it under control. He asked Preuss to get out and walk with the chronometer, to save it from getting wet.

Preuss, scandalized at the risk Fremont was taking, tried his best, but the sheer walls made passage impossible. He was forced back into the boat. He put the clock into a bag around his neck, took firm hold on the log book, and away they went.

Once the boat was in the current their puny efforts at control were totally useless. The men on shore felt their arms jerked from their sockets, and two loosed their hold on the rope. The third man was yanked from his 12-foot ledge into the churning waters. He was pulled after the racing boat like a fish on a line, his head a black spot that appeared and disappeared in the white water.

A moment's ease in an eddy allowed them to reel in the half-drowned man before they were off again, careening through the rocks. As the seconds passed and they continued upright, they began to enjoy the thrilling ride. Laughing, shouting a Canadian boat song, intoxicated with the danger and excitement, they bounced along.

Then it happened. The boat struck a boulder and flipped over.

Fremont came up sputtering, his first thought that three of the five in the boat could not swim. Preuss surfaced downstream, still clutching the book, and somehow all made it to the rocks of shore, from where they watched their books, boxes, instruments, blankets, and clothes continue downstream with the current.

Luckily there was a quiet bend not too far downstream, and as they searched the banks and shallows they recovered some of their belongings. Miraculously, the Platte gave up all but one of Fremont's registers and journals. They found one gun, a blue capote, some hides and the tent. But the sextant, telescope, compasses, food, ammunition and all other guns were lost.

They left the battered boat where it lay and climbed out of the canyon. All were half-naked, and Fremont stumbled over the rocky and cactus-strewn ground with only one moccasin.

They were fairly close to the island rendezvous, but there was one thought in their minds as they clambered through rocks and up and down the canyons between. They had been expected hours before. What if the others decided they had missed connections and moved on downstream? The thought of several days march without food, arms, or proper clothing spurred them on. Just as the summer sun was setting, they mounted a ridge from which they could see the island. Thank God! The train waited.

The hungry men gorged themselves on buffalo and recounted the excitement of their narrow escape. Charles Preuss said little to the others, but in his diary he wondered how Fremont could have been so foolhardy. And when Fremont, in his tattered uniform, managed to look dignified and martial for a formal entrance into Laramie, he shook his head and decided that "a young lieutenant is always a strange creature."

Not a man to give up easily, Fremont later made a bull boat of hides and willows, and once again tried his luck on the Platte. The boat, loaded with four men, drew only four inches, but the autumn Platte that had nearly drowned him upstream, would not float it. He left the craft grounded on a sandbar, and with it his final hopes of navigating what Preuss called "this scoundrel of a river."

They followed the Platte on to Bellevue, Preuss counting the days, thinking only of wife, child, bread, and coffee.

By October 29 John C. Fremont was back in Washington. A few days later Jessie gave birth to a daughter, and John spread her bed with a worn and ragged flag. "This flag was raised over the highest peak of the Rocky Mountains," he told her. "I have brought it to you."

He also brought back the most accurate and complete knowledge of the trail west the country had even known. And, with his literary flair and Jessie's assistance, he produced a report of his journey that glowed with his enthusiasm for the West. It was widely read and did much to counteract the stigma of the Great American Desert. He had not broken trails, but he had marked them. Others would find higher mountains in the Rockies, but the map he and Charles Preuss produced would be the standard for years to come.

Charles Preuss accompanied Fremont on two more expeditions, complaining and criticizing every step of the way, but doing his job all the same. The melancholy man who wanted nothing more than to stay home and tend his garden continued to make his living mapping the wilderness. In 1854, suffering from ill health and despondence, he hung himself in a neighbor's orchard.

John C. Fremont made four expeditions after his first journey up the Platte. One named and delineated the Great Basin, and one ended in frozen death for 11 men in the San Juan Mountains. He was hailed as the liberator of California in the Bear Flag Revolt, served as Senator from California, and was the Republican candidate for President in 1856. He rose to major general in the Civil War, and was governor of Arizona Territory from 1878 to 1883.

But he also was court-martialed for insubordination, was removed from his Civil War command, and was reduced from millionaire to pauper by railroad speculations. Somehow his reach seemed always to exceed his grasp, and he was continually embroiled in controversy. In the end he had only his faithful Jessie.

Intelligent, resourceful, energetic, and literate, he never conquered the impetuous nature that had imperiled his whole mission when it led him to launch a boat into the white water of the upper North Platte.

Calling Cards on Laramie Creek

Even before John Fremont's report could be distributed, the Oregon Trail was cut deeper into the landscape by the Great Migration of 1843. Nearly 1,000 emigrants, some recruited and led by Marcus Whitman, marched for Oregon in a train 10 times the size of any the Indians had seen before.

A year later the migration was almost as large, and the Pawnee, Sioux, Cheyenne, and Arapaho who frequented the Platte found the wood had vanished, the grass was disappearing, and the game had been driven away. The Pawnees preyed on the trains in a small way, stealing horses, mules, and anything else left unguarded, but the powerful Sioux and Cheyennes threatened real trouble.

In 1845, with some 5,000 emigrants on the road, the government sent Colonel Stephen Watts Kearny up the trail with 250 Dragoons to impress the natives with the advantages of peace. Guided by Broken Hand Fitzpatrick, Kearny marched to Fort Laramie, demonstrated the power of his howitzers, and told the impressed Indians that the road must remain open. He repeated the message to the Cheyennes and returned to Fort Leavenworth, convinced similar periodic expeditions would keep the Indians peaceable.

But if the rattled sabers kept the Sioux off the Oregon Trail, they did not keep them from the Pawnee villages. Repeated Sioux attacks during the summer of 1846 drove the missionaries back to Bellevue, and the struggling, squabbling mission to the Pawnees was no more. The Pawnees, pushed south of the Platte by the Sioux, and north of the Platte by the emigration, were left virtually homeless. They moved off south on their semi-annual hunt, leaving the shores of the Platte to men of a very different heritage.

Francis Parkman spurred his horse up the small hill and read the letters burned into the rough plank thrust into its grassy surface.

MARY ELLIS
Died May 7th, 1845
Aged two months

He had become accustomed to seeing grave markers along the trail since he had left the settlements, but this one touched him enough that he pencilled it in his journal. As he and his cousin Quincy Adams Shaw broke camp the next morning, they could see a line of wagons silhouetted against the horizon.

Bostonian Francis Parkman was intrigued and puzzled by this mass migration. He himself was going West, but he traveled without wife, children, and all his worldly possessions piled in a wagon. He did not seek land or fortune of the usual kind. He sought knowledge. That placed him in a decided minority among the plains travelers.

Though Francis was only two years out of Harvard, he had already set his mind on his life's work. He wanted to write history. Specifically, he intended to compile the history of the French-English struggle in the settlement of the East. As the Indians played a major part in that conflict, he wanted to learn all he could about Indians in their primitive state. For this he came West in the spring of 1846. He had interviewed the old Astorian Robert Stuart, and he had consulted with the guide Broken Hand Fitzpatrick in St. Louis. Then, with his cousin Quin as companion, he hired a hunter and guide and joined the stream of population that flowed out from the settlements.

With the emigrants he shared experiences of broken harnesses, shattered axle trees, muddy beds, meals of biscuit and salt pork, unnumbered mosquitoes, visiting snakes, drinking water enriched by tadpoles, and disgustingly regular afternoon thunderstorms. But he had no desire to share their company.

Francis was a real Boston Brahmin, with wealth and family position behind him, and engraved calling cards rested even now in the pocket of his notebook. To his aristocratic eye the emigrants were rough, ignorant, and uncouth—the lowest segment of the frontier population. Yet he had to admire their courage and admit that some seemed manly and intelligent.

If Francis thought little of the emigrants, he thought even less of the Pawnees. When they crossed the great trail left by the tribe as they moved off on their summer hunt, Francis labeled them ''treacherous, cowardly banditti'' who deserved anything that happened to them, and he listened with relish to the story of a Sioux warrior who had dropped through the smoke hole of a Pawnee lodge and dispatched the sleeping inhabitants one by one.

At dusk the same day they rode through the sand hills that bordered the Platte Valley, and Francis found it a strange and striking sight. He could not call it beautiful, but he was impressed by the vast expanse of wild solitude; the level sands, broken here and there by long, coarse grass, the scattered jumbles of prickly pear, and the lizards that darted between the bleaching bones of buffalo.

Past Ash Hollow Francis' small party came upon an encampment of emigrants. The men of the camp came out to meet them—hostile and suspicious—afraid they might be a party of dreaded Mormons. All spring there had been rumors of a Mormon migration, and the emigrants from Missouri and Illinois had a hearty fear of meeting them on the prairie. When they found Francis' party of four offered no threat, they welcomed them in, and Francis found them to be fine and generous fellows—evidently hailing from the least barbarous counties of the frontier.

Descending from the pass at Scotts Bluff, Francis found some Indians more to his liking. Old Smoke's Oglala Sioux were nooning at Horse Creek, and the meadow was alive with children, dogs, and horses. These were the Indians that Francis had come so far to study, and he found them strong and attractive. But, as he scribbled notes on their appearance, a procession of emigrant wagons lumbered across the creek, and Francis realized he was seeing both the past and the future. For he expected the Sioux would be swept from the face of the earth before another hundred years had passed, crowded out by the people who were driving their creaking wagons across Horse Creek.

His feeling of impending conflict was even greater at Fort Laramie, where he watched emboldened Sioux demand food and presents from the intimidated trains. He thought that troops should be stationed at Laramie, to guard the trains from the increasingly indignant Sioux.

But—whatever happened on the trail—Parkman was determined to carry out his research. This meant living for a time in one of the Indian villages, and with the help of his guide he made friends with the Oglala. When he heard they were planning to go to war against the Snakes, the young scholar was delighted. Here was a chance to observe all the rituals and ceremonies of war. By the first of July, Francis and his cousin were camped with the village of The Whirlwind, where the Chugwater flowed into the Laramie, waiting anxiously for the impending conflict.

But it was not to be so simple. Francis found the Sioux society to be loosely organized and totally democratic. No one gave orders and demanded obedience. Each warrior was basically free to do as he pleased. He could make up a small party and go out on his own, or he could stay home. There was still talk of war, but little action. And to complicate matters, Francis, who had never had a strong constitution, fell victim to dysentery. With no treatment available but rest, he spent days lying in weakness or staggering faint and dizzy around the village.

Then The Whirlwind's village decided to move. Not to make war, but to make meat. Francis, so weak he could scarcely sit his horse, went on a wild goose chase across the prairie, in a futile search for another village that would go to war. Finding none, he decided to retrace his steps and try to catch up with The Whirlwind.

At this point his cousin balked. Having had enough of Indians, he returned to Fort Laramie, while Francis, with one hunter for company, set out after the Oglala village.

It was a lonely, dangerous journey. At night, wakened by pain, Francis would lie listening to the whisper of grasses, and wonder if he heard stealthy footsteps. A wolf would howl, and then another. He knew there were Crow war parties in the vicinity, and every day they saw tracks of grizzlies.

But in spite of the hunter's protests, he insisted on tracking the village. Vulnerable to attack by any passing party, so debilitated that he had to crawl up the slopes when his horse couldn't carry him, he persisted. When at last they came on the camp between the Medicine Bow and Laramie Ranges, the Boston scholar thought no home had ever looked as good to him as the smoke-darkened lodges of the Oglala village.

As he settled into village life, Francis' conception of the noble red man was shaken by reality. He discovered they could be incredibly brave, self-sacrificing, generous, and deeply religious. But they could also be petty, jealous, cruel, and dishonest. Having expected too much, he had a hard time forgiving them for being human.

As he moved with the buffalo camp, Francis' illness recurred. At one time he was so sick that he realized he might never leave the prairie. But when a herd was spotted and the Indians moved out for a surround, he rode along. He watched the scouts signal the location of the herd and the hunters leap from their tired riding horses to their fresh buffalo ponies. Eagle feathers flying in the wind, they rode down from all sides on the startled herd.

In a moment all was uproar and confusion, as Indians, horses, and buffalo milled in the dust. Then buffalo raced out from the center in all directions; the yelling Indians after them, firing arrow after arrow. Francis had resolved to be only a spectator, for his own sake and for his horse, but he couldn't resist joining the chase. He galloped after a cow and shot her just as she tumbled into a ravine, but the shot hit too far foward, and she lumbered off after the herd.

That night there was feasting in the camp, and for days after the squaws worked at drying meat and tanning hides. They saved the sinews to lace together the hides that covered their lodges, and as Parkman noted how the buffalo provided them with everything from boats to glue, he thought the Indians must follow the buffalo into extinction.

But now the tribe was well-supplied with hides, and they moved on to gather poles for next year's lodges. Francis accompanied the tribe as it flowed through the Laramie mountains to an area of tall, slender pine. Soon piles of white poles lay drying in the sun.

Summer was passing. Francis lived with the Indians, but he could not become one of them. He hunted elk and mountain sheep, shared the pipe in their councils, ate their food and slept in their lodges, but he felt there was an impassable gulf between him and the red man. He could not become a savage, and he could not see them as anything more. Yet there were two among the tribe he counted as real friends, and when time came for him to leave for Laramie, he felt reluctant to go.

He saw that the stream of migration through the country would destroy the buffalo and weaken the tribes, and that whiskey and the military would effectively finish the destruction. Then travelers might pass secure in their country, but ''its danger and its charm will have disappeared together.''

Francis' small party was reunited at Fort Laramie, traveled south to Bent's Fort, and then down the Arkansas to the settlements. He collapsed on returning home, and his eyesight began to fail. In spite of these difficulties, he dictated an account of his adventures, and *The Oregon Trail* was published in 1849. He was the first writer to actually live with the Indians, and his book became an immediate success: a classic equally valuable to the gold seekers of the 1800s and students of the Old West today. Although Parkman fought sickness and blindness the rest of his life—he wrote with a wire frame and a black crayon—he accomplished his goal by producing the eight-volume *France and England in North America*. His exhaustive research and literary style rank him pre-eminent among American historians, and his work in the field of horticulture produced *The Book of Roses*, a standard reference. He was never able to return to to the wilderness, but an Oglala shield and war bonnet still hung on the wall of his study when he died in 1893.

Come, Ye Saints

While Francis Parkman endured cramps and chills in a Sioux tepee in the summer of 1846, an English violinist named William Clayton was suffering similar agonies in a primitive village 500 miles to the east. This village was on Indian land beside the Missouri River, but it was not peopled by Omaha or Potawatomies. It was peopled by Saints—or as Francis Parkman would have labeled them, Mormons— followers of Joseph Smith in the body of the Church of Jesus Christ of the Latter-Day Saints.

ASA BATTLES

William Clayton had come many miles to lie in misery among the Saints. His trail began back in England, where he had been converted and then served as a Mormon missionary. In 1840, Clayton had headed a company of new Saints on their voyage from England to the Mormon city of Nauvoo, Illinois. There he had used his musical talents as a member of the Nauvoo Brass Band, and he had become a trusted secretary to Joseph Smith, his church's founder.

When Smith was killed, and religious persecution forced the Saints to flee Nauvoo early in 1846, they headed west in search of a new place to settle. Clayton assisted the church's new leader, Brigham Young, as head of a company on the trail. With the accustomed obedience of any Mormon, he had left his pregnant third wife behind and worried his way across Iowa to the Missouri River.

It had been a three-month journey, miles of struggle with meager provisions. When possible, the band made side trips to play for settlers along the way, and they used the money or produce they received in payment to replenish their shrinking supplies.

All the way William Clayton worried about Diantha, the wife he had left behind, and when he finally learned she had delivered a healthy son, he wrote a hymn in celebration. It was "Come, Come, Ye Saints," and it became the great camp song of the migration. Music was the Saints' great joy, and the band and Clayton's song helped make the miles go faster.

But William, and all the Saints, had many more miles to go. They knew the camp where they now rested (Winter Quarters near the present Mormon Bridge in Omaha), was only a stopping-off point on a longer journey, one that would put them out of the United States, far out into the wilderness, beyond the persecution of the Gentiles (their label for any non-Mormon). Behind them lay their sacked and ruined city of Nauvoo, their desecrated temple, memories of the painful, frozen journey across Iowa, and a trail of graves that would continue to mark their passing as they moved west.

Behind them also they left permanent camps with log cabins; fields that were not only plowed and fenced, but planted; bridges, wells and roads. For they knew they were only the first of many companies who would take the road to Zion.

As William Clayton had doled out supplies,

kept inventory, bickered with teamsters, and recorded each day's happenings in the official journal, he had played his part in the most organized migration in the history of the West — possibly of the world. The Saints were grouped into tens, fifties and hundreds, each with its captain and lieutenant placed in a chain of command that reached up to President Brigham Young. And each company not only cared for its own, but fulfilled assignments that would make the way easier for those who followed.

It had cost the summer and all their energies to get some 4,000 of the people to the Missouri. Many, like William Clayton, lay in their tents and wagons, weakened by the journey, sick with dysentery and malaria, ill in spirit at the loss of so many loved ones. There was not time, equipment, or the will to go farther. They would have to winter on the Missouri.

The question of how and where was answered in a strange way by the government that had watched them driven from their homes without raising a murmur of protest. The United States was raising troops for the war with Mexico, and it asked the Saints for 500 of their men to form a battalion. The Saints' first reaction was shock, indignation, and anger. Why should they give their young men to a country that had served them so ill?

But Brigham Young could see possibilities in the situation. When he got through negotiating, the army had its men, but the Saints had permission to winter unmolested on Indian land. More importantly, there was hard cash advance wages to buy supplies for the winter.

And so the gathering of wagons on the west bank of the Missouri took on the look of a permanent camp. Cabins of log and sod went up, laid out in 41 long, narrow blocks. Some who couldn't manage cabins made dugouts, and some remained in tents and wagons. They raised a meeting house and a gristmill. They had order, they had each other, they had their faith, but they had little else.

Weakened by cold and malnutrition, they fell to dysentery, tuberculosis, whooping cough, mumps, scurvy, and pellagra. Their gums softened, their faces sallowed, their eyesight failed, their legs turned black and the flesh fell off in rotten clumps. Of the 3,483 Saints who began the winter, 600 lay in graves before spring thaws greened up the pigweed and wild onions. Many of the graves took only a little ground, for 150 were for children not yet six years old.

Spring of 1847 did come at last, and it was time for the Pioneer company to be on the road. Brigham Young had decided to send a party of 144 men out first, to make the road toward that spot in the wilderness they found to be Zion. They would also get a crop in the ground so the new colony would have food for winter. Uncharacteristically, Young bowed to his brother's wish that his family be allowed to go, and then he added one of his wives and one of another apostle to the train, so that three women and two children joined the men.

William Clayton did not expect to go. He was lying on his bed nursing an aching tooth when Brother Brigham walked in and told him to rise up and accompany the train. In three hours he had bid his wives—and a second new son—goodbye, and left Winter Quarters behind.

He went willingly. As he stood on the bluffs above the Saints' ferry on the Elkhorn River, his eyes followed the April green of the Platte bottom that stretched to the west as far as he could see. Somewhere out there, he hoped, the Saints would find a home where they could live in peace.

They moved out up the north bank of the Platte. The 72-wagon train marched with accustomed Mormon organization, beginning the day at 5:00 a.m. with a bugle call to prayer, and ending with another at 8:00 p.m. Except for his throbbing jaw and the cold that penetrated his quilt at night, William traveled in relative comfort. He often walked ahead of the wagons, rifle on his shoulder, but when time came to make road, he bent his back with the others.

If the days were filled with labor, evenings around the fire were made sweet for him by the serene voice of his violin floating off across the Platte. As the official historian of the camp, he spent many hours with his writing desk on his lap, keeping a meticulous record of their journey.

The Saints had made a leather boat for use on the trail, which they called the *Revenue Cutter*. At the first opportunity they used it to seine for fish in a small lake. Their initial attempt swept up five turtles, two catfish, two suckers, and one squawking duck, but later efforts saw the net filled with fish.

William's jaw was growing worse, until the whole side of his face was frozen in pain, and every time his foot met the trail new jabs shot through his head. When the train stopped and set up the anvil to repair wagon tires, he convinced

a friend to try to pull the tooth.

Once the gum was lanced, nippers jerked out half of the infected molar, but half was left in the jaw, and that night he could not sleep for the throbbing.

They passed the deserted Pawnee mission and farm, where hay, fodder, plows, and drags had been left where they stood, and William climbed up to see the Pawnee graves on the bluffs above. From there he could also see the Pawnee corn fields, yellowed stalks from the season past still standing.

One of William's responsibilities was to estimate and record distances between campsites on the trail, and he suggested a wooden cogwheel that measured distance be fixed to a wagon hub so that his map would be more accurate. Everyone thought it sounded like a good idea, but the hierarchy took no action.

As they passed Grand Island the country took on a new identity. The wind blew hot and dry, laden with bitter alkali dust. Lizards skittered across the trail. Wolves loped by. William's writing desk began to split with dryness, and his lips cracked and bled. Then someone shot a hare, and for a moment his mind was back in the green English countryside.

But England had no buffalo like the herds the Saints were seeing now. Clayton counted 72 through the spy glass he rested on a brother's shoulder, as the envious but obedient men watched the chosen hunters race off on the exciting hunt. Even the hunters did not have carte blanche, for Brother Brigham forbid shooting more of the Lord's cattle than they could use.

In spite of Clayton's repeated suggestions, no one made a move to construct his coveted cogwheel. It went against his precise nature to rely on estimates—especially when estimates varied widely from person to person—and he was finally driven to do something about it. He measured the wheel of Brother Kimball's wagon. It was exactly 14 feet 8 inches in circumference. Providentially, such a wheel made exactly 360 revolutions per mile.

William was delighted. The next morning he tied a rag on a spoke and walked beside the wagon all day, counting every revolution of the wheel. His measured mileage was 11¼ miles, plus 20 revolutions. With a real feeling of satisfaction he pounded a cedar post into the ground at the campsite. "From Winter Quarters 195 mi. May 8

61

'47. Camp all well. Wm. Clayton.''

Feeling he had proved the value of accurate mileage (some had estimated 14 miles when they had actually gone 11¼ plus 20 revolutions) Clayton continued to press for his cogwheel. But as they passed the forks and turned up the North Platte he was still counting. For two more days he counted doggedly, and perhaps very audibly, but on the twelfth of May, Appleton Harmon whittled and installed a roadometer—a wooden screw turned by the wheel, the screw in turn activating a wheel of 60 cogs that turned once every mile.

William's delight was tempered when he heard that Brother Appleton Harmon was claiming the invention as his own, and brotherly love gave way to carping in his journal.

It was still a long way up the Platte, with dust in their throats and blisters on their heels, their faces often black with the ashes of prairie fires. They found a mammoth bone, entertained a Sioux chief in camp, and named bluffs and streams along the way. But mostly they plodded on day after day. The strain was beginning to tell on all of them. When at length they came to Chimney Rock and the promise of the mountains to come, their peevishness gave way to giddiness, and the camp was full of men dancing and playing cards, ignoring the call to 8:30 prayers.

By the time they were opposite Scotts Bluff, Brother Brigham, who had not felt much like preaching so far on this mission, suddenly felt the call. He climbed up on the *Revenue Cutter* and lectured them roundly for the ''low, mean, dirty, trifling, covetous, wicked spirit'' dwelling in their bosoms. Like naughty children they welcomed the scolding and pledged their faith anew. William Clayton felt as if they ''had emerged into a new element, a new atmosphere, and a new society.''

Whatever their spiritual state, they were entering a new country. On May 31 they found firewood for the first time in 215 miles, and on June 1 William was pounding a mileage post into the river bank opposite Fort Laramie. When they ferried over to the fur trading post, he could see snow on Laramie Peak, and a climb up a high bluff netted him a view of a succession of high ridges stretching to the north, south, and west. They were through with the plains.

At Laramie the train was reinforced by a contingent of Saints from Mississippi, 17 souls who had wintered at Pueblo and then come north to join the pioneers. But theirs were not the only

wagons on the trail. From here on the Saints, forced south of the river by seemingly impassable bluffs, would have to share the road with Gentiles, and word came that 500 Gentile wagons were approaching Laramie.

The Saints pushed themselves to ferry all the wagons over and keep ahead of the Gentile migration, but by June 5 two Oregon trains had passed them. With water and campsites scarce, there was nothing to do but share the trail through South Pass. And, in spite of mutual fear and suspicion, there was some contact. A few Missourians had heard of the roadometer and came to view it. William Clayton listened as they expressed curiosity about his device, but as they didn't address any questions directly to him, he didn't volunteer any information.

The first few days out of Laramie were good ones, with camps boasting clear streams, rich grass and currant bushes in tangles of bloom. Mint crushed by their boots perfumed the air. William was charmed by the beauty of the country. On La Bontes Creek, where Francis Parkman had waited hopefully for warring savages the summer before, William wrote a letter to his family, longing for the day they would all be together in their new home.

At Deer Creek camp the flash of silvery fish in the water brought out his fishing gear, and he landed 24 grayling in the evening and rose at 4:00 a.m. to try for more. Somehow the cool dawn, the flowing stream, the calls of birds, and the comfort of timber brought on a homesickness for England even sharper than that the arid plains had aroused.

But they could not remain in the shaded glen.

Ahead of them lay the crossing of the Platte. Its mid-June waters were 15 feet deep and 100 yards wide, and it rolled out of the mountains with a wicked current. The invaluable *Revenue Cutter* could carry the wagons' loads, but the Saints worked for three days to get the wagons themselves across. Up to their armpits in icy water, fighting wind and thunderstorms, they tried one method and then another, while a crew worked to build a substantial ferry of planks and logs.

By the time the ferry was ready, the Saints' wagons were nearly over, but Brother Brigham knew there were many more who would want to cross the Platte that summer. He left a crew to man the ferry for the Saints to follow, and in the meantime to help the Gentiles across—for a price. Even before the Pioneer Company started on, the Gentiles had paid $400 into the Saints' coffers.

As they pulled away from the Platte for the last time, they plunged suddenly from friendly to forbidding country. Gray sage replaced the green of the valley, and the creeks changed from fresh-flowing streams to foul-smelling poisonous pools. They camped at the foot of a cliff in what William thought was "one of the most horrid, swampy, stinking places I ever saw." Hordes of mosquitoes fed on man and beast, and the ground was so soft that they woke to find two oxen sunk to their nostrils in the mire.

There was no temptation to linger here, and they were on the trail early the next morning for the pull to Independence Rock. William, and many others, easily clambered up the fizzured surface to find hundreds of names and dates painted on with red, yellow, and black paint. The cleft of Devil's Gate rose six miles to the west, and the horizon was broken in every direction with gray ridges, buttes, and scattered ranges. William thought it looked like land where giants had dumped wheelbarrows of clay haphazardly around the landscape and left them where they fell to be hardened into rock by the ages.

Still measuring and mile-posting as they moved, William found another kind of marker on the trail. This one read

Matilda Crowley
July 16, 1830
July 7, 1846

He stood at the barren grave and was reminded of his own family and the miles between them and their new home.

But they did not yet even know where that home

was to be. They crossed and recrossed the gentle Sweetwater, and on June 27 Clayton had the satisfaction of seeing the current of a small creek run west instead of east. A few miles through the pass the trail also divided, and on the advice of a mountain man named Moses Harris, they took the trail south toward Fort Bridger and the Great Salt Lake.

They found Jim Bridger himself before they found his fort, and they pulled into camp so they could benefit from this encyclopedia of the wilderness. With William and others keeping careful notes, they heard Bridger recommend the Bear Valley or the Utah for settlement. He thought the Salt Lake Valley itself was too cold to allow the raising of corn. But his descriptions, like his experiences, ranged all over the whole of Oregon, and the precise William was hard put to decide what parts of the rambling conversation were significant "from the very imperfect and irregular way he gave his descriptions." He finally concluded that they would know best what they found out for themselves.

By the end of July they had found out for themselves. William, who celebrated his thirty-third birthday with his "heart filled with blessings" in the bottom of rock-strewn, willow-filled, all but impassable Echo Canyon, climbed out of the chaos on July 22 and saw the Great Salt Lake glimmering in the distance.

To his eyes the hard-baked valley, spotted with bunch grass, and the white-rimmed sterile lake looked fertile, rich, and handsome. His only objection was the lack of timber, and even before he slid down from his perch he was picturing houses of Spanish adobe or lodges like the Pawnees. He "had no fears but the Saints can live here and do well." William Clayton was at home.

Two weeks later he took the long road back to fetch his family—measuring all the way with a new roadometer—to find the family ill but intact, except for the brother he would lose in November.

In 1848 Clayton authored *The Latter-Day Saints Emigrants Guide,* the most accurate and complete guide of the 1,032 mile trail, which would be used by Saints and Gentiles alike for years to come.

Clayton spent the rest of his life in Salt Lake City, holding several important offices in the church, contributing his talent, and fathering over 30 children by his several wives. When he died in 1879, the chapel resounded with the hymn he had written on the trail up the Platte to Zion.

Separate From All These, Forever

While the Saints worked to move their population up the Platte and far past the borders of the United States, those borders suddenly expanded westward. The settlement of the Mexican War placed California, New Mexico—and the Saints' new Zion—in the United States territory. If, at first, this seemed unimportant; if it seemed the vast distances would still provide isolation; it was because the Saints could not conceive of a world gone mad for gold. That a few yellow flakes in John Sutter's California millrace would wake a hunger that would pull tens of thousands of people out of the States and up the Platte road seemed incredible. It was incredible. But it was happening.

The trail that had supported 4,000 emigrants, mostly Mormon, in 1848 was clogged with 30,000 people in 1849. Fledgling Fort Kearny, just established at the head of Grand Island to aid and protect the migration, was hardly more than a half-dozen soddies when the torrent of gold seekers washed over it. They came in all ages, sizes, and conditions, with only this in common: they were headed for the gold of California, and they were in a hurry.

n June 2, 1849, when 4,400 wagons had already rolled past Fort Kearny, Sarah Royce, her husband Josiah, and her two-year-old daughter Mary had yet to cross the Missouri River. It had taken the month of May to get across Iowa, as Sarah, Josiah, and an elderly companion, "utter strangers to camping life," had spent the miles unloading the mired wagon so it could be driven out of a mud hole, loading it again with their rain-soaked possessions, and driving it half a mile so they could repeat the performance.

Sarah had spent the winter anticipating this great adventure, but the reality of the first camps, without even a tree or a bank to provide shelter from the brooding sky, filled her with fear. At first she lay awake at night in the unfamiliar straw of the wagon bed, feeling terribly vulnerable and homeless, but soon the exertions of the day made insomnia a forgotten luxury.

They knew they were late. News of the trail ahead was a discouraging mix of unavailable supplies, vanishing grass, and raging cholera. But when they drove down the draw that sheltered the scattered cabins of Council Bluffs, they found a city of wagons still waiting a turn on the ferry that crossed the Missouri.

For four days they waited, Sarah and little Mary two of only a handful of females sprinkled among the men of the wagons. At last on the eighth of June their turn came, and they ventured their lives and their possessions on a fragile-looking ferry on the unfriendly Missouri. Safely across, Sarah and Mary enjoyed a last civilized meal in the Indian Agent's home at Trader's Point before their train organized and rolled out. They knew they were nearly the last to cross the Missouri, but everyone remained hopeful as they "launched forth upon a journey there was not the least chance of turning back."

They were scarcely on the trail when the elderly man who shared their wagon began to feel ill. Before long he lay in the wagon bed, shaking with spasms of pain. The captain of the train examined him and gave him a dose of medicine, but there was nothing more they could do until they arrived at the Elkhorn. Here they scouted the other camps for a doctor, and when they found one they heard the dreaded diagnosis. Asiatic cholera.

Sarah shuddered, her worst fears confirmed. Fighting panic, she did what she could to make him comfortable. In three hours he was dead.

Unwilling to sleep in the contaminated wagon, Sarah and Josiah managed to borrow a small tent for the night. As there was not room for three of them to stretch out, Sarah sat up. (Josiah had stood guard the night before and badly needed sleep.) She was dozing fitfully, her head on Mary's pillow, when a sudden storm broke over the camp. As rain pelted the tent, misting through the canvas, she lifted the tent flap to watch the storm.

There beside the wagon on a rude bier lay the old man's body, covered with a white sheet that flapped in the wind. Off in the distance she could see shadowy figures around an Indian fire, and the chant that rose above the wind was so mournful she knew it must be a death dirge. Chilled in mind and body, she dropped the flap and huddled closer to the warmth of the sleeping Mary and Josiah.

Morning brought sunny skies, but it was hard to feel cheerful when their first task was to bury the old man. They interred him on an adjacent hillside, and then they emptied the wagon and Sarah washed the bedding and aired all their belongings. Before the quilts were dry, the wagon was rafted across the Elkhorn and they left the grave behind.

But they did not leave the cholera. June 14—two more men in the train were down. By nightfall one was dead. The train was encased in gloom. Everyone knew what cholera could do. Reports flew between the trains of families struck down—children orphaned—whole companies reduced to half their size by the swift killer. The road on the south side of the river was lined with graves, and they had hoped to avoid the plague by taking the north route. But here it was in their midst.

Sarah lay awake in the night. What if Josiah died and left her a widow on this trail? What if she died and left Mary without a mother? What would happen to Mary, if—God forbid—they both were taken? Hoping God would forbid, she prayed for strength and placed her family's lives in His hands. Then she slept.

Whether or not the Lord heard Sarah's prayers, the capricious cholera did not take any more lives on their train. But they continued to hear of cases before and behind, and nearly every mile hasty, pitifully inadequate graves served as a reminder of its deadly presence.

They worked their way along the Platte to the Loup crossing, only to find it swollen and dangerous. A man had drowned trying to cross just before they pulled in, and the Royce train decided to wait for the water to go down. For three precious days they waited. Then they began to drive the wagons over the always tricky, quicksand ford. Sarah clutched Mary and the wagon seat. She could feel the quaking sands and see the wheels settling into the current, but quick action pulled them out of the hole and safely across.

Sarah was grateful to be through with river crossings for awhile, but the next peril came by land. When the company pulled into camp June 20, the Royce's wagon was parked next to the opening left in the circle so that livestock might be driven inside for the night. After the stock was bedded down in the center, chains between the two end wagons held them secure.

In the early morning hours Sarah was awakened by rain on the canvas. Then there was a stab of lightning, and a strange rushing sound began. Scarcely awake, Sarah felt the wagon shake and then move. Before she could rise it was pushed, lifted, and thrown over, and she, Josiah, and Mary tumbled with boxes, trunks, and cooking pans, as the livestock stampeded their way out of the circle.

Luckily the chain holding the two wagons broke and they were pushed aside rather than trampled. But when they had picked themselves up, checked for broken bones, and comforted the terrified Mary, they found one of their wheels completely smashed.

Two wheels of the adjoining wagon hung broken and useless. When the train captain surveyed the damage he shook his head and swore. ''Three wheels broken all to smash and 50 miles from timber!''

Perhaps it was relief, perhaps incipient hysteria, but his expression struck Sarah funny. She began to laugh and Josiah joined in. They clung together beside their damaged wagon and the jumble of their belongings in the rainy dawn and laughed until they could hardly stand.

If the captain found it humorous he didn't say so. He consulted with a blacksmith member of the train, persuaded two families to give up heavy boards they used for tables, scrounged the rest of the wagons for scraps, and—with two more days gone—the wagons were moving again.

Sarah had with her John Fremont's guidebook of the trail, and now she began to watch for Lone Tree, one of the few landmarks in the monotonous central valley. When she saw the cedar rise against the horizon, she walked out ahead to be near it. To her green-starved eyes it took on

importance all out of proportion to its value, and she speculated about its history. She even caught herself talking to it as if it could answer, and when the train had slogged slowly past and it was time to leave, she kept looking back until it disappeared, feeling as if she were leaving a living creature behind.

After they turned up the North Fork, scrub cedar began to dot the bluffs and Sarah was encouraged. They celebrated July 4 opposite Court House Rock, with Chimney Rock in the distance. When Laramie Peak rose before them, Sarah thought it was a cheerful sight, and, if the snow on its crest reminded her of mountains to be crossed that still stood hundreds of miles away, she didn't voice the worry in her diary.

There were continuing reminders of their lateness. The camp at Deer Creek that William Clayton had found so idyllic was eaten bare. They had to drive the cattle 15 miles upstream before they found sufficient grazing.

Yet Sarah continued to savor her adventure. She had long before determined to ascend Independence Rock, and with another woman, her two sons, and Mary (''that she might have it to remember and tell of'') she scrambled to the top. Finding themselves congenial, the two families dropped behind the train, took a day to observe the Sabbath, and then traveled on alone together.

Where others plodded on unheeding, Sarah continued to recognize the significance of their journey. Her sense of history was fully aroused at South Pass. She ''had looked forward for weeks to the step that should take me past that point'' where the waters flowed east to where she had spent her childhood, and ''where all I loved, save, O, so small a number, lived, and now I stood on the almost imperceptible elevation that, when passed, would separate me from all these, perhaps forever.''

She wanted to mark the spot with a pile of stones labeled ''Ebenezer'' to signify ''Hitherto hath the Lord helped us'' as Samuel had done in ancient days. She knew nobody but the Lord would understand, but that didn't matter. She scanned the barren pass for materials for her marker.

There were no stones—no sticks—no bushes— no shrubs—no trees that she could use. Unable to do more, she marked the spot with the shadow of her body until the wagons were far down the road. Then she ran after them, leaving the pass marked only by her presence.

On August 30, in spite of warnings from the Saints who knew first hand of the Donner tragedy three years before, the Royce's left the "snug dwellings and thrifty gardens" of Salt Lake City for the last leg of their journey. Following a handwritten, two-page guide to the gold mines, and accompanied only by an elderly gentleman, they braved the desert.

For six weeks they struggled, lost their way, retraced their steps, starved and thirsted, until Sarah's only prayer was "Let me not see the death of the child." Finally across the sands and about to attempt an impossible crossing of the Sierras, they were met by a relief party sent out by the government to assist late travelers.

They left their wagon, packed what they could on two government mules (Sarah saved her Bible, her Milton, and her lap desk) and rode over the pass to California. As they neared the pass, Sarah spurred her mule ahead, to have first look at the fabled Sacramento Valley and to offer a prayer of thanksgiving.

She had much for which to be thankful. A few days later the snows began and the pass was blocked for the winter. Sarah was sure God alone had put them on the right side.

By October 27 Sarah had set up housekeeping in a tent at a gold camp, one of only two women in camp. It was the first of several primitive homes. Wherever she was, Sarah took what there was and began to build. She worked for schools, churches, and libraries and saw to it her four children were well educated.

She and Josiah never did strike it rich. But as she raised her children (one of whom — also named Josiah — became a professor of philosophy at Harvard), she taught them that "experiences of heart and mind...bring a delight to the soul" that can never be matched by worldly goods — not even the glittering but elusive gold of the California mountains.

ASA BATTLES

Most of the 30,000 souls who shared the trail with Sarah Royce in 1849 were only passing through the valley of the Platte. But the United States government sent a contingent that intended to stay. On June 17 a dust-gray column of cavalry rode into the trading post at Laramie. Nine days later the old fort was signed, sealed, and delivered to the United States Army for the sum of $4,000. The fur traders, their era all but ended, established a new post a few miles east of the fort. With Fort Kearny to the east, the stars and stripes were now firmly planted at the two most strategic locations along the Platte.

The Indians were not blind to the implications. The flag that now flew daily at Laramie was only the most recent sign the Platte country was suffering drastic changes.

The 30,000 Forty-niners were followed by 50,000 gold-seekers in 1850, and the trail that had been an irritation became an intolerable burden for the country and the Indians. There seemed to be no end to the trains, no limit to the destruction of their hunting grounds. The trail etched a widening scar across the prairie; barren of grass, stripped of timber, devoid of game, obscenely decorated with the litter of overloaded pioneers. The great masses of bison that had centered on the Platte were split into two shrinking herds, their traditional routes destroyed. Their way of life threatened, the Indians' concern turned to resentment and hostility.

The People of the Prairie Gather

Tom Fitzpatrick, who had guided both settlers and soldiers since 1841, was now serving as agent for the plains tribes. By 1851 he had been the Indians' champion for five years, and he could see a confrontation would not be long in coming. Envisioning only one hope to keep the peace, he began promoting a conference with all the tribes. The aim of the conference would be a treaty that protected both white and Indian rights. Word went out that the big talk would begin at summer's end at Fort Laramie, and from all parts of the country individuals turned toward that crossroads of the West.

The army recruiting officer had scowled up at young Percival Lowe and given him fair warning. "If you take this step you will regret it only once, and that will be from the time you become acquainted with your position until you get out of it!" But Percival Lowe had been primed for adventure—filled to the brim with Fremont and Bonneville and anything else he could find to read about the West. He had been determined to join the mounted service. And he had done so.

As he rode out of Fort Kearny in August of 1851, after a year of "beans and hay," he had no regrets about his decision. He had watched the gold-seekers trundle by, escorted the paymaster to Laramie and back, met the fabled Broken Hand Fitzpatrick, slept in a Sioux lodge, and spent a peaceful, lazy month on the green banks of the sparkling Laramie River. Now he was riding again to Laramie, again one of an escort party. But this trip he would have no time to loll on the river bank. This trip Corporal Lowe of the First Dragoons would find himself in the midst of 10,000 Indians and part of the most incredible spectacle ever witnessed in the valley of the Platte.

In the carriages escorted by the Dragoons up the trail now empty of emigrants, were a newspaper editor, a young lawyer, a fur trader, an army general, and Colonel David D. Mitchell. Mitchell had won respect for his service in the Mexican War, and he had served for 10 years as an Indian Agent. He was now Superintendent of Indian Affairs in the western states.

As Corporal Lowe rode behind the carriages into Laramie on September 1, he gazed around in amazement. The fort was surrounded—nearly lost in a forest of tepees. They lined the rivers, covered the plain, and spread to the foot of the bluffs. Lowe marked the lodges of the Oglala and Brulé Sioux, gathered in from the nearby plains. The "agile, intelligent and brave" Cheyennes had trailed up from the south, as had the Arapaho, in lesser numbers, led by a handsome young brave named Friday. With dogs and horses by the hundreds, women, children, and the old ones, the chiefs had gathered their people into the largest congregation of tribes that would ever be seen.

As Lowe wound his way into the fort, he wondered if the Indians really had anything to gain from the touted conference. To him they seemed happy as they were, and he thought perhaps the manufacturers of Indian goods, the merchants, and the freighters would profit more than anyone. But he decided, "whether it led to tragedy or ended in a farce, here was a well-laid plan for the largest assemblage of Indians ever gathered."

It was also the most dangerous. For the white men were asking the Indians to share the same campground with tribes who had been enemies as long as they could remember. The plains tribes were at least nominal friends, but Jim Bridger was bringing the Snakes from the Green River, and the horse-hungry Crows would be down from the Powder country.

About noon one day, Lowe, camped above the fort, looked up to see a long plume of dust hanging to the west. Soon forms became visible, and he could make out a line of mounted Indians, arms ready, led by a lone figure. The line advanced slowly and deliberately on the camp.

As others spotted the approach a wave of excitement rolled through the tribes. It was the Snakes. The Sioux, camped below the Dragoons, raced in to see their ancient enemy. Squaws began to keen for those lost to Snake arrows, and braves felt a rush of adrenaline as they thought of exacting vengeance.

Knowing the danger, outnumbered by thousands, the Snakes came on. They rode proudly on their war horses, the sun flashing off their finest ornaments, with Chief Washakie in the lead, and the women and children, well-guarded, at the rear.

The Dragoons watched tensely. The government had promised safe conduct for all, and it was their responsibility to preserve the peace. Corporal Lowe had a sudden flash of what chance 195 soldiers would have in this mob of Indians if anything went wrong. Then "boots and saddles" sounded and Lowe mounted his horse, one of the handful of men who were all that stood between the Snakes and the Sioux. The Snakes reached the brow of a hill less than a mile away, and Washakie began the descent.

Suddenly a Sioux brave gave a wild yell. He leaped on his pony and galloped for Washakie.

The Snake column immediately halted and raised a scream of defiance. As a French interpreter jumped on his horse and raced to intercept the Sioux, Washakie took in the situation. He walked his horse a few steps forward and raised his rifle at the oncoming enemy.

Before he could fire, the interpreter caught up with the Sioux. He flung himself at the mounted

brave and knocked him to the ground.

Washakie and the Snakes cooly held their fire, ready for whatever might happen, but refusing to be provoked. The Sioux brave, thwarted in his attempt to avenge his father, was escorted back to his camp, and the spark that might have ignited wholesale slaughter cooled and died.

From that moment Percival Lowe "became a Snake." He could not forget the discipline, confidence, and self-reliance the Snakes had shown under stress. A soldier himself, he thought it a "lesson for soldiers who might never again see such a grand display of soldierly manhood." He was delighted at the chance to escort Jim Bridger and his charges to camp, and he asked permission to stay with them. That night half the Dragoon troop stood guard around the tribe, and calls giving station number, time, and "All's well!" floated through the camp every half hour.

It did seem all was well, and that the conference could proceed. But with thousands of horses and people, the grass around Laramie was gone. They would have to choose a new location for the campsite. Fitzpatrick suggested Horse Creek, 35 miles down the Platte, site of good grass, clear water, and ancient trade fairs. Better yet, it was also two days march closer to the Missouri and to a tardy supply train that carried all the trade goods for the Indians. They had come to expect presents as part and parcel of every council with the white man, and Mitchell and Fitzpatrick were embarrassingly empty-handed until the train arrived.

On September 4 the Dragoons led a procession that included heavy supply wagons and dogs pulling travois, dogs by the hundreds and horses by the thousands, dignified chiefs and squawling children, boys racing horses and girls leading pack animals, and the spindly-wheeled, elegant carriages that contained the government dignitaries.

Mid-afternoon of the next day the parade streamed into the council grounds, and tribes were assigned their special areas. Two days were spent in feasting, dancing, and ceremony, while the women erected sun shelters of lodge poles and skins for the coming meetings.

The boom of a cannon reverberated through the valley at 9:00 a.m. September 8, and the people began to gather for the formal opening of the meetings. Each tribe moved as one, dressed for the occasion in its best ceremonial attire, filling the air with its own song. The people of the prairie, bedecked with the rich variety of skins, claws, feathers, and horns of its wildlife, spread themselves in a sparkling kaleidoscope across the tawny valley grasses. Led by the chiefs, braves following, women and children to the rear, they gathered in a great semi-circle. As they settled themselves to the ground, one after another, the songs faded and died, and the valley was filled with an expectant hush.

Superintendent Mitchell rose to begin the conference. The pipe was smoked, and Mitchell explained, through interpreters, the government's position. The Indians would be paid $50,000 in goods per year for 50 years as compensation for the damage to their land. In return they must allow the white man to build forts and to have unobstructed passage over his roads, must agree to tribal boundaries that would end tribal warfare, and each tribe would be expected to choose a chief who would be head of his nation and responsible for its conduct.

Then Tom Fitzpatrick spoke. For nearly 30 years now he had moved among the tribes, and they knew him to be worthy of respect. As a slight breeze lifted his white hair, he spoke briefly but earnestly to the assembled leaders, urging them to talk over the matter among themselves and to be sure they understood what the government wanted.

What the Indians understood best was that they were hungry and the white man was offering food. Peace between the tribes had its attractions, and the other requirements did not seem overly important. After some of the chiefs responded, the council adjourned to the joys of feasting and dancing and reciting coups. The Cheyennes gave an exhibition of mounted maneuvers that left Lowe and his fellow Dragoons in open-mouthed admiration.

But the circle of Indians was still not complete. In the cool of the morning on September 10, a delegation of Crows marched down the valley. Every tribe present was their bitter enemy, and they made the most of their entrance, surpassing even the Snakes in the magnificence of their horses, the lavish sweep of feathers in their headdresses. Undoubtedly some in the murmuring crowd recognized a cherished mount that had been appropriated by the Crows in days past, but, in the spirit of the conference, all held their peace.

Toward evening the next day, a new delegation rode out of the sunset. Escorted by the indefatigable Father DeSmet, 31 Assiniboine, Minnetaree, and Arikara chiefs joined the assembly from the area of the northern Missouri. Known and respected by many of the tribes from the Missouri to Oregon, Father DeSmet's presence had been requested by the government, and the Indians gave him a royal welcome.

Somewhat thinner—he had suffered a nearly fatal attack of malaria on the way to the conference—he still put forth his best effort to promote peace and understanding between the tribes. He moved among the lodges, baptizing Indian children, and in a special ceremony, he baptized Andrew Jackson Fitzpatrick, the new son of his old guide Broken Hand.

For Broken Hand it was a time of joyful reunion. He could listen again to Bridger's yarns, knowing there was more truth than imagination in the tales of their trapping days. He could watch Friday, his waif from the desert, move among his people with strength and confidence, for his adopted son had returned to his own people to work for peace from Arapaho campfires. He could obtain the blessings of Father DeSmet for his new son and the

wife he had taken at the age of 50 years. Surpassing all of these, there was the satisfaction of seeing all the tribes smoke the pipe at the conference, and the real hope that a lasting peace would result.

Still empty-handed, unable to provide concrete assurances of their sincerity, the white commissioners begged the Indians' indulgence and took up the difficult question of tribal boundaries. Without Fitzpatrick and Bridger's knowledge of the territory it would have been impossible, but gradually a settlement was worked out that was acceptable to the tribes. Then the Sioux demanded the right to hunt south of the Platte—in Arapaho and Cheyenne territory—and finally it was agreed all tribes had hunting privileges through the entire region. So, in the end, the Indians retained their freedom to roam, and the boundaries were fixed largely in the minds of the white men.

The business of choosing one chief responsible for all proved a problem, especially to the Sioux, who had several autonomous bands. When they told Mitchell that choosing one chief was impossible, Mitchell chose one for them. He named a popular, respected chief, The Bear, and in spite of The Bear's protests that it was an impossible job, and the rest of the tribes' marked reluctance, The Bear became spokesman for the Sioux.

By September 17 the treaty was ready for signing. A final grand council was called, and Colonel Mitchell read the treaty sentence by sentence, pausing while each sentence was translated into the language of every tribe present, and answering questions that arose. Then he and Tom Fitzpatrick signed for the government, and each chief in turn touched the pen to the paper opposite his name. It was agreed.

But still the train of goods had not arrived. The sweet green banks of Horse Creek had long since turned to dusty powder that hung in the air after every step, and the refuse of 10,000 people and thousands more animals raised an incredible stench. Percival Lowe and the Dragoons moved two miles downstream to breathable air, but the rest of the whites, already chagrinned by the continued lack of gifts, remained with their guests, sharing dwindling supplies and feasting on dogs, the only meat still available. "No epoch in Indian annals," wrote Father DeSmet, "probably shows a greater massacre of the canine race."

At last, on September 20, the long-awaited

71

train pulled into camp. For two days the Indians remained orderly and cheerful as the goods were dispensed. The chiefs disappeared into Mitchell's tent and emerged in generals' uniforms; ribboned, sabered, and bemetaled, complete but for the boots they rejected for their own more comfortable moccasins. They stood proud in their new finery, innocent of its incongruity with paint and braids and moccasins. Corporal Lowe, who a few days before had been moved by their wild beauty, dropped his eyes and choked back a laugh.

Lesser uniforms went to lesser head men, and each clutched a ribboned document attesting to his character. Then the food, knives, blankets, beads, tobacco, and other goods were parceled out to the people. As the huge pile of supplies disappeared, band after band struck their lodges, loaded their travois, and left the valley.

Eleven of the Indian leaders accepted Fitzpatrick's invitation to visit Washington, D.C. and meet with The Great Father, and with Mitchell, DeSmet, and most of the white delegation, they moved east down the Platte.

Corporal Lowe watched the campground empty until only a few scavengers were left, picking over the jumbled refuse. Then he bid Bridger a reluctant goodbye, ''he was a genuine article with no alloy,'' and the Dragoons moved back east to Fort Leavenworth.

Lowe had found the West all he hoped it to be. He remained there after his enlistment ended, working in the Quartermaster Department and in the freighting business. He joined the gold rush to Pikes Peak and built one of the first frame stores in Denver. In 1877 he would return to the Platte with a herd of cattle, sent to feed what remained of the proud tribes he saw at Horse Creek in 1851.

The Duke and the Artist

The days turned into weeks and still nobody came. The bitter cold clamped around his tepee. His provisions disappeared. Snow piled on snow and hunting was impossible. The wolves skulked ever closer around the camp. He dared not sleep at night because of them, and they roamed through his dreams when he fell into exhausted sleep at dawn.

As the colorful mixture of Council delegates left Ash Hollow on their journey east, they met a much smaller, but equally distinctive party heading west. In an open wagon, accompanied only by each other, rode two German citizens.

One was the hefty, full-faced Duke Paul Wilhelm of Würtemburg. At age 54, the adventurous German nobleman was making his third journey into the American wilderness, where he had already ventured as early as 1822 in search of specimens of natural history. Since that time he had explored Mexico, Texas, the sources of the Mississippi, California, and the River Nile, and now he was squeezing in a quick survey of the Platte.

With him rode a 26-year-old artist who had come to America determined to spend his ''entire life in the romantic, alluring, primeval wilderness.'' Orphaned at an early age, unable to afford college or an army career, Heinrich Baldwin Möllhausen had fled the mundane life of a farmer for adventure in the American West.

Though the Duke had promised him only that life on the trail would be miserable, he had badgered his countryman until he finally won a place as Paul's companion. The Duke, scorning danger from Indians, never traveled with more than one or two companions, and, with an impulsive disregard for the lateness of the season, the Germans had set out in mid-August, and had only reached Ash Hollow when they met Fitzpatrick's party in late September.

Heinrich Möllhausen had already found life on the trail miserable. He grew more homesick with every mile, concluding, as the empty distances piled up between them and civilization, that neither one of them would ever return alive. Determined not to show his fear, he put up a good front for the Duke. But as they passed the trading post called Fort John south of Scotts Bluff, he came down with a fever. And, as his health changed, so did the weather. Sudden cold wind swept down the valley, filling the air with clouds of dust, and chilling the already shaking Heinrich.

Sympathetic to a point, the impatient Duke pushed on for another week, past the barren meadow that had held the council, past the new post of fur trader James Bordeaux. But, when he reached Fort Laramie and both Möllhausen and the weather continued ill, he conceded the expedition had reached its limits. On October 6 they

began the return journey to the States.

In spite of his illness, Heinrich sketched as they traveled. Back near Scotts Bluff he sketched the trading post of a trader named Robidoux, while Robidoux's Sioux wife and relatives made the Germans a tepee, and the blacksmith repaired the spokes of their wagon. Then it was on down the valley; the weather wet and cold, Heinrich shivering in his blanket, and the Duke voicing his exasperation that he had hired a useless artist instead of a healthy Creole.

Once again at Ash Hollow, they faced the forbidding slope of Windlass Hill, but this time they would have to go up instead of down. Unable to pull the grade, they were forced to unload the numberless cartons of plants, skins, rocks, and fossils, and carry load after load up the slippery hill on foot.

It was near dusk when they reached the South Platte, and more trouble waited beneath the swollen waters. At the Duke's insistence, Heinrich rode into the current, searching for the safe ford. The Duke ramrodded the wagon at his heels, and Heinrich led him straight into quicksand.

The wagon stuck. The Duke refused to leave it. Heinrich spent the night alone on the bank with the horses, an ax handle his only weapon. The Duke spent the night in the wagon in the middle of the Platte. A cold, persistent rain deposited its blessings on them both.

Morning brought an amused party of Cheyennes, who offered to help—for a price that got larger by the moment. They wanted coffee and sugar, then more coffee and sugar. They erected their tepee and settled in to smoke and reduce the coffee supply, while the Duke sat fuming in the river. Luckily for the intimidated Heinrich, a coach came along, and the Cheyennes decamped. The driver pulled the wagon out of the river for his own price—$10.

Three days later it was an Oglala war party. Duke Paul—who was never intimidated—gave them vinegar instead of the demanded whiskey, and in retaliation a brave snatched Heinrich's knife.

The Duke's advice to Heinrich was to ride over and demand his property before the Indians decided to take anything they pleased. Heinrich looked at the painted Oglala and swallowed hard. He thought his life was of more value than any knife, but he did as he was told. He got the knife back, but the angry brave took a shot at him as he returned to the wagon, and his cap fell to the ground, neatly punctured.

This was too much for the Duke to take. He marched over and told the Oglala what he thought of such cowardly actions. He suggested they'd be better off saving their bullets for their enemies the Pawnees. While Heinrich watched open-mouthed, the admiring Oglala not only listened to the Duke, but presented him with some meat in apology. The matter settled, the Duke spun on his heel and returned to the bemused Heinrich, congratulating him for having passed out of the ranks of the greenhorns.

Next it was 18 Kiowas, who parleyed in a friendly fashion, and then suddenly seized the men, held arrows at their throats, tomahawked a horse, and emptied their wagon.

Again the unflappable Duke brazened it out. He berated the braves for attacking two helpless men, calling them squaws and cowards. The tactic worked. The Kiowas released them and returned everything, but Heinrich's diary and some sketches got lost in the shuffle.

Just past Fort Kearny and beginning to feel safe, the pair met up with the Pawnees. This time the Duke's stratagem was not so successful, and they lost most of their supplies.

By now Heinrich was so used to being threatened by Indians that he wished for another diversion. It came. A prairie fire chased them into a ravine, where they crouched in the smoke and cinders as it rolled over them.

A few days later the heat from the fire would have been more than welcome. The November snows had come, catching them south of the Platte near the Big Blue River. One horse had already been killed by the Kiowas, and now another mired in a bog and was frozen by morning. They struggled on with a mule and an Indian pony, but by November 25 the pony was dead. Travel on foot was impossible, so they made camp where they

were with a faint hope that they could stay alive until help might come along.

One cold morning in late November they heard the sound of horses and the rattle of wooden wheels. It was a mail coach from Fort Laramie, bound for Independence. They were saved! They whooped and hollered and waved it down.

But the coach was full. The Duke managed to buy one seat with a $100 saddle and the mule, but not even he could squeeze out room for two. The Duke and Heinrich drew lots for the seat. Heinrich lost. Duke Paul swung onto the coach, promising to send back help. Heinrich stood in the road and watched the coach until it disappeared in the whitened distance.

Figuring it would take two weeks for help to reach him, Möllhausen settled in to wait. He packed snow around the walls of the tent for warmth, gathered wood and water, and divided his stores of buffalo, rice, coffee, and corn into 14 allotments.

But again his fever struck, and his joints became sore and swollen. Soon he was so lame that he was forced to crawl for wood and water. Searching through the wagon he discovered some laudanum and some quinine. The quinine helped the fever, and the laudanum helped the endless days drift by.

The days turned into weeks and still nobody came. The bitter cold clamped around his tepee. His provisions disappeared. Snow piled on snow and hunting was impossible. The wolves skulked ever closer around the camp. He dared not sleep at night because of them, and they roamed through his dreams when he fell into exhausted sleep at dawn. Finally he shot one that became too brazen for safety, and then he gnawed on the dry, sinewy meat, tough as the hides of his tepee. But he was cheered. It was edible. At least he would not starve. And, gradually, his illness loosened its hold.

One day he forced himself out of camp and up a hill for observation. What he saw was two Pawnees creeping up on his camp, unaware that he was not there. His heart pounding, he watched them shoot five arrows into his tepee—aimed to strike any sleeping occupant. He realized that, however miserable, life was still dear. He loaded his rifle and fired, killing one brave and wounding the other.

When he had walked shakily back to camp and viewed the bodies, he was stricken by what he had done. He decided to try to nurse the wounded

75

brave. After weeks of solitude any presence seemed welcome, and his mind painted romantic pictures of the friendship that would ensue. But when he reached to turn the wounded man, the Pawnee stabbed at him, slicing open his arm. Instantly Heinrich reacted. He sunk his knife in the Indian's chest, and there were no more possibilities of friendships.

That night, the most dreadful of his life, Heinrich lay alone, his wounded arm throbbing, while he listened to the wolves tearing at the corpses of the Indians. He had found adventure on the prairie, but it was not quite so romantic as he'd imagined.

A month of notches on his tent pole told him it was Christmas, and he celebrated with a pipeful of willow leaves and tea. He had given up on rescue, but he was beginning to believe he might survive until spring. Then—when 43 notches scarred the pole—a band of Otoes came on his camp and befriended him. They even offered to drag the hapless wagon back to their village.

Heinrich's body and spirits quickly recovered as he spent the winter between the Otoes, the Omahas, and Peter Sarpy's post at Bellevue, happily learning of Indian life and painting Indian style on buffalo skins. When spring came he rejoined Duke Paul in St. Louis. Four days after he

had left on the stage, the Duke had hired an Indian to go bring Möllhausen in. The Indian was never heard from again.

Möllhausen returned to Germany, but he took part in two more expeditions in the American West, serving as a naturalist and artist. One was a surveying expedition along the 35th parallel, and another went to explore the Colorado River. He produced a large volume of work depicting the country and the Indians he observed. In 1858 he sailed for Germany, where he spent the remainder of his life writing about the American frontier. He produced over 100 novels and stories, and some considered him the German James Fenimore Cooper.

His love for the prairie never faded. In 1904, at the age of 79, he wrote, "One would like to push back the inevitable onward march of civilization, before which the shaggy buffalo and the brown hunter disappeared, and, with them, the last of the romance of the 'Far West.' "

The greater part of his paintings of the West was destroyed during the bombing of Berlin in 1945. But some of them had been photographed by American historians, and thus copies were preserved. Through Heinrich Möllhausen's pictures, historical sites such as the Robidoux trading post near Scotts Bluff have been positively identified.

While Heinrich Möllhausen suffered through the winter of 1851-52 on the plains, Fitzpatrick and his delegation of Indians were being entertained in Washington, D.C. Denied a smoke with the Great Father (there were ladies present and it simply wasn't polite) the chiefs nevertheless left the capital impressed with the unbelievable strength of the white man's numbers.

Tom Fitzpatrick returned with the Indians to the frontier, where he soon faced the disagreeable job of negotiating changes in the treaty with the ink scarcely dry on the original. The Senate saw fit to reduce the period of annuities from 50 to 15 years, and Fitzpatrick had to visit the tribes in 1853 to win approval for the changes. He was shocked by the obvious deterioration of the people.

Convinced that penning Indians up on reservations to die of disease and famine was nothing short of murder, Fitzpatrick saw but one possibility. He thought that opening up the whole Indian territory to hard-working settlers might teach them the virtues of civilization (to counteract

the vices they already knew) and gradually they might be assimilated into a farming economy.

But Tom Fitzpatrick was not to have a voice in the final solution. In Washington that winter on government business, he caught a cold that developed into pneumonia. On February 7, 1854, the man who had survived every challenge of the wilderness died in a bed of Brown's Hotel. He was 55.

The young Irishman who had sought his fortune in the mountains had grown up with the West he helped to open. Unsurpassed in the skills of a mountain man, an enthusiastic explorer, a sought-after guide, he was something more. He had a clear vision of the problems and possibilities of the West and the ability to express his views and concerns in lucid prose. He was equally at home in the halls of Washington's bureaucracy and in the skin lodges of his Indian charges. He earned the respect of white and Indian alike, and in later years, the Arapahos would say, "We had but one fair agent; that was Major Fitzpatrick."

The Yelling Soldier

Every season saw fewer buffalo. Many Sioux, Cheyenne, and Arapaho were actually starving. "Their women are pinched with want and their children constantly crying out with hunger," Tom Fitzpatrick had reported to Washington.

Six months after Fitzpatrick's death, in mid-August of 1854, Man Afraid of His Horses rode south down the North Platte and joined the mixed throng of Sioux that spread down the valley below Fort Laramie. He was hungry. They all were hungry. Some of the tribes had been camped here as much as a month, waiting for their agent to arrive so that the annuity promised by the Great Council might be distributed. The goods sat even now in the warehouses of the fur company nearby, but the white men would not open the doors until the agent came. Every day there were hopeful rumors of his approach, and it was one of these reports that had brought the tall Oglala chief to Laramie.

But the agent was not there. There were some 600 lodges of the Brulé, Minniconjou, and his own

Oglala, and there were a few of the white-topped wagons still trundling along the Holy Road—their drivers tight-lipped and silent as the road threaded through the Indian camps. They were people with a different look to them than many of the wagoners, and they spoke in a tongue that Man Afraid of His Horses had never heard before.

The young men of the tribes watched the white men's horses and their evening campfires with covetous eyes, and joked—half-seriously—that one good war whoop would set them all to flight and leave their riches to fill empty Indian bellies.

In fact the first story Man Afraid of His Horses heard around the camp was how a Minniconjou named High Forehead had shot a footsore cow that had strayed from the train—shot her and faced down her frightened owner—and invited all his friends to feast on what meat the poor stringy beast had left on her bones.

They had all enjoyed the feast, but now some of the leaders began to have second thoughts. The Bear, the paper chief named in the Great Council, knew that the tribes were under obligation to pay for any damage to travelers on the Holy Road, and if the Indians didn't behave as promised the agent would withhold the annuity. He hurried to Fort Laramie to speak to Commandant Hugh B. Fleming and offer to pay for the cow.

It came to nothing. The Bear offered a horse in payment—worth at least two healthy cows (and this one had been sick and dying)—but the cow's owner refused to be satisfied. The young soldier chief seemed bored with the whole business, and The Bear returned to camp with nothing settled.

After a lengthy council, the Indians tried again. The next morning Man Afraid of His Horses was asked to go to the fort and see what to do about the cow. But when he got there he was told the soldier chief was asleep, and he was sent to the store, where a disinterested clerk assumed he wanted rations and parcelled out the usual provisions.

Finally a young officer rushed in waving a paper, and Man Afraid of His Horses heard him say "Minniconjou." The interpreter asked Man Afraid of His Horses what he knew about a cow being killed, and when Man Afraid of His Horses confirmed that it had happened, the officer rushed out of the store, red-faced and shouting.

There was much noise and confusion. Soldiers began running from building to building, and Man Afraid of His Horses saw them pull out two wagon guns and begin to work over them.

He went out near the wagon guns and asked interpreter Auguste Lucien what was happening. Lucien shook his head helplessly and told him the young lieutenant named Grattan was going to arrest the cow-killer.

Man Afraid of His Horses was shocked. Indians did not willingly give up their freedom. They equated capture with torture and death. Only last summer three Minniconjous had died rather than let themselves be ''arrested'' over a trouble at the Laramie ferry. And now this yelling soldier was going to try to arrest the cow-killer.

Man Afraid of His Horses stepped up and caught the attention of the officer named Grattan. Through the interpreter he offered to go himself and try to get the cow-killer.

Grattan would have none of it. ''No,'' he snapped at Man Afraid of His Horses. ''Do not go. If you get there and tell the news, the Indian who killed the cow will run off.'' He ordered the Oglala to remain at the fort until the soldiers were on their way.

Smarting under Grattan's insulting manner, Man Afraid of His Horses turned away. A hot wind swirled across the open ground, stirring up dust around them, and preparations continued. Lucien began to groan that he was going to die, and Grattan proceeded to stick him playfully with his sword, prodding him to hurry.

Lucien continued to wail, saying he wanted a drink before he had to die, and someone handed him a bottle of whiskey. He took a few swallows, and then Grattan prodded him onto his horse and swung himself into the saddle.

Man Afraid of His Horses tried once again. ''You had better not go tonight,'' he warned Grattan. ''There are a great many Sioux.''

Grattan stared down at him. ''Yes,'' he replied haughtily, ''that is good.'' Then he spurred his horse after the cannons and wagon load of infantry that were already splashing across the Laramie. There was nothing for Man Afraid of His Horses to do but mount and ride after them.

As they moved along the trail Lucien continued to drink. By the time the column had reached the warehouses that held the annuities, four miles down the valley, he was racing his horse back and forth, screaming insults at the Sioux who lounged about. Grattan tried to quiet him with little effect. But when he saw that Lucien had another bottle, Grattan managed to snatch it away from him and smash it. Some of the white traders at the post asked Man Afraid of His Horses what the trouble was. Frustrated and angry, he told them they were white like the soldiers, so they had better ask the soldiers.

The group now ascended a bluff and the lodges of the Oglala were spread below them. Man Afraid of His Horses tried to reason with Lt. Grattan. "Look, my friend," he gestured at the hundreds of tepees, "do you not see a heap of lodges?"

Grattan saw them. He also saw the Oglalas were rounding up their horses and preparing for action. But he brushed off Man Afraid of His Horses' warning. Instead he issued a warning of his own. The Oglalas were not to leave their camp. If they did he "would crack it to them." Dramatically, he told his men he would arrest High Forehead even if he had to die in the attempt. While he didn't expect resistance, he "hoped to God they would have a fight." Gleefully the interpreter translated for the Oglala chief, and Grattan ordered his troops to load and prime their weapons.

Within a few minutes they reached James Bordeaux's trading post, and Grattan called out the stocky Frenchman. Bordeaux was a familiar figure to Man Afraid of His Horses. His wife was Brulé and the Brulé lodges were gathered around his post. When Bordeaux saw the detachment of soldiers and the cannon, he looked puzzled and apprehensive. And, when the drunken Lucien proceeded to race his horse before the assembling braves, wave his pistols, and promise to eat the hearts of the cowardly Sioux, his pudgy face paled with horror. He huddled with Grattan, gesturing worriedly at the swaying Lucien.

Man Afraid of His Horses, conscious of the glowering Sioux and of the nervous grasp of the troopers on their rifles, felt some relief when a rider was dispatched and returned with The Bear and two other chiefs.

Grattan spoke to them without preamble. "I have been sent to get the Indian who killed the cow. I want to take him to the Fort and keep him until your Father the Agent comes, and then will send him back to you."

The Bear drew back in surprise and anger. Then he turned to Man Afraid of His Horses. "You are a brave, what do you think of it?" he asked.

"You are the chief," parried Man Afraid of His Horses, not willing to express an opinion. "What do you think of it?" He knew that Grattan was asking an impossible thing—that High Forehead

was a guest in The Bear's village, and that The Bear had no authority to tell him to surrender.

The Bear chose to equivocate. "I must go and put on my dresscoat before I give an answer."

But the dresscoat and a hurried conference still did not provide the impatient Grattan with an answer. As The Bear tried to explain his position to the lieutenant, word came that High Forehead refused to surrender. He would die where he was.

At this word Grattan's face hardened. He repeated that he would have High Forehead or die. Then he demanded to know which lodge belonged to High Forehead, and he moved his men toward the village, ordering his troops to be ready to fire.

Bordeaux, who had done most of the interpreting to this point, gave quick warning to the chiefs when he heard the order. They must give up the man and they had better do it fast.

But The Bear was expecting to parley. Grattan had not yet expressed his demand four times, as was Sioux custom. He expected the lieutenant to observe Indian protocol.

Grattan, more red-faced with every delay, moved determinedly toward the village. Bordeaux pulled at his sleeve and said something Man Afraid of His Horses could not understand. In answer, Grattan patted the holsters of his two pistols. Then he rode on. Bordeaux spun on his heel and scurried back to his post.

Grattan pulled his men up before The Bear's lodge. The chiefs had followed, and now both soldiers and Sioux sat down for another parley. Grattan was now dependent on the obnoxious Lucien to interpret, and Lucien took advantage of the spotlight to add color to his insults.

Man Afraid of His Horses, driven at last to action, hurried back to Bordeaux. "My friend, come on," he begged. "The interpreter is going to get us into a fight, and they are going to fight if you don't come."

With marked reluctance, Bordeaux borrowed a horse and lifted his bulk into the saddle. He rode with Man Afraid for a few paces. Then, complaining his short legs could not reach the stirrups, he turned back.

When Man Afraid of His Horses returned alone to the tense council, Grattan asked him to speak to High Forehead. Man Afraid of His Horses entered the Minniconjou lodge to find High Forehead and five warriors stripped and painted for battle. Man Afraid of His Horses asked them to smoke and they agreed, but they would not agree to surrender.

They reminded the Oglala of the Minniconjous killed at the ferry the summer before. "We want to die also."

Man Afraid of His Horses reported back to Grattan and The Bear. Alarmed at Grattan's agitation, The Bear tried again to placate the officer. He again offered a horse for the cow. Then two horses. He begged Grattan to wait for the Indian Agent to arrive, sure he could settle the matter.

Grattan refused to bend. And now The Bear's attitude began to change. "It was only a poor cow," he insisted. "Today the soldiers have made me ashamed. I was made a chief by the whites and today you come to my village and plant your big guns."

Lucien added to the tension with continued insults. The Sioux took his words for those of a drunken man, but he was the only link between them and Grattan. Desperate, Man Afraid of His Horses galloped again to Bordeaux's. "Come quick!" he yelled. "I am afraid it will be bad." Seeing Bordeaux mount and start toward the village he dashed back to the council. "Stop!" he called. "Bordeaux is coming!"

Both white and Indian were now on their feet, tempers out of control. The Bear shouted furiously and stalked toward his lodge. Suddenly a soldier stepped forward and fired. An Indian fell.

After the echo of the shot all was silent but the sound of Bordeaux's horse as he retreated to cover. Man Afraid of His Horses shouted to the Sioux, "Do not fire! They have killed one man and might be satisfied."

But, having come so close to war, the lieutenant did not know how to retreat to peace. He ordered the riflemen to fire, and The Bear crumpled into the dirt with three gaping wounds. The Minniconjous answered with a volley. Then the howitzers boomed, but their charges only tore through the tops of the lodges. The air was filled with arrows, and Grattan fell, five men with him.

The other soldiers scattered in panic. Several climbed into the wagon and whipped the team wildly as they dashed toward the road. Others rode the limbers of the howitzers. Lucien and a soldier who had grabbed Grattan's horse galloped through the lodges toward Bordeaux's. From behind a bluff hundreds of Brulé pounded into view. They rode to intercept the frantic Lucien, cut down his horse, and silence his voice forever.

The wagon and limbers, bouncing crazily

through the sage, had nearly made the road when they disappeared in a mass of Sioux horsemen. All that remained of the command, a small group of riflemen, managed to keep the Indians at a distance as they retreated toward a rocky hill. But when they had to cross an open area, the horsemen swarmed in upon them, and the last man fell to lance and tomahawk.

Man Afraid of His Horses had been narrowly missed by a Brulé arrow when the fighting exploded. He turned his horse and galloped to his own Oglalas. They stood in a long line, watching the battle.

"They are killing the soldiers!" he screamed as he reined in his horse. "Have we no brave men? Do you not see that they are killing all the soldiers? What do you stand looking for? Do you not see they are nearly all dead? Are you going to let them all die?" Impulsively he turned his horse back toward the battle.

An Oglala reached out, grabbed his horse's bridle, and held him in line. In a few moments it was all over.

Then the Oglalas joined the excited Brulé on the battlefield as they counted coups and fired arrows into the corpses. Afterward the warriors turned their attention to the traders and Fort Laramie. Bordeaux knew resistance meant death, and he surrendered his goods to forestall attack. The young braves urged attack on the fort, but Little Thunder, Man Afraid of His Horses, and other chiefs spoke against it. Luckily for those at the fort, darkness fell before an attack could be organized. Commander Fleming, with 32 men away from the post at the army farm, would have found he had only 10 men to defend the post had the attack materialized.

Realizing the government would now refuse to release their annuity issue, the Indians broke into the storehouse and took what they wanted. They did no further killing. By August 23 the Brulé had headed east and north to the Niobrara, where The Bear, dead of his wounds, was raised on a burial scaffold.

Before he died The Bear tried to pass his position as paper chief on to Man Afraid of His Horses, but the Oglala chief was not hungry for power. He refused to be raised above the other leaders, and with them he spent the long winter months in serious discussion, wondering how and when the Great Father would answer the bloody ground along the Platte.

The Avengers

But there were others among the Sioux who would not wait for the white man to react. The Bear was dead. Struck down before his own lodge by men who had pushed him into being chief and then shot him down when he could not answer their impossible demands. If the honor of the Brulé were to be upheld, The Bear must be avenged.

Early in November the brothers of the dead chief, Red Leaf and Long Chin, painted themselves for war and made a farewell ride through the Brulé village. With them rode a cousin of The Bear, a respected warrior named Spotted Tail, and two younger boys. To the sound of the women's strong-heart songs, the five rode out of the village on the Niobrara to make war against the whites.

They rode steadily south toward the whites' not-to-be-touched Holy Road and scouted it for something to attack. It was late in the year for travelers. The shrubs along the river bed had lost their color, and the valley lay empty under a gray sky. But after a day or two the Indians saw the dust of wheels to the east. It was a mail wagon, rattling along the trail with only four men to guard it.

Spotted Tail and his companions hid behind the river bank—not far from the ground of the Great Council that had made The Bear a reluctant chief. When the wagon rolled into range they fired. The driver pitched to the road, and then the man on the seat beside him fell. Two from inside tried to run away, but swift arrows dropped one to the ground. The other, an arrow through his leg, scrambled to cover, and the Indians let him go. The Bear was avenged. It was enough.

Inside the coach they found a heavy metal box, and when they had hammered it open, piles of shining gold pieces tumbled to the ground, with many pieces of paper that began to blow in the wind. They saved some of the small green papers for smoking, gathered up the gold, and continued up the trail to Bordeaux's.

There they spent some of their new wealth and laughed at the trader's bulging eyes when he saw their new smoking papers. Curious, they walked over to see how the bones of the soldiers they had killed with Grattan were already poking up from the shallow grave. Then the little party returned to their tribe, showing the gold they could use to buy guns, and telling of the ease of its taking.

Talk of war with the whites now filled many councils. The young men were eager for action. They scorned the older chiefs' caution. They had destroyed Grattan's force, and now the mail wagon, and still the white men did nothing. When spring came the road would be lined with wagons—there would be coups and horses and scalps for everyone.

There was some cause for worry. Word from the people who lived near the fort was that the Great Father was angry and would send his soldiers in the spring. However, months went by and nothing happened, and when spring came the Sioux held their Sun Dance and Spotted Tail led a band of warriors against older and more attractive enemies, the Pawnees and the Omahas. War with the whites was forgotten, and the wagons rolled up the Platte with only minor harassment from the Indians.

It was late summer before word came from the new agent at Fort Laramie. The soldiers were on their way to punish the killers of Grattan and the attackers of the mail wagon. All friendly Sioux were to come south of the Platte and proceed to Fort Laramie, where they would be safe. But those who had murdered whites were known, and they could not come in. They were to be punished.

The news brought a dividing time to the Sioux. Man Afraid of His Horses led his Oglalas to Laramie and some of the Brulé followed, but most of the Brulé and all of the Minniconjou stayed above the Platte.

Spotted Tail was in the Southern Brulé camp of Little Thunder on the banks of a creek called the Bluewater, just northwest of Ash Hollow. When word came from the agent the chiefs counciled on what to do. They had been told twice to move. But the camp was full of fresh buffalo meat, not yet dry enough to pack. And Little Thunder was known to the whites as a friendly chief who wanted peace. He had worked hard the night of the Grattan trouble to keep the braves away from the fort. Surely that was enough to show he was for peace. Little Thunder did not move his camp. And he did not send Spotted Tail and the others away.

One morning when the dew of early fall lay shining on the lodges, the Brulé awoke to see a force of soldiers marching up the creek toward their camp. In a moment the whole camp was astir, as the women raced to strike the lodges and retreat before the troops. Hoping to avoid trouble, and to buy time for the women and children, Little Thunder and Spotted Tail rode out to meet the soldiers, carrying a white flag and asking to parley.

The soldier chief called Harney agreed to a council, but as they talked the soldiers continued to move toward the village. Little Thunder told the soldier chief who he was and how he had worked for peace, but Harney insisted he must give up all those who had been in on the Grattan killing. When Little Thunder said it was impossible—that there were many, nobody could name them all, and some were far to the north—Harney rose in anger. He shouted at Little Thunder that the parley was over and they must fight. As the chiefs galloped back toward camp the infantry began its charge.

While the chiefs were engaged in the talk, the women had begun to retreat up the canyon. Scrambling up the creek with her two children, a Brulé woman suddenly saw more soldiers. They were horse soldiers, and they lined the canyon bank, cutting off the way of retreat. She ran back to warn the others of the trap, and the village broiled in panic and confusion. Many, seeing no other escape, climbed the canyon wall and sought shelter in small pockets of brush and shallow caves.

Spotted Tail, unarmed for the council, was caught in the first charge and lost his horse. Afoot in the melee, he wrested a saber from an attacking soldier, knocked him from the saddle and leaped on the horse. Then, sword singing through the air, he cut his way through the troops, slashing again and again, until many soldiers lay on the ground where he passed. Fighting furiously to protect the women and children, he did not withdraw until the last, and when he did he carried two bullets in his body, and blood flowed from two gashes of a saber.

The field he retreated through was a carnage. Harney's wagon guns had zeroed in on the cliffs where the people crouched and blasted them from their hiding places. The horse soldiers and their guns poured fire on all who tried to retreat up the creek, and then thundered after the people fleeing through a break to the east. Old people were cut down by the cannon fire, and mothers died shielding the dead bodies of their children.

Spotted Tail, dizzy with pain, followed the trail of his people. It was an easy trail, marked by blood-soaked clothing, abandoned lodge rolls, scattered parfleches, robes, and cradleboards. When the shattered tribe came again together in the safety of the sand hills, he found his wife and baby daughter were not among them. They—and nearly 70 others—were prisoners of the soldiers, taken by the wagon road east to Fort Kearny. And 86 Brulé braves would not fight another battle.

Never had a Sioux village suffered such loss. Their homes, their food, their robes, and many of their horses were gone, and over half their people were dead or prisoners. Harney the Wasp had indeed stung them badly, and Spotted Tail could do nothing but lie quiet while he waited for his wounds to heal.

Then came news that the Wasp was still not satisfied. He would have the warriors who attacked the mail wagon. Until he had these murderers there would be no peace and no safety for the Indian villages.

It was a difficult decision for Spotted Tail, Red Leaf, and Long Chin. They knew Harney called

them murderers, and they knew the whites hung murderers by the neck until they were dead. It was not the way for a warrior to die.

But the safety of the people was the most important thing, and so on a bright autumn day Spotted Tail and the two braves rode into Laramie on their finest ponies, dressed in their garments of war, singing their songs of death. Behind them came the wives and children who were not already prisoners, and before long the little group had been escorted down the Holy Road to Fort Leavenworth—Spotted Tail riding not proudly on his war horse, but in a wagon with iron chains around his hands and a heavy black ball that rolled against his ankles.

Subdued and resigned to death, Spotted Tail rode through the territory of the enemy Pawnees and on south of the Platte to country he had never seen. Whites were everywhere. Many seemed new to the area, building houses and working on the land, and every day boats on the river carried more whites upstream.

Fort Leavenworth itself seemed huge, lined with large, strong houses and filled with more soldiers than there were braves in Spotted Tail's tribe. When he learned this was only one post, and the soldiers had many others, Spotted Tail began to realize the true power of the whites.

After a month at the fort, the Indians learned their agent had secured them pardons, and they would not be hung after all. In the spring they would be free to return home.

Freed from the shadow of the gallows, Spotted Tail responded to the friendly overtures of white officers and their wives. Reunited with his young wife and child, he gave personal thanks to the officer who had picked the baby from the battlefield. While Long Chin sulked and Red Leaf sank into depression, Spotted Tail remained alert and open, observing the ways of the white men and drawing intelligent conclusions.

When they left Leavenworth in the spring on the journey home, it was to move through vast armies of whites, some settlers in wagons and some troops moving west. By the time Spotted Tail reached his own people near Laramie, he was a changed man. He had offered his life for his tribe and it had been given back to him. But the Brulé warrior had also been given a vision of the futility of war against the whites. He joined the camp of Little Thunder, to take up the new and difficult position of advocating peace with the white man.

The Lord Will Open the Way

Spotted Tail, impressed as he was with the white man's numerical superiority, had seen only the beginning of the white invasion of his country. The Kansas-Nebraska Act of May, 1854 had opened the Indian lands west of the Missouri to settlement—the Indians along the Missouri powerless to do anything but sell what the white man demanded. By September of 1854 Omaha City had 20 houses, a post office, and a newspaper, and promoters were organizing sites at Plattsmouth and Bellevue.

The Saints who were still in the vicinity were not eager for Gentile neighbors. But nevertheless in 1855 the land around them was surveyed, platted and incorporated with the pretty new name of Florence.

People would be coming—were coming—from all over the East and beyond the Atlantic. Some were Gentile and some were Mormon. The Gentiles intended to stay in Florence; the Mormons did not. Some who decided not to stay would pay for their decision with the most incredible suffering ever endured on the trails up the Platte.

In May of 1856, John Chislett strode up the gangplank of the good ship *Thornton* in high spirits. He was sure the journey he was embarking on was inspired by the Lord. John was 24, newly converted to the Mormon faith, and he and the 763 other Saints who crowded aboard from the Liverpool docks had eagerly grasped this chance to emigrate to Brigham Young's settlement in the Salt Lake Valley.

John, like most of the *Thornton's* passengers, could not have been there but for a new and unusual plan Brigham Young had suggested. It had been a bad year for the Salt Lake colony. Grasshoppers had stripped the crops and a severe winter had further reduced their resources. The church simply did not have the funds to provide the wagon trains that usually transported its converts to Salt Lake. And the converts, drawn from the mills and factories of Europe, could not pay for their own wagons.

But they were anxious—even frantic—to go, and when Brigham Young declared that all those who were sincere in their desire to come to Zion had only to "gird their loins and walk through," the faithful saved their tobacco money, forewent their tea, and flocked to Liverpool to begin the journey.

The plan sounded simple. They would travel by ship and train to Iowa City, as usual. Then they would walk the 1,400 remaining miles to Zion, pulling their belongings on a handcart. It would not only be cheaper, but faster, and they would be demonstrating every step of the way the strength and enthusiasm of their faith.

Except for bouts of rough weather, John found the voyage a pleasant experience. The Saints were organized with Mormon efficiency; divided into groups, assigned places, and carefully scheduled. There was a time to cook, a time to clean, a time to pray, and a time to dance. At night the ship sounded with song. The new Saints, still shepherded by the missionaries who had converted them, were on their way to Zion, and they couldn't have been happier. Ushered off the ship and onto a train to Iowa City, they were sped on their way in relative comfort.

But it was June 26 before they reached Iowa City, and here they found a cog in the system had failed. The church's agents at Iowa City were not prepared for more emigrants—they had already outfitted over 800 souls and sent them on their way—and lumber and other supplies were exhausted. When, on July 8, the 856 passengers of the *Horizon* swarmed off the train to join the *Thornton's* waiting hundreds, the agents were faced with outfitting 1,600 people for a two-month trip across the plains.

They managed as best they could. While the English and Scottish immigrants sweated in the muggy Iowa heat, and the weakest began to fall with fever, they threw together one two-wheeled cart for each five persons, stitched up tents that would hold 20 people, piled a wagon with provisions for each hundred, and hurried the trains on their way. On July 15 John Chislett threw his weight against the crossbar of a handcart and stepped into line with the 500 Saints of a company under James G. Willie.

The Willie Company was divided into the usual hundreds, and John Chislett was asked to captain one of the five divisions. Twenty handcarts, five tents and one wagon became John's personal responsibility, a responsibility the intelligent young Englishman welcomed. He was strong both in body and in faith, and he was glad for a chance to serve.

John was also unencumbered by family, but his charges were of different status. Families with six to eight children were common, many with fathers approaching or over 50. There were widows with young children, and men and women in their sixties. The Willie Company included one woman of 75, and at least 10 babies one year or younger. Several carts were pushed by teen-aged girls. In the entire 500 there were fewer than 75 able-bodied men between 17 and 50.

They were city people, pale from long hours in the factories and totally unprepared for life on the open plains. They were used to hardship, but they had never walked 1,400 miles pushing and pulling a cart that weighed nearly 300 pounds, even though baggage was strictly weighed and limited to 17 pounds per person.

For nearly a month they toiled across Iowa, and by the time they limped into Council Bluffs and were ferried over the river to Florence, practically every cart was in need of repair. The axles and spokes were of green wood. The wheels and axles were unprotected by iron. Even this, the easiest part of the trail, had taken its toll. John and the other men spent another week making repairs.

It was now August 17, and some raised the question of whether they should try for Salt Lake so late in the season. When they heard of the dissension, the elders called a meeting of the 500 to see if they preferred to winter in Florence and finish their journey the next spring.

John, like the crowd, was swept with uncertainty. He did not believe in taking foolhardy chances, but he longed to finish the journey and be finally in Zion. Of the 500, only four men had been over the trail before, and three of these spoke in favor of going on.

One voice only was raised in dissent. Levi Savage, captain of one of the hundreds, rose to speak against the risk of going on. He looked around at the old, the women without husbands to help them, and the congregation of children and babies. He told them they could not go so late in the season without much suffering, sickness, and death. In two weeks it would be September, and September meant snow in the mountains.

But 496 of them had never challenged a trail that could exhaust them in the stretch of a mile, had never seen a real mountain, had never experienced a plains blizzard. The elders assured them they would be walking with the Lord. He could hold back the storms until they were safely through. Rising on a tide of emotion they voted—all but Levi Savage—to be on their way.

Savage bowed to their will. "Brethern and sisters," he said sadly, "what I have said I know to be true; but seeing you are to go forward, I will go with you, will help you all I can, will work with you, will rest with you, will suffer with you, and, if necessary will die with you. May God in his mercy bless and preserve us."

Levi's somber words sobered the crowd for a moment, and John felt uneasy about the wisdom of their decision. But he shook it off in the flurry as the camp prepared to move, and by the time they trailed out of Florence the long line marched with cheerful confidence.

For awhile it seemed the majority had made the right decision. Evening camps were full of song, in spite of the fact that each cart now carried an additional 98-pound sack of flour, and the extra weight caused the axle of cart after cart to snap off at the shoulder. The pilgrims bent their backs to the load, trying to protect their axles with tin plates, leather cut from their boots, and grease from the bacon they should have been eating.

Food was scarce. The flour ration averaged a pound a day, milk from three or four cows was shared by 100 people, and there was only an occasional issue of fresh beef from the small herd. Then one evening as they camped at Wood River their beef and oxen stampeded with the buffalo, and in spite of a three-day, hopeless, horseless search, they never again saw two-thirds of their animals.

They were left with one ox team for each of their five wagons. When the oxen were unable to move the heavy wagons, they hitched up every animal they had left, including the milk cows and two-year-old heifers. Still the wagons would not budge. There was nothing to do but distribute part of the wagons' flour among the handcarts. Each cart was loaded with another sack of flour, and the Saints, without their beef ration or their milk supply, bent to even heavier loads.

One day as they crept up the Platte, they were overtaken by a party of church elders, traveling in fast carriages. One of them was Franklin D. Richards, president of the European Mission, who had recruited and organized the handcart migration. He stopped long enough to rebuke Levi Savage in public meeting for his lack of faith, and to assure them that "the Lord will keep open the way." He promised to send supply trains from Salt Lake to meet them on the trail. Then he consented to feast on the fattest calf from their dwindling herd.

Some of the Saints were moved to tears of joy by his presence. But John thought of the labor and sacrifice his people had made to come this far—of the already pitiful condition they were in—of the long miles yet to walk—and he wondered how Richards could swallow his beef. It was easy enough to urge others to faith and confidence when you had a full stomach and a fast horse. When the carriages headed west in a whirl of dust, John stared after them, his face hard with resentment.

At Fort Laramie, where they had hoped to pick up supplies, there was only a barrel or two of hardtack. Knowing they could not hope for resupply from the valley before they reached South Pass, they cut the flour ration to 10 ounces.

And as they passed Laramie and began to climb, the October nights took on the bite of winter. Distant mountains wore snow from peak to base, and the clouds moved down the slopes. Their allotment of clothing and bedding was not enough to keep them warm. They bedded down in everything they had, but mornings found them numb and haggard instead of rested.

John Chislett watched his people begin to fall.

Hungry, cold, spending themselves in labor day after day, the old and infirm began to die. They left the Platte and crossed to the Sweetwater, where the icy water sapped their strength as they were forced to wade it time after time. John pondered on the attraction of its crystal waters, but he found the ache in his legs drove out thoughts of beauty and divine aspiration, leaving "a void, a sadness, and—in some cases—doubts as to the justice of an overruling Providence."

Now dysentery struck and added its miseries. They had no medicine, and soon the young and strong—or those who had been young and strong—were adding their graves to every camp-ground. John watched fathers pull their sick children in a cart all day, only to die themselves before the next morning. There was no panic. The people died with the calm faith and fortitude of martyrs. "Life went out as smoothly as a lamp ceases to burn when the oil is gone."

But every death weakened the train. John could not raise enough men to pitch the tents at night. He drove himself to exhaustion and past, trying to care for his hundred. He had to carry the sick from the wagon to the fire every night, from the fire to the wagon every morning. He dug graves for the dead, as well as he could, and interred them with a desperate prayer for help to the God who was watching them suffer.

The day came that they issued the last ration of flour. And then snow came from gray October skies, catching them 16 long miles from wood or water. Against a sharp wind they struggled on, while snow stung their faces and the children cried with cold and exhaustion.

As they fell to the ground for a brief rest that noon, a light wagon materialized out of the west. It carried two young men from the valley, one of them Brigham's son. John thought his prayers had been answered. Help was on the way! The men encouraged the Willie Company to push on west to meet the rescue train, while they drove

farther east in search of the Martin handcart brigade and two more wagon trains, which had left Florence even later than the Willie Company.

Renewed in faith and hope, the Willie Company stumbled on to camp and settled in to wait the rescue train. But by morning the snow was more than a foot deep, several cattle were dead, and five more Saints had died in the night. There was little food but the barrel of hardtack, which was divided among the hundreds, leaving a few pounds of sugar and dried apples, a quarter sack of rice, and 20 pounds of hardtack in the commissary.

As the company was helpless to move on to the rescue train, Captain Willie and another man rode out to find it and bring help. But before he left, Willie chose John Chislett to take charge of the commissary, with orders to distribute what there was to those in the worst need.

Captain Willie was gone for three days, and it was a three days John Chislett would never forget. They killed some cattle, but the meat was so poor it would not satisfy their hunger, and for many it only increased the agonies of dysentery. John had to visit the sick, the widows, and the aged, making decisions as to who would eat. He tried not to listen as proud men begged him for a morsel for their children. Every face he looked into stared with naked want, and he prayed to God for strength to do his duty. Fighting pity—seething with anger at the conditions which made him do it—he refused them bread. The faith that had brought him so many miles began to die.

At last, as the setting sun turned the cold drifts to flame, the wagons drove in with Captain Willie at their head. Those who had the strength shouted for joy, while others stood weeping, and the smallest children stood confused, not knowing whether to laugh or cry.

The young men from Salt Lake, almost over-powering in their strength, soon had dragged in wood and cooked a hot meal. They had flour for bread, and potatoes, and even onions. But it was

too late for some. Even with warm clothes, blankets, and marvelous, heavy buffalo robes, with tents pitched and fires blazing, with songs and prayers again filling the night, nine more Saints died before morning.

Fed and rested, the survivors in the Willie Company continued west. The weakest were put into wagons, but still progress was painfully slow. Some of the Saints were so sunk in exhaustion and apathy that they could not be pulled back to life. Two or three died every day. When they began the climb of Rocky Ridge (25 miles east of South Pass) Captain Willie asked John to take the rear and help the stragglers.

John went from one cart to another, doubling up the labor, moving one cart ahead and then going back for another. But the stragglers kept increasing. By dusk nearly 40 people were lagging, and there was a creek that had to be forded. The cold was intense, and people dropped along the trail with frozen fingers, frozen ears.

One man, whom John called Old Man James, lay beside the trail while his 14-year-old son stood helplessly by. John tried to lift him and help him walk, but it was impossible. So John took the quilt from his own shoulders and wrapped it around James. He was frantic. One man could not help so many. Knowing the people would soon freeze where they lay, he ran up the trail to find help.

But he could find no one in the growing darkness. He couldn't imagine how the train had gotten so far ahead. The cold air wrapped his lungs in pain as he ran on, with boots frozen so stiff that he stumbled and fell again and again.

Picking himself up from an ice-hard drift, he remembered an elder's words at that fatal meeting back in Florence when they had voted to go on. ''I'll eat all the snow that falls on the train between Florence and Salt Lake,'' he had promised. But John did not have the strength for either tears or laughter. He plunged woodenly on through the bitter cold, not allowing himself to think that he might have missed the camp, might be running in the wrong direction.

It was 11:00 p.m. when he finally found the camp and reported the need for aid, and it was 5:00 a.m. before the last straggler had been brought in. Old Man James came in alive, but in a stupor. By morning he was dead. Old Man James was 46.

John's first task the next day was to collect the dead. By the time he had finished he had 13 frozen corpses. He helped dig a large square hole, and they laid in the bodies three or four abreast and three deep. One that wouldn't fit was put in crosswise. John read a prayer over the grave, but most of the relatives were too numb to even attend the services. Before nightfall two more were dead.

Still the nightmare was not over. The next day John had to bury two more men of his company, and as he worked the stench of these more recent victims made him nauseous. He knelt on the frozen ground and vomited again and again, until he thought his turn, too, had come to die.

But he did not. One of the bodies wore a pair of still-good shoes, and looking at his own disintegrating boots, he argued with himself about taking the shoes. At first he could not do it, but at the urging of one of the elders he conquered his disgust and took the needed shoes.

Now, as they crossed South Pass, they met more relief wagons, with good fat beef to fill their stomachs. And now the weather warmed. At Fort Bridger they met enough wagons to hold them all, and John Chislett had a ride for the first time since Iowa City.

The Willie Company arrived in Salt Lake City on November 9, 1856. Sixty-seven of their 500 were dead. Behind them was an even more horrible story. The Martin Company, which came in November 30, had lost 135 to 150 of its people. Many of the survivors of both trains were maimed by freezing, and fingers, toes, feet, and legs fell to amputation. The new Saints had achieved their Zion, but at a terrible cost.

The elders of the church who had led the Saints to slaughter—whether through ignorance, incompetence, or excessive religious zeal—did respond nobly when they learned the trains were in trouble. They gave freely what they had and mounted the massive relief effort in two days' time.

The rescued Saints were grateful, and John Chislett later wrote that the rescuers could not be too highly praised for their kindness. But John's faith in the hierarchy of the church was too badly eroded. He could not forget or forgive the suffering he had witnessed on the journey up the Platte, and he renounced his faith in the Mormon Church.

Years later he was still haunted by the horror of it all. When he wrote the story of his experience with the handcart brigade, he repeated assurances he had received from members of his hundred that he had done all any man could do. It was as if he were still trying to assure himself that it was true.

The Newspaper in the Attic

Three years after John Chislett's one hundred had marched out of Florence to learn the unforgiving nature of the plains, another young man prepared to leave the environs of Omaha City. He, too, was headed west to seek his destiny, but instead of a pauper's handcart, he struggled to force two heavy wagons through the mud of Omaha streets. Twice the second wagon sunk up to its hubs in muck, and twice the sweating, heaving men had to unload its cargo, push out, and load up again. But the cargo that sat momentarily beside the bottomless street was not the ordinary emigrant's outfit. And instead of the usual "Pikes Peak or Bust", the letters on the mud-splattered canvas read "Rocky Mountain News."

William Newton Byers was joining the gold rush to the Rockies, and while he certainly wouldn't have objected if he ended up with a gold mine, he was going primarily to establish the first newspaper in the gold fields.

It was rather a strange ambition for a man who had no formal schooling, no training or experience in journalism, and who up to now had made his living as a surveyor, but William Byers was always one to welcome a challenge. At 28 he had already crossed the continent to Oregon, laid out section lines in Washington and Oregon, worked as a logger, visited the California gold fields, crossed the Isthmus of Panama and toured New York City, drawn the first map of Omaha, served as Alderman of Omaha and as a member of the Legislative Assembly of the Nebraska Territory, and co-authored a widely circulated guide to the Pikes Peak gold fields. Now, as he had promised in his guidebook, he was following his own advice and heading for the new settlements at the far western end of Kansas and Nebraska Territories.

With a partner, a printer, three of his wife's

brothers, and assorted others, Byers slogged up the spring-swollen Platte. If it didn't snow it sleeted, if it didn't sleet it rained, but the form of precipitation did not really matter; they all made for heavy going. They crossed one creek by felling trees and teetering across with what they could carry. Then they swam the oxen over, threw back ropes for the wagons and the Reliance press, and pulled them through the flood. The second-hand press did not take kindly to such treatment. It began to rust and the men began to feel their own joints stiffen in the constant wetness.

They were far from alone in their misery. Everywhere, ahead on the trail, behind in the mud, and before them at every campground, moved a population the Platte Valley hadn't experienced since the Forty-niners had raced for California. These argonauts did not have as far to go, but if anything they had higher hopes and poorer preparations than their predecessors. The wild reports of gold that had scattered them from the Missouri frontier like buckshot had even less validity.

But William Byers and his crew were hopeful as they turned up the south fork and stopped at the ruins of Fort St. Vrain. While the other men spread out to pan along the Cache la Poudre (Byers own guidebook speculated that the gold fields probably ran as far north as Laramie) Will rode on toward the settlements at Cherry Creek to check the situation.

As he rode south a crowd appeared in the distance. They were mostly on foot, devoid of equipment, and obviously angry as they marched back down the Platte—away from Cherry Creek and away from the touted gold fields.

When they drew nearer Byers could begin to pick up words. They were harsh words. Pikes Peak was a hoax. A humbug. There was no gold. There was nothing but a few ratty cabins. They had come all the way for nothing. You couldn't pick fist-sized nuggets out of the creeks or scrape gold from the hillsides with a sled. You couldn't do anything but suffer and starve. And the men who had told them different—men like Byers in his guidebook—ought to be hanged.

They were disheartening words—frightening words if your name was Byers. The young editor-to-be had already had one experience at trying to persuade a mob against action, and he had finished that day with his right shoulder permanently lamed by gunshot. Preferring to be hanged in

effigy rather than in person, he kept his counsel and threaded through the crowd of angry men.

Around him fellow travelers began to slow and stop, discouraged at the reports and questioning whether they need go farther. Some actually turned and joined the malcontents, and the crowd of go-backs gained in size and volume as it grumbled on north.

Byers' spirits sank. The journey that had begun so full of promise now seemed nothing but a fool's errand. But having come this far, he decided to go on and see for himself. He continued on to Cherry Creek.

He rode down the hill to the settlements where the creek flowed into the Platte about noon of April 17, and while there was nothing prepossessing about the 300 tents and mud-roofed cabins that lined the creek on both sides, Will was used to frontier settlements. He had laid out the streets of Omaha and built one of its first houses. The dirt, the crowds, the whack of hammers, the wagons clogging the streets, the crack of the bullwhip, and the shouts of men in a hurry were not new, but they were still exciting. Obviously not everyone had given up on Pikes Peak country. Will decided to find out who was right.

He walked to the river bank and picked a likely spot. Then he began swirling the waters of the Platte over a handful of gravel in his pan. Was there gold here? Or had he unknowingly advertised a hoax?

The first two pans yielded about twenty cents in dust. Byers began to relax. Up and down the Platte he ranged, picking his spots with care, crouching in the cold water and patiently watching the circle in his pan. Nearly every pan yielded something. Some only a penny's worth. Some as much as ten cents. Satisfied that a man who wanted to work could probably earn two dollars a day—and that the area had a future—he straightened his cramped legs and went to find a home for his press.

The only space available was the attic over Dick Wootton's saloon in Auraria (the name of the settlement on the west bank of Cherry Creek). Byers was a temperate man, but he couldn't afford to be particular. And when he learned that another journalist was already setting up in Denver (the name of the settlement on the east bank of Cherry Creek) he sent hurried word to his party to bring the press and come on. They had competition.

It was nearly dark when the press wagons

groaned in on April 20, and the heaviest immediately stuck in the sandy bottom of Cherry Creek. So the *News* team ended their journey as they had begun, unloading the press and type cases from the stranded wagon, and carrying load after load across the creek and up the outside stairway to the attic of the saloon. In the chilly, dank, dark cubicle, bumping their heads on the slanting roof, they coaxed the rusty press into working order, arranged the type cases, and made ready for the next day's work.

William Byers had no experience at printing, so he left the setting of type to his partners and prepared to serve as reporter. It was not a difficult task, as word of their intentions spread rapidly through the community, and Byers was quickly surrounded by volunteers bearing news. When the people realized there was a race in the making — that Editor Jack Merrick was rushing his *Cherry Creek Pioneer* to press in Denver, and that the crew of Auraria's *Rocky Mountain News* fully intended to be first on the street — they laid wagers and streamed back and forth to watch the progress of the battle.

For two days the printers of the *News* labored over the type, squinting in the flickering candles, fingers numb with cold. Water from a spring snow dripped through the roof to run down the backs of their necks, wet the forms, and spot the paper stock. Finally they rigged a tent over the press area to save the press, the paper, and their tempers. They ran out of periods and had to use commas. They ran out of k's and had to run other letters upside down. They had to substitute italic face for Roman. And somehow, in the midst of it all, Byers listened to a miner's plea and printed up a flyer about a lost horse and dog.

After dark the evening of April 22, the last line was set and the page forms were locked. Byers gave the honor of inking the forms to a little old mountain man named O.P. Wiggins; a black named Jack Smith bent his weight to the press level; and, to the cheers of onlookers, a proud William Byers pulled the first sheet of the *Rocky Mountain News* off the press. It was dated for the next day, April 23, 1859.

Across the creek Jack Merrick ran a close second. Twenty minutes later the first and last issue of the *Cherry Creek Pioneer* hit the streets. If Jack Merrick knew that Will Byers had been playing with a stacked deck — that the two outside pages of his *News* had been composed and locked

up way back in Omaha, and only the two inside pages had needed to be filled at Cherry Creek — he didn't quibble. Deciding the gold mines looked more promising than the type cases, he sold his whole outfit to his competitors for $25 and headed for the hills, leaving the field to William N. Byers.

Byers gladly took it. He fell in love with the Rockies, and when Denver and Auraria joined forces in the spring of 1860, he became the quintessential civic promoter. For 19 years he edited the *News*, lending its pages to enthusiastic, but basically factual, reporting. When new strikes were reported in the spring of 1859, he personally visited the sites to be certain of their potential and then trumpeted the news that changed go-backs to turn-arounds. Tirelessly he publicized the promise and potential of the Pikes Peak country.

If he was the area's self-appointed chamber of commerce, he also was its civic conscience. Time and again he upbraided the community for its sins. He was shot at, kidnapped, and caned for his efforts. With incredible energy he promoted agriculture (planted the first wheat, fruit trees, and grape vines), prospected (he never did strike it rich), enjoyed the Rockies (climbed mountains, fished, collected wild flowers and geological specimens), organized and promoted towns (Greeley, Longmont, and Hot Sulphur Springs), established a telegraph line (personally staked the line from Denver to Santa Fe), and promoted the theater, the railroad, the Humane Society, the first university, an electric tramway, a fish hatchery, a mountain resort, oil exploration, and conservation of nature.

There was one notable case where his native enthusiasm outran his grip on reality. For three months in the fall of 1860 Byers tried to believe that the Platte was navigable. He began a column called "Shipping News" to detail arrival and departure times of various scows, and looked forward to the day a steamship would pull into the docks of Denver.

It never happened. Not even William Byers could change the Platte. But his energy and enthusiasm did much to change the grubby settlements at Cherry Creek. He died one of the most influential and respected citizens of Denver, his name memorialized in a mountain peak, a small plains town, and a junior high school. The **newspaper he founded in the attic of the saloon is** still being published 125 years later.

The Pony Rider

    While William Byers was busy staking out the streets of Omaha in the spring of 1857, a young boy some miles to the south in Kansas was facing a crisis. He had just buried his father, and now, at age 11, he was the sole support of his mother, five sisters, and baby brother.

    But the death of his father, blow though it was, was only the climax to three years of trials for the boy's family. After filing the first homestead in Kansas Territory in 1854, the Isaac Cody family had become embroiled in the dispute over whether slavery should be allowed in Kansas. Isaac had been stabbed while promoting free-soil at a proslavery rally, and for two years the family had been subjected to threats and harassment. With Isaac spending most of his time hiding away from home, the rest of the family saw their chickens killed, their cattle run off, their pigs slaughtered, and very nearly had their house blown up around them. When Isaac, weakened by the stab wound which had never completely healed, finally died in 1857, 11-year-old Will became the man of the Cody family.

ill was a frontier boy, and he knew how to ride and shoot as well as plow a field and herd cattle, but 11 was a pretty tender age for a boy to seek serious employment even among the self-sufficient settlers. For a while he drove an ox team to Leavenworth for fifty cents a day, and then he applied to a local freighting firm for work.

Here, at last, Will was lucky. His family's home was near the headquarters of the giant freighting firm of Russell, Majors, and Waddell. Though the freighting partnership was only two years old, the pastures for miles around were filled with the freighters' oxen, and the whole valley teemed with the activity of the enterprise as trains were formed to carry merchandise across the plains.

Alexander Majors was friend and neighbor to the Codys, and he knew the family's situation. When Will appeared in his office and asked for work, Majors not only hired him, but he promised the round-faced boy a man's wages if he could do a man's work. He hired Will to carry messages and herd cattle for the company's trains.

Will proved he could do a man's work. In the next two years he went west with three of the Russell, Majors, and Waddell trains, and he hunted, scouted the trail, and twice fought Indians alongside the older men. He spent time at Fort Laramie with Kit Carson and Jim Bridger, learned to speak Sioux, and trapped in the Laramie mountains.

It was a life that suited him. He loved the freedom of the open spaces, the challenge, the danger—the chance to go for months without a bath. Faithfully he took his wages home to his mother and the sisters who welcomed him with open arms—after they had tubbed him, cut his matted, buggy hair, and burned his odoriferous clothing.

The family also shamed the swaggering young frontiersman into a few months of school. Will had always done his best to avoid book learning, but when his mother watched the 13-year-old boy sign for his man's wages with an X, she burst into tears and Will spent part of that winter in school. He became at least semiliterate and soon the wagon covers, tents, and oxbows of the company trains wore the practiced brand of "Will Cody" and "Billy the boy messenger."

The excitement of Pikes Peak gold bought Will's release from school, and he and a friend spent two months prospecting in the Rockies. Without knowledge or experience, Will and his friend had no luck, and they soon joined the go-backs that so disgusted William Byers.

But Will Cody did succumb to one of Byers' predilections. Near Denver the boys built a raft, and they boated down the Platte successfully as far as Julesburg. There they wrecked, and like so many before, found themselves standing soaked and provisionless on the banks of the Platte. Lucklily a freighter's train happened along, and the boys were able to hire on for the trip back to Leavenworth on the less romantic but more reliable form of transportation.

After a trapping expedition in the fall of 1859, Will returned to Leavenworth at loose ends. But his old friends Russell, Majors, and Waddell were about to launch a project that had more appeal for Will than even the gold of Pikes Peak. They were to inaugurate a cross-continental mail service that would be faster than anything yet imagined. Running in relays from station to station across the country from St. Joseph to Sacramento, ponies would carry the mail in 10 days or less. Riding these ponies, they wanted "young, skinny, wiry fellows not over 18." They must be expert riders. Must be willing to risk death daily. Orphans were preferred.

It was a job tailor-made for Will Cody. He could ride, he was experienced on the trail, he enjoyed danger, he was at least half an orphan, and, at 14, he was still well below the 125-pound weight limit. Also the $100 or so per month that the riders would be paid was more than twice what he could earn anywhere else.

Will again applied to Russell, Majors, and Waddell for a job. He was younger by two or three years than any of the other applicants, but his record with the company was good, and one of his old wagon bosses agreed to give him a chance as a rider. Will again signed the oath required of all Alexander Majors' employees, promising not to swear, drink, gamble, fight, or be cruel to animals, and with a pair of Colt revolvers, a rifle, and a Bible, he took his station near Julesburg and waited for his leg of the race to begin.

Will was given a short route of 45 miles, with two changes of horses along the way. When the rider from the east galloped into his station, Will caught the specially made leather mochila that held mail in four pockets, tossed it over his saddle, mounted, and galloped west. In an hour he was at the next swing station, and it took only seconds for him to switch the mochila to the fresh horse that stood waiting. Another hour gained another station, and in the third hour the last 15 miles swept beneath him. He flung his mochila to the next rider and stopped to catch his breath.

He felt bruised and shaken clear through. He had never galloped a non-stop 45 miles before, and the incessant pounding was hard on his insides. But he was also exhilarated. When the pouch from the west came through, he pushed to make even better time on the return leg, and he wrote his family that he had found a life he loved.

After two months on the Julesburg segment, Will took time to visit his consumptive mother and then found an opening in Joseph A. Slade's division west of Fort Laramie. It was one of the loneliest parts of the route, and this time his assignment stretched from Red Buttes to Three Crossings, a distance of 76 miles. In that distance he had to ford the North Platte as it ran a half mile wide and work his way through the canyons and cliffs of the broken country. Sometimes he rode by day; sometimes through the black night. By now most of the riders had discarded their rifles as unncessary weight, and they depended on the speed of their ponies in case of attack.

Will left Red Buttes station one day after a few weeks on the route, and as he rode through a sandy ravine a mile west of the station, a band of Indian warriors rose in ambush. With shots whizzing by his head, Will clamped his heels into his pony and the animal managed a burst of speed. With the Indians howling in his wake and bullets kicking up sand under the pony's hooves, he lay on the horse's neck and made for the next station.

Gradually Will's grain-fed horse pulled away from the grass-fed Indian ponies, and he had a lead of two miles when he clattered into Sweet-water Bridge station, yelling a warning to the stocktender.

But there was no answer. The station stood deserted. The corral was empty. And the stock-tender's body lay in the dirt.

Knowing the Indians could not be far behind, Will had to force his tired horse on toward the next station. It was an agonizing effort for both boy and horse, and had the Indians persevered they likely would have caught the rider. But not realizing their advantage, they abandoned the chase, and Will rode into Plant's Split Rock station with his hair still on his head.

That was fortunate, for that hair was to become his trademark; one that was known around the world. When the Pony Express was discontinued in October of 1861, Will returned home to see brief service in the Kansas border wars and to serve the Union Army as a hospital orderly. After the war he did some scouting for the cavalry and shot some buffalo to feed the railroaders. He might have spent the rest of his life in relative anonymity on the ranch he had begun at the forks of the Platte. But a writer named Ned Buntline was in search of a hero for his dime novels, and when the real hero he approached refused his proposition, someone suggested Will Cody.

It was a good suggestion. Will was still only 23. Handsome. Adventurous. A crack shot. And not at all adverse to some publicity. By the end of 1869 Buntline had launched Will's career as Buffalo Bill, and for the next 48 years Will did his best to live up to his reputation.

He had sound instincts as a showman, and the Wild West Show he created played for years, both in the United States and Europe. If he was some-times foolish, and sometimes used poor judgment as he made and lost several fortunes, he was always kind, always generous with his friends, and always the support of his large family. He gave the West a glamour it didn't know it possessed. And when he died in Denver in 1917, old and broke and exhausted, communities fought for the right to enshrine his body.

Keeper of the Wire

The ponies of Will Cody and his cohorts could outrun the Indians, but they could not outrun the lightning. In the spring of 1861 the docks on the Missouri River in Omaha were piled high with heavy reels of galvanized wire, crates of glass insulators, thick green bottles of battery acid, kegs of nails, shovels, axes, and carefully boxed sending and receiving instruments. For while the ponies raced from station to station, crews building the transcontinental telegraph line would race from east to west toward Salt Lake City.

Construction engineer for the eastern half of the line was Edward Creighton, son of Irish immigrants, who had already erected lines in the east. Capable and efficient, he divided his men into three crews—one to dig post holes, one to cut and set poles, and one to string wire. Soon the prairie sprouted 24 poles per mile. Three months and eleven days after they began, Creighton's crew strung wire into Salt Lake City. On October 24, 1861, the line from the west was connected, and communications between east and west moved from a pony's back to a slender wire. The dashing pony riders would have to be replaced by other young men with a different kind of skill.

On a Sunday in early October of 1861, even before the telegraph line had been completed, Oscar Collister kept an appointment in the office of the Western Union Telegraph Company in Cleveland, Ohio. Oscar was not yet 20, but he and the three young men with him had come to seek jobs with Western Union as telegraph operators in the West.

Oscar had first hoped to work for the railroad,

but he was small and sickly and the railroad would not hire him. Determined not to be excluded, he had learned telegraphy by working as an unpaid messenger boy, and then had served the railroad in that capacity. But even this job had not lasted, as his employer decided the strain was damaging his health and dismissed him. Thoroughly frustrated, Oscar applied to Western Union. Evidently all Western Union required was that he be alive and breathing, for by Monday morning they had signed him to a contract requiring a year's service and put him on the first train west.

Some days later Oscar alighted stiffly from the stage and peered through the darkness at his appointed station. It was called Deer Creek, and it perched on the North Platte some 100 miles west of Fort Laramie. He could make out a huddle of buildings, a large stable, and a stockaded corral. He could just see where the telegraph line dipped to one of the primitive cabins, and he knew that was his new home. As the stage clattered off into the night, he settled his few belongings in the barren cabin.

Morning brought the old French trader Bissonette to the door, and one look must have convinced him that here was a soul who would need some nurturing, for the Frenchman immediately began shouting orders to his Sioux wife and family. Before long he had Oscar's cabin fixed up better than any of the others, and he arranged for Oscar to take meals with men who had Indian wives to cook for them. At night the old Frenchman took to visiting, and through the stories of the Indian trader, Oscar began to learn the ways of the West.

Unfortunately his education was not yet complete when he ran into a Pony Express rider named Bond. Deer Creek had been a Pony Express station as well as a stage stop, and with the Sioux Indian agency just three miles up the creek, there were often travelers passing through. Oscar happened to engage Bond in conversation, and somehow the discussion wandered to President Lincoln's inaugural address. Bond made a statement that Oscar knew to be in error and in all innocence corrected him.

There was instant silence in the group of men. Bond turned his back on Oscar and stalked across the road. Men standing near Oscar began to back away. A path cleared between him and Bond, but still nobody spoke.

Oscar stood alone and puzzled. He knew something was going on, but what it was was a mystery. All eyes were on Bond. For a long, tense moment nothing happened. Then the cook stepped to the window and called Oscar inside.

There he found out he was lucky to be alive. Everyone else had expected Bond to shoot him for the "insult." His tenderfoot status was all that had saved him, and Bond sent word that Oscar had better not cross him again.

Oscar, who had never intended to "cross" him the first time, took to his cabin for some sober reflection. Ohio and his friends and family might as well have been in another world, and he wondered if he could survive the dangers of the one he had chosen. He resolved to profit by his experiences, but still he felt vastly relieved when the last mochila cleared the line soon after, and Bond left the station.

Now Oscar's job as telegrapher began in earnest. He was responsible for keeping the glass bottles of the cumbersome bluestone battery at the proper solution by adding vitriol and rain water, replacing the copper and zinc plates as necessary, checking the connections from the main line through his key and out again, and maintaining the galvanized wire for 40 miles in each direction. With buffalo rubbing against the poles until they snapped, Indians vandalizing the wire, emigrants and Indians alike using the wood-capped insulators as targets, and the weather of the high plains winter to consider, it would be no easy task.

Oscar had been on duty only a short time when builder and superintendent Edward Creighton passed through Deer Creek and stopped for the night. When he got a look at the sub-100-pound Oscar, his reaction was different from Bissonette's. He told Oscar he was too young and too delicate to handle the job and he could not understand how a sickly boy had ever been assigned to Deer Creek.

After Creighton left, Oscar spent the days in dread of being replaced. He liked his job, and he wanted to stay in the West. He was tired of being judged too young, or too small, or too frail to carry adult responsibilities.

Then the line to the east of Deer Creek went dead, and Salt Lake sent him orders to go find the break. He had no real experience on the prairie. It was nine miles to the next station and nearly dark, but Oscar saddled his horse and left immediately.

Before he was halfway there the trail was lost in

blackness, but he managed to follow the glint of the wire on into Boxelder Station. There he grabbed a few hours' sleep, and was off again at daylight. He rode another 16 miles before he found the break, but he fixed it without difficulty and returned the 25 miles to Deer Creek. When he reported his success to the Salt Lake Office, they recommended that he be kept in his position, and Creighton assented. He had saved his job.

Sometimes that winter he wondered why. As the weather closed in, time hung heavy on his hands. He had promised his mother never to gamble, and the French traders seemed to know no other amusement. But he kept his promise. He did find a congenial chess partner in former Indian Agent Major Thomas Twiss. And at Oscar's suggestion they taught the traders' wives to dance. With a man named Wheeler on the fiddle, and Oscar shouting directions and demonstrating turns, the squaws were soon dancing old-fashioned quadrilles.

Oscar liked the Indians. He respected their customs and enjoyed their interest in his telegraph. He relayed Sitting Bull's requests for newspapers, and arranged for Little Owl to "talk" to Chief Washakie, noting that the Indians were "almost as superstitious as the witch-burning founders of our great city of Boston."

When the giant Man Afraid of His Horses came for a demonstration, he gladly obliged. Man Afraid of His Horses was deeply interested in the telegraph and awed at its ability. As he towered over Oscar and listened to the click of the key, he smiled and said, "The little man is good medicine."

In April of 1862, two stage coaches rolling west of Deer Creek were attacked by an Arapaho war party. The nine men traveling in the coaches managed to fight off the Indians without suffering any deaths, but the attack caused panic along the road. Every tribe was suddenly suspect. Ben Holladay ordered his coaches pulled off and the line closed from Sweetwater Crossing to Horseshoe Station until he was guaranteed protection. Oscar received orders from Ed Creighton to withdraw with the stage people when they came through, bringing with him everything that was portable and burning what he had to leave.

Oscar had his orders, but he hesitated to fulfill them. He knew the telegraph was a lifeline of information for the west coast as well as the scattered settlers along the route. He thought

the Indian danger was being exaggerated. He consulted Bissonette. The old trader, long used to sporadic Indian troubles, agreed their real danger was minimal. He said he would stay if Oscar stayed.

Collister made his decision. He wired Creighton that he would stay and keep the line open. Creighton allowed him to use his own judgment, and Oscar remained at Deer Creek, nominally in charge of 250 miles of line. Fortunately no breaks occurred before the other operators were back at their posts.

The restless Indians continued to harass the white man's road. In July of 1862, Sioux warriors pulled down miles of telegraph line west of Sweetwater Bridge, and Oscar and another operator began the 80-mile ride to Sweetwater Crossing to serve as relief operators while the line was being repaired. The trip was almost too much for Oscar. He had to be helped on and off his horse, and he arrived almost unconscious. But once there he recovered quickly and worked for five days until the line was open again.

With his station strengthened by a detachment of the Ohio Volunteer Cavalry—which was pulled out of Civil War service and rushed west to fortify the trail—Oscar didn't expect any more Indian problems. But he underestimated their growing bitterness. In the fall he strolled unconcerned into a lodge of Sioux who had come in to trade, dressed, as he usually was, in army boots and jacket (there was no other clothing for him to buy). There was an instant response to his appearance from the circle of braves, and as Oscar looked at the white-faced trader, he realized he was in great danger. Quickly he presented himself before an old chief he had met before, and when the chief recognized him and explained who he was, the braves relaxed. But it had been a tense moment, and Oscar was shocked at the quick hostility his blue uniform had aroused.

The hostility Oscar Collister felt in the fall of 1862 was to fester and grow, but he left Deer Creek before it exploded into war. After 2½ years of service on the Platte, he asked for a transfer on west to the Salt Lake Division. In later years he worked for the railroad at Sidney and Potter, Nebraska, and was the Union Pacific Agent at Carbon, Wyoming. In 1929, when Oscar related his adventures as a telegrapher in the West, the "sickly boy" was 88 years old.

Reach of the Rebels

A. BATTES

At the same time Oscar Collister was beginning his occupation as a telegrapher, a young woman in Denver was contemplating a new direction her life was taking. "I never thought to be the wife of a soldier," Mollie Dorsey Sanford confided to her journal the evening of October 5, 1861.

In the year and a half since she and her new husband Byron Sanford had left the Nebraska settlements for the Pikes Peak gold fields, 22-year-old Mollie had done many things. She had driven a wagon up the Platte road, placated threatening Indians with sugar and biscuits, lived in tents and shanties, earned her keep as a seamstress, followed By to the mine fields, fought homesickness and discouragement, and finally, just when things were beginning to ease, she had lost her first-born and almost her life in childbirth.

Now, still weak and grieving for her child,

attractive, dark-eyed Mollie listened to the excited talk that flowed through Denver. The trouble that had long festered between the North and South had broken into open conflict at Fort Sumter and Bull Run. It was war. And it was reaching toward the settlement at Cherry Creek. Confederate forces in Texas were forming for a march on the gold fields. Governor William Gilpin, governor of the new Colorado Territory, was calling for volunteers to defend against the Rebels. By Sanford had been offered an office in the First Regiment of the Colorado Volunteer Infantry.

Mollie's husband By had been a teamster, a blacksmith, and a miner, but she had never expected him to be a soldier. She turned to the journal she had kept faithfully since her family left Indianapolis to homestead in Nebraska. In its pages she had changed from a romantic schoolgirl to a responsible young woman, and to it alone she had confided the loneliness and heartbreak of her months in the Pikes Peak country.

But its pages also bore witness to the faith and courage that had helped her endure her pain and joke about the makeshift ways of their uncivilized life. Now there was a new development to ponder. She felt dazed that a war she had heard predicted for years was to come in her time and to take her husband.

By October 5, 1861, By Sanford was a second lieutenant in Company H, Colorado Volunteers, and he left for Central City to recruit more men. Mollie walked through the confusion of Denver's streets while bands paraded and the fife and drum sounded at all hours. The Southern sympathizers, of whom there were many in the beginning, had either left or subdued their expressions of loyalty as the new territory swung to the support of the Union.

On a few acres of bottomland two miles up the Platte from Cherry Creek, Governor Gilpin established Camp Weld, and before November 1, Mollie and By were settled into the new barracks. The fresh smell of recently milled lumber was heavy on the air, but Mollie had a floor under her feet, and after the succession of dwellings she had survived, she was truly grateful.

Mollie, who always seemed to be the one called when anyone was ill, served in the improvised hospital. Eager to please, she spent hours reading to the patients, and she cut up her green silk parasol to make eye shades for some snow-blinded soldiers. Warm, impulsive, and naïve, Mollie was

hurt when an officer's wife criticized her activities, warning her about "chasing after those rough men." Still she took a sick boy she knew from the mine fields into her home to die, because he so dreaded going to the hospital.

At first there was little for the Volunteers to do. Once in a while scouting parties were sent out to look for hostile Indians, but most of the activity consisted of endless drilling on the parade ground. Guard mount, company drill, battalion drill, and dress parade were spaced through the day, and the citizens of Denver often drove out to watch the evening ceremonies. Mollie had to admit that By looked handsome in his dress uniform, with sword and regimental sash, and she watched proudly as he marched with the men.

But drills did not long occupy the energies of the young miners, who had volunteered to fight, not to march in pretty squares. Realizing the guard was always picked from the left rank, they formed in a shambles that had no "left," or they stood in large circles. By and the other officers were hard put to control the restless roughnecks, and the citizens of Denver found they needed some protection from the soldiers.

Just before Christmas, orders came that cheered the soldiers and disheartened Mollie. Companies H and G were to go to Fort Wise (later renamed Fort Lyon) down on the Arkansas River, 200 miles closer to the Rebel threat.

Mollie could have gone home to her parents in Nebraska, but she chose immediately to go with By. She knew what the hospital facilities were, and she knew By would need her care if he were wounded. She determined to stay with him as long as possible. Trying to be philosophical, she wondered what kind of life she was going to, but kept her expectations low. The vagaries of their fortunes the past year had taught her that much. The day after Christmas they pulled out of Camp Weld, traveling without tents or other shelter, and two weeks of frozen prairie later they were home in the stone barracks of Fort Lyon.

Suffering as she often did from bad teeth and neuralgia, Mollie made her bed on the floor and prayed that the war would be short. The windows of her quarters were large and deep, but they looked out on a level plain completely devoid of trees, dwellings, or other people.

Mollie had strong religious convictions, and she did not play cards, drink, or dance. As these were the main amusements at the fort, her social life was limited. But as the dark days of February dragged by, she consented to learn cribbage—to keep By out of the sutler's store, away from cigars and whiskey. And she had to admit she found it fascinating. She also whiled away the hours learning to play a guitar and visiting with the great-granddaughter of Daniel Boone, though Maggie Boone's deafness made it a ''little hard to converse.''

Mollie and By celebrated their second wedding anniversary by spending the afternoon in quiet reminiscence. They laughed over the way Mollie had cried the first time she heard By swear; the time By drank water Mollie had used to rinse his socks; the time By had refused to trade Mollie for a pony, because the old Indian who offered the pony had never done him any harm. Mollie remembered how By had walked 10 miles from his gold diggings to be with her on their first anniversary. By remembered his young wife gamely trying to cook for 20 miners over an open fire, until she collapsed from the effort. They both remembered the shock and grief of losing their first son. Soldier and soldier's wife—unable to plan for the future—they pledged to ''love and live for each other.''

Then on March 1, 1862, came word that the Rebel forces under General Henry Sibley were on the move. They had already captured Albuquerque and Santa Fe, and they were advancing on Fort Union in northern New Mexico. The Colorado Volunteers had something to do at last. The women must return to Denver.

Two days later By and Mollie stood on the Arkansas plain in the crush of a thousand soldiers and tried to say goodbye. There was no place or time for a private word. Mollie was sick. An infected tooth ballooned her jaw. She had no money. The regiment had not received a cent of pay. She was being sent to Denver, where she had no place to live. And she was three months' pregnant.

As she stood fighting her tears and trying to comfort By, his captain learned of her plight and offered her a place with his wife at Camp Weld. Giving By a last embrace, she mounted one of the three wagons that would take the women to Denver. Clinging to the lurching wagon, shivering in a bitter March wind, sick and miserable and full of fear for By, Mollie rode back to Denver. They were compelled to spend the nights in saloons full of drunks and Rebels, and along the way she was

forced to sell a box of dishes—all that she had in the world except the clothes in her trunk.

At Camp Weld she was taken in by the captain's wife, and they spent the days wondering about their husbands. Late in the month they learned their men had been in a battle with the Rebels at Pigeons Ranch. The Coloradans had won, but five of the Volunteers were dead.

For three days they waited word of who had been killed. Mollie refused to wail and carry on. She tried to stay calm and cheer the others. Only to her journal did she admit it might be her soldier who had fallen. ''O! I dare not think!'' she wrote.

At last the messenger rode in, and the wives gathered anxiously to hear the fearful news. Mollie steeled herself for whatever would come, but this time they were all lucky. Only single men had been killed, so there were no widows or orphans among them. Mollie's happiness was tempered by the five names on the death list. ''Yet,'' she thought, ''they were someone's sons and brothers.''

The Battle of Pigeons Ranch was an important victory for the Volunteers. It and other successes stopped the Rebels well out of reach of Colorado gold, and the threat was ended. Mollie had a few more days and weeks of waiting and By was home. She recognized his step on the walk one night after dark, and the next day she wrote in her journal, ''And now our life begins again, and if we have but little of this world's goods, I feel so rich! So rich!''

Mollie was rich, for her husband had survived the war, and in September she gave birth to a healthy baby boy. The next years were not easy ones; she found herself housekeeping again in a tent; she and By bought a ranch and lost it to a plague of grasshoppers. They lived through fires, Indian troubles, and floods, and when a daughter was born to them in December of 1866, Mollie closed her journal. ''Altho hard times are with us, and troubles surround us, we are happy. Life now has much in store for us.'' She promised to keep the little book as ''a reminder of the past, and a help for the future.''

Mollie and By Sanford spent the rest of their lives in Denver. By was employed by the United States Mint for 40 years and served as a trustee for the University of Colorado. Mollie's journal, recopied by her in 1895, was willed to her grandson, in the hope that it might be some help to her posterity, and with the very human wish that she not be forgotten.

Bluecoats Come to Cottonwood

Few in the West were directly involved in the Civil War as were Mollie and By Sanford, but the war was to affect them all the same. Thinned by calls to bolster Union forces in the East, soldiers became part of a token army. Unaware that the balance of circumstances which had kept peace on the plains was beginning to tilt, settlers pushed farther up the river valleys. Hungry, angry, and increasingly desperate, the Indians watched.

In the seven years since his release from Fort Leavenworth in 1856, Spotted Tail had led a relatively peaceful life, but it had not been easy. Little Thunder's band of Southern Brulé spent most of its time along the Republican and Solomon Rivers, south of the Platte, and with the advent of the Pikes Peak gold rush they found themselves surrounded by whites. Traffic flowed heavily along the Platte to the north and the Arkansas to the south, and when the whites began a stage line up the Smoky Hill River to Denver, the wheels rolled directly through their hunting grounds.

Still convinced that a war with the white man could not be won, Spotted Tail tried to make the best of his changed world. Instead of buffalo and antelope, the valley of the Platte held the telegraph and its operators, stage stations, and the ranches of traders. Every 10 to 15 miles from the Missouri through the Rockies, some white man had planted himself beside the trail.

Spotted Tail was learning how to deal with the white man. He spent weeks on horseback traveling to and from the Sioux Agency at Deer Creek to attend to tribal business. Some things had not yet changed, and he took great pleasure in directing many successful attacks against the enemy Pawnees. As Little Thunder aged, Spotted Tail took the position of war-shirt wearer, and his standing and influence in the tribe increased.

But in 1863, when Spotted Tail and the Brulé rode to Deer Creek to pick up the goods that made up their annuity, they heard disturbing news. This year—and from now on—there would be no guns or ammunition given out. The whites were afraid of another uprising like that in Minnesota, and there would be no more guns. Instead, the agent smiled, they could have plows and hoes and tools for farming. The tame tribes who lived around Laramie had agreed; the outlying tribes were to have no voice.

Spotted Tail was furious and he soon found his voice. His people lived by hunting, and they could not survive without guns and bullets. The buffalo were already difficult to find and bring down, so scattered and frightened were they by the whites' trespass. The skimpy annuity goods would not feed his people through the winter. And he would starve before he'd grub in the earth like the white man and the Pawnee woman. What's more, he thought the agent was cheating his people— stealing from the store of goods that was theirs by treaty.

The argument was loud and long. The sweating agent retreated behind his counter and kept his hand near his pistol. But in the end the Indians made their marks on the white man's papers and took what he gave them—except for the farming tools. They were left to rust until the agent could find men little enough to use them.

Spotted Tail took his disgruntled people back south of the Platte for an uneasy summer. The settlers at Cherry Creek were spreading up the South Platte, and runners from the Arapahos and Cheyennes who hunted the South Platte valleys told of their clashes over horses, women, and game, and of the white chiefs' increasing pressure to make them sell their land and move south of the Arkansas.

More and more of the young men began to talk about war. Here and there small parties of raiders struck at the whites. Warriors from above the Platte carried the war pipe to a council with the Southern Cheyennes, Sioux, and Arapahos. But with pressure from the chiefs still for peace, only the Cheyennes accepted the pipe.

In mid-October of 1863 Spotted Tail learned that yet another soldier fort was being built, this one where Cottonwood Canyon ran down to the Platte (present-day Fort McPherson National Cemetery). Here the sweet water of the springs and the brush of a large island made for good camping summer or winter, and Spotted Tail had often stopped there. Now the Bluecoats would join the traders already there, and perhaps the Sioux would no longer be welcome.

The Indians kept watch as the soldiers cut logs and snaked them down the canyon, stacking them together until they had four large houses for themselves and one for their horses. By the time of the snows, the soldiers had finished their houses and had pulled two wagon guns up the Platte from Fort Kearny. The Sioux found out what their welcome to the post would be when the friendly Oglala chief Bad Wound and his people stopped on the island one afternoon and cannon shells began exploding around them.

Winter's cold kept the Sioux in their camps and the soldiers in their forts, but spring thaws brought new pressures on Spotted Tail and the other peace chiefs. Fort-watchers told that even more soldiers had marched away to the war in the East. The young braves could see no reason they should not join the Cheyennes, and now the Arapahos, in a war that would drive the whites from their country.

Then word came that the soldiers wanted the Sioux to come to a council at their new fort at Cottonwood. Assured they would not this time be used as targets for artillery practice, Spotted Tail and Bad Wound brought their people in to the fort. There they were imperiously ordered to camp no closer than two miles from the post, while the soldiers made a big show of guns and guards and marching.

When the time came for council, the Sioux donned their finery and rode toward the half-finished building that had been chosen for the talks. While most of the people stayed back, Spotted Tail and the other chiefs put down their weapons and walked into the council site. They seated themselves in a semicircle on the ground. The soldiers, resplendent in their finery of red sashes and shiny metals, also removed their swords and guns, but they sat on wooden boxes instead of the ground.

For several moments they sat in silence. Then Spotted Tail took out his redstone pipe and began the smoke with the usual homage to the earth, sky, and the four directions. When each one had put the pipe to his lips, Spotted Tail rose and asked what their white brother wanted.

After the long, rambling talk of the soldier chief was translated, they found out what was wanted. From now on they were to stay out of the Platte Valley.

There was instant response. A huge Indian called Big Mandan rose and threw off his robe. He began to recount the history of the Sioux's westward journey—from the big lakes to the Missouri—from the Missouri out into the plains—pushed along always by the greed of the white man for Sioux lands.

Another rose to speak of the people's hunger, of the constant struggle to fill the children's bellies with buffalo so few and the other game driven away. A third stood to speak of the troubles white man's whiskey brought into Indian camps: quarrels, and killings, shaming of women, a lodge full of hard-won skins gone in an evening's foolishness.

But to each complaint the soldier chief had an answer. The Sioux had no right to all the land; an Indian shouldn't expect to hold 10 times the land allowed a white man. And it wasn't the government's fault their people were hungry. The government gave them food. They should make it last longer. If they would give up their way of life and live like the white man they would have no problems. They brought their troubles on themselves.

The debate went round and round, like the pipe as it made its circle, until finally Spotted Tail rose again to ask, "Why are we here?"

The soldier chief explained the paper they were to sign. They must promise to stay out of the Platte Valley. They could hunt to the edge of the hills, but no farther. If they wished to cross the valley, they must ask for an escort of soldiers. They must restrain their bad men. In return they would get more blankets, bacon, and corn, if the government decided they needed them. But, above all, they must stay out of the Platte Valley.

A murmur of protest swept the Indian circle and began to grow. Then Spotted Tail spoke and the braves subsided. He was not an orator, like some of the others. He stood with arms folded and spoke simply and quietly for his people. The Sioux were a great people, he said, and they did not need the whites to tell them where they could go. They did not care to hunt in the Platte Valley, because there was no game left to hunt, but they would come in to trade when and where they pleased. The Platte Valley was theirs—used by the white man for a road only by Sioux permission—and they would not give it away. If the white man wanted the Platte Valley he could pay for it, in a regular treaty. He must promise to close the road along the Smoky Hill River and to stop a road survey even then working on the Niobrara to the north. When these conditions were met, the Sioux would consider another treaty.

At that the soldier chief snapped that he would not ask the Indians what they wanted to do; he would tell them what they were going to do. And if he had to he would put a soldier behind every blade of grass from the Missouri to the Rockies to keep the Sioux out of the Platte.

Spotted Tail, in rising anger, answered the bluff. The Sioux nation would match the whites warrior for warrior, he promised. They were not afraid to fight.

With the conference at an impasse and tempers dangerously high, the soldier chief adjourned the meeting. He fed the Indians beef and bread with molasses, and the Indians staged a feast of fat puppy in return, but the Sioux left the valley with hardness in their hearts, and Spotted Tail began to think of war instead of peace.

He did not really believe they could win a war, but when the young braves stood in council to ask him what they had won with peace—as they were sure to do—he would have no answer.

Winter of Horror

For the Cheyennes, the decision had already been made. Through the spring and early summer of 1864, they were harassed by the Colorado cavalry, who could not, or would not, distinguish between friendly and hostile tribes. Finally the peace chief Lean Bear was shot down before his people as he rode out to parley with some soldiers, and there was no more hope of holding back the young warriors.

Small parties began to strike in Kansas and along the South Platte road, stealing stock and killing ranchers and freighters. They were soon joined by their Arapaho allies, and when the Sioux saw these camps rich with plunder, the white soldiers seemingly unable to retaliate, more and more Brulé and Oglala defied the wishes of their chiefs and joined the war against the white man.

Early in August the tribes combined for a huge attack on the Platte road, and in two days every ranch and station from Fort Kearny to Julesburg lay under siege. A train of freighters attacked at Plum Creek was wiped out, a dozen men killed and a woman and child taken into captivity. Station after station was left in smoking ruins. As the telegraph flashed news of the danger up and down the line, settlers abandoned their houses and fled into the forts for protection.

But south of the Platte, in the valley of the Little Blue, there was no telegraph to carry a warning.

In the heat of the sultry Sunday afternoon, two young women sat engaged in conversation. Lucinda Eubank fanned herself lazily, as she watched her three-year-old daughter Isabelle at play in front of their cabin. She was glad the baby had finally settled into sleep, so that she could visit with her friend Laura Roper.

Laura was only 16, but she was female company, and that was always welcome among the scattered settlers along the Little Blue. Lucinda's glance swept up and down the valley, vivid green along the edge of the blue water and dotted here and there with groves of oak. It was a beautiful place for a home. They were not far from a stage station, and with the constant travel on the road, she did not feel as lonesome or vulnerable as she had expected. Developing a farm was proving to be hard work, but working with her husband's father and brothers, they were making good progress.

The sun had swung toward the west, without any real reduction in heat, when Laura Roper stood, stretched, and said it was time for her to be going home. Lucinda picked her son out of his cradle and offered to see Laura home. She called to her husband Will that she was going, Laura took Isabelle's hand, and the women started off across the fields, with Will's assurance he would not be far behind.

When they had strolled nearly past the bluff that edged the river at the Narrows, Lucinda turned to check on Will's progress. He was on his way, but he had stopped. He leaned over, doing something to his boot. Lucinda was about to suggest to Laura that they wait for Will, when a loud yell split the air and Indians appeared. Howling wildly, painted for war, they rode down on Will and on the house.

At the first yell Will straightened. He whirled to run for the house and his gun, but the Indians were there before him. Cut off, he turned toward the river bank. He was leaping down the bank when an arrow thudded into his back. Lucinda watched in disbelief as he crawled onto a sandbar and then lay still.

Screams from the house pulled her attention away from Will, and she watched Will's sister Dora run from the house and fall under a tomahawk. More screams told her the Indians had found Will's younger brothers.

Frozen in horror, Lucinda and the children had not yet moved. But suddenly she realized their only chance to live was to hide. Somewhere. Anywhere. Nauseated with terror, she grabbed the children and pushed them into the rushes of a buffalo wallow. They threw themselves into the muck and tried to be invisible.

For a few minutes it seemed they might be safe. The Indians were concentrating on the house, mutilating the bodies of Will and Dora, searching for guns and horses. Then a brave rode out near the wallow and the terrified Isabelle cried out. In an instant they were dragged out of their sanctuary, pulled up on Indian ponies, and ridden back to the house.

Lucinda tried to shield Isabelle's eyes from the bloody body of her father, but they had to ride directly past the spot where Dora's body lay sprawled in the weeds.

The next two hours were a nightmare. Yelling Indians waved the fresh scalps of Will and Dora in their faces, and Lucinda discovered Will's brother had also been killed when he resisted capture. Not knowing if they would live or die, almost past caring, they watched the Indians wreck the Eubank house. They split open feather beds, smashed dishes, and broke up furniture. Then they loaded everything they could use onto their ponies and put a torch to the buildings.

By 6:00 Lucinda was behind a brave astride an Indian pony, riding away from the smoking ruins of her home and what was left of the body of her husband. She could only clutch her baby and concentrate on staying on the pony. It didn't do to think about what was going to happen to her and her children. Trying to keep track of Laura and Isabelle, she discovered that her six-year-old nephew was also a captive.

For four days the Indians rode south and west, stopping only for brief rest periods, until Lucinda's bruised and aching body could scarcely stay upright on the horse. The only food the Indians offered was dried buffalo, and that only increased her frantic thirst. Her arms that held the baby knotted in cramps, but she dared not complain or ask for help. She was sure they would kill him if he caused any trouble.

When they met another band, Lucinda and Laura were given their own horses, and Isabelle rode with Laura. She cried for her mother, but the Indians thought she belonged to Laura and wouldn't allow Lucinda to comfort her.

On the fourth day, Lucinda saw the smoke of a village in the distance. The Cheyennes paused to apply their paint and don some of their stolen finery. Then, yipping and shrieking, the Indians drove them into the center of the large camp on the banks of the Smoky Hill River. Some 2,000 Cheyennes and Arapahos surged around the terrified women and children, and they soon found themselves in a circle of squaws who stoned and beat them. As Lucinda collapsed under the force of the blows, she had her last glimpse of her daughter, her nephew, and Laura Roper. Dragged to the lodge of an old chief, she was raped by him and taken as his wife.

It was only the beginning of a winter of horror. After a few weeks she was sold for three horses to a Sioux named Two Face. Later it was another called Black Foot. Then Two Face took her again. Weak and ill, beaten at every excuse, forced to do all the heaviest work of the squaws, often hungry, she would have welcomed death if it had not been for her baby. Through it all she clung to him. The Indians tried to force her to wean him, but she refused, feeling sure if she did she would never see him again.

After she was sold to the Sioux she was taken to the north, where the band ranged along the upper North Platte. Braves returning from successful raids along the Platte would wave fresh white scalps before her face and taunt her with their victories.

A few weeks after the snows had begun, the Cheyennes visited the Sioux camp and tried to buy her and her son. Hard as life was with the Sioux, she found it worse with the Cheyennes, and she was relieved when Two Face refused to sell her. Then she found out why the Cheyennes wanted her. They had intended to burn both her and her son to death.

Stunned with horror, Lucinda stared at the departing Cheyenne warriors. What had she done, what had her baby done, that they inspired such cruelty? She huddled miserably against the lodge of Two Face and wondered if there was any chance she and her baby would survive the winter.

Even if Lucinda Eubank could not understand the Indians' implacable hatred, the Cheyennes thought they had good reason. The raids that had cost Lucinda her home and family had virtually ended by the last of August, as the Indians had to stop warring to put up meat for the winter. The chiefs, who had never wanted war, again exerted their influence, and the Cheyenne Chief Black Kettle met at Camp Weld with Colorado officials to negotiate for peace. Though there were still hostile Cheyenne bands about, and some like Lucinda Eubank were still prisoners, Black Kettle pledged his tribe for peace, and he settled his people into winter camp on Sand Creek near Fort Lyon.

On November 29, 1864, the unsuspecting village was attacked by some 700 members of the Colorado Cavalry under Colonel John M. Chivington. With orders to spare no one and take no prisoners,

the troops spent the day in slaughter, until over 150 Cheyennes lay dead, two thirds of these women and children. The village was destroyed, and the survivors fled into the icy hills—wounded, naked, without food or shelter.

When the pitiful remnants of the band stumbled into the Cheyenne hunting camps along the Smoky Hill River and told their story, there were few who could still refuse the war pipe. Spotted Tail of the Brulés, Bad Wound of the Oglalas, and the Northern Arapahos joined the Cheyennes in declaring war on the whites. Gathering in a great camp on a branch of the Arikaree through the snows of December, they planned their strategy. Their villages were not safe on the southern plains. They would have to move north and join the other fighting tribes. On their way north they would cross the Platte River road at Lodgepole Creek.

A Glorious Indian Campaign

The boys of the 7th Iowa Cavalry, snug in the new adobe post at Julesburg, where Lodgepole Creek enters the Platte, were not much worried about Indian attack. The raids of the summer of '64 had been bad, but they were over. They knew the Indians didn't like to fight in the cold any more than they did. The battle would probably be rejoined in the spring, and until then they worried more about the outcome of the November elections, Price's raid in Missouri, and the cost of cavalry boots than they did about Indians.

In January, when the lieutenant of Company F, Eugene F. Ware, left Fort Sedgwick (as the new post at Julesburg was christened) to struggle with a batch of recruits waiting at Fort Cottonwood, he only hoped the new men would equal the old. They had begun service green, wild, and overconfident, but they had proved to be good troopers, and the 23-year-old Ware felt a fatherly satisfaction with their progress.

He was not anxious to father a new brood. Looking with a jaundiced eye at the 116 baby-faced neophytes who lined up for his inspection at Fort Cottonwood, he suggested to his superiors that his services might be better used by his own Company F.

His suggestion brought no response, so Eugene turned his attention to his young charges. He told them they were just in time to get in on a glorious Indian campaign. Then, in the cold January wind,

he began drills that ran from breakfast until supper. As yet horseless, the recruits had to practice their cavalry drills on foot, and their feet had soon covered much of the territory around Cottonwood.

At night he called them to class in the headquarters building and demonstrated cavalry calls and movements with charcoal on a wrapping paper blackboard. In Indian country the cavalry depended entirely on the bugle to relay orders, and he knew from past experience that the men were inclined to forget the calls.

Lieutenant Ware had tackled his assignment in his usual thorough and efficient manner, but when new orders came on January 6, 1865, he was jubilant. Not only was he relieved of training duty, he was to receive a nice promotion. He was to report to Omaha and General Robert B. Mitchell, whom he would serve as aide-de-camp.

Looking forward to his new assignment with delight, Ware was packing for his journey the next morning when the telegraph line began to chatter. Indians had struck Fort Sedgwick and Julesburg.

Immediately Ware was ordered to take 40 men and artillery and march to the relief of Fort Sedgwick. As he prepared, additional reports came in of strikes both west and east of that post.

With 32 of his recruits in wagons and 12 cavalrymen, Lieutenant Ware rode all night into an icy wind. The recruits were initiated to the glories of Indian campaigning when they had to take turns running at the tailgate to prevent their feet from freezing solid before they had covered the 40 miles to O'Fallons Bluffs. Ware, knowing his company was under attack, pushed hard.

But at O'Fallons new orders waited. They were to return to Cottonwood. Facing the 40-mile return march, Ware gave his men a chance to eat and sleep a couple of hours, and before they could get underway, the orders were changed again.

This time their destination was to be Alkali Station, farther west, which reported Indians threatening. Again they marched west.

At Alkali Station everything was still peaceful, but Ware learned that his company at Fort Sedgwick had been in a big battle on January 7 with 1,000 or more Cheyennes and Arapahos. Fifteen of his comrades were dead. Anxious to go on west to his company's aid, he waited impatiently for time on the telegraph line to report his position and request orders to proceed to Sedgwick.

When he finally got through he was ordered back to Cottonwood. He protested. He even deliberately misconstrued an order and sent his command back without him, but in the end he was forced, frustrated and fuming, to return to Cottonwood.

However, in a week's time most of Company F had left Fort Sedgwick and joined him at Cottonwood. General Mitchell arrived to lead the Iowa and Nebraska forces in an expedition to hunt the Indians.

Thinking the hostiles were still camped on the rivers to the south, Mitchell's men marched through the bitter cold for 12 days. They found no Indians, and when the troops returned to Cottonwood, 50 soldiers had to be discharged for frostbite and injuries, and 100 horses had been ruined. Still glory eluded them.

Two days later the wire was again hot with news of Indian attacks both west and east of Sedgwick. Lieutenant Ware and the captain of his company, Nicholas O'Brien, took a howitzer and the 10 men of Company F still at Cottonwood and began another march to Fort Sedgwick. At the sod corral that was Alkali Station, they agreed to escort a stagecoach that was trying to open the stage route to the west. The employees of the stage line and additional troopers made them 25 strong as they left Alkali.

But signs of Indians were apparent all the way up the valley. Smoke signals rose from the hills, and pairs of braves were observed several times on the north side of the Platte. Feeling attack of the valley was imminent, they left men at various ranches along the way.

As they neared Julesburg on February 2, they saw droves of cattle across the river, herded by Indians instead of settlers. Other braves rode the hills on their side, without offering to attack or even appearing concerned at their presence. The settlement at Julesburg was hidden from view by a high point of land, but with his field glasses Lieutenant Ware could see black dots moving in the Lodgepole Valley.

It was a puzzling situation. They halted the command to discuss their position. They were reduced to 15 men—four of these civilians—and every moment made attack seem more likely. Nervously, Ware checked the howitzer to be sure it was ready for use.

Everything was in place—except the priming wire. Horrified, Ware looked again. Frantically he searched the chest of the howitzer. It was not there. It had been lost somewhere back along the trail! Without it the gun could not be fired.

Ware's mind raced, trying to think of a substitute, and his glance fastened on the telegraph wire. He sent one of his men shinnying up a pole, to swing out hand over hand and pull the wire to the ground. He couldn't bring it down far enough, and several more men added their weight. Still there wasn't enough slack. Finally they took an artillery hatchet to a pole, and when it fell the line sagged to the ground.

Ware felt their need of the wire was critical, but he also knew the importance of the line to communications. He cut the wire and tied one end to the coach, driving the horses forward until the wire was stretched to its limit. Then he stretched the other segment, and when he was through they had an extra two feet of wire. Sharpening this for their primer, they rejoined the ends of the telegraph line and made ready to move.

But while they had been working over the wire, smoke had begun to billow from the other side of the bluff. Captain O'Brien sent Lieutenant Ware up the bluff to reconnoiter. Ware saw nothing unusual as he rode up the slope, but when he reached the top, inched to the crest, and peered through the cactus, his heart nearly stopped.

Indians were everywhere. They splashed across the river, they bunched on the far side, they circled the stage station, blacksmith shop, and telegraph office—all of which were in flames—and they rode by the hundreds on the broad plain around the fort.

Ware plunged his horse down the sandy slope of the bluff and reported to Captain O'Brien. What could they do? They could not hope to make it back to Alkali. There was no place nearby that they could defend successfully. Their only chance (and it looked impossible) was to get through to the fort.

Captain O'Brien ordered the howitzer loaded with canister, and with Ware in the lead they probed cautiously around the point of the bluff. Using the land for cover where possible, and aided by the dense smoke from the burning buildings, they crept within a mile and a half of the post. Then they dug their heels into their horses and ran for the gates of the fort.

Stage rattling, howitzer bouncing, the men yelling like banshees, they raced in a line through the startled Indians. Ware had a glimpse of the burning stage station, where Indians carried off corn and chickens pinned to the ground with arrows still fluttered. The howitzer boomed and cleared a brief path in front of them, but Indians began to close in on the sides. The troopers drew their sabers and galloped on, ignoring the pistol fire on their flanks.

Indians began to group again between them and the post. Then the troops in the stockade aimed their howitzer in the direction of O'Brien's force and dropped shells in front of them. Before the Indians could regroup, the stage, the howitzer, and the 11 cavalrymen had exploded into the fort. Almost as astonished as the Indians, Ware and O'Brien checked their men. They found not one had suffered a wound in their mad dash for safety.

But their relief was only quantitative. In the beleaguered post were some 50 members of Company F and 50 civilians—a force of 100 to face 1,500 Indians. Their huge camp was in plain view up the Lodgepole, and those in the fort could only expect another attack.

Lieutenant Ware and Captain O'Brien decided the large haystack in the northwest corner of the sod enclosure offered the best observation post, and they burrowed into its top to spend the night, being careful first to see that buckets of water were spaced around the bottom of the 30-foot-long stack.

Ware swept the valley with his glasses and found it a scene of destruction. The telegraph line was down for miles, everything but the fort was in ruins, and across the river the Indians drove large herds of cattle and horses into their camp. The Indians' fires, fueled with telegraph poles, grew as the night darkened, and Ware could clearly hear the thump of the drums and the chants of the dancers.

He was absorbed in their wild celebration when a shooting star arched and fell across his view. In another instant he realized it was not a shooting star, but a fire arrow, and it had landed in his haystack. He turned to pound on the flames with the butt of his carbine, and at the same time a soldier threw a dipper of water. It was a perfect shot. The fire sizzled and died.

Across the river the Indians' fire began to spread, but the wider it grew the more dancers there seemed to be to surround it. Then for a few minutes the smoke obscured Ware's view, and when it lifted he could see Indians no longer. They had disappeared.

Alarmed that this must mean attack, O'Brien had the bugle sounded and every man took his place at the wall. For the rest of the night they stood waiting.

Even dawn brought no Indians. Smoke wafted from their camp across the river, but nothing else moved in the cold quiet.

When it was fairly light, and still no Indians appeared, the troops ventured out to probe the countryside. The deserted camp was littered with broken bottles, whiskey kegs, abandoned loot, and the heads of 156 beef cattle. Tracks of a great herd headed north up the Lodgepole, interspersed here and there with the narrow, wavering lines left by loaded wagons.

Ware took eight men with him and scouted west for nine miles. He found the ground burned over, an abandoned train of mining machinery, and a prairie dotted with white where the Indians had dropped flour sacks. But no Indians. When he reported this to the fort, and other scouting parties' findings were the same, many of the civilians at the post celebrated their deliverance by getting so drunk they had to finish their celebrations in the guardhouse.

But the soldiers had work to do. Reinforcements arrived the afternoon of February 3, 1865, and they began preparing for an expedition to follow the Indians' trail. Lieutenant Ware was anxious to be included, but when a train of telegraph poles arrived, he was assigned to help repair the line to Denver instead. He protested that he wanted to fight Indians, not set telegraph poles, but by midnight of February 11 he was marching out with the repair crew.

Working in fours, the men swung their picks into the stump of a pole, jerked it out, pushed the new pole into the hole, tamped it down, and moved on to the next pole. Behind them a man attached the insulator and strung the wire, and a wagon pulled it tight. From midnight of February 11 until 8:00 p.m. of February 12 the men set poles, without stopping to sleep. By afternoon of the thirteenth, they were exhausted and nearly frozen, but they had the line to Denver open. It was a substantial achievement, but not the kind that won medals for soldiers.

Eugene Ware returned to Sedgwick to find he was again ordered east to become General Mitchell's aide-de-camp. He left for one more long, cold, miserable ride along the Platte to join the general and see if battling the South might offer a more generous serving of glory. The two of them arrived at Fort Leavenworth just as the Civil War was ending.

A year later Ware left the service to become a newspaperman in Iowa and Kansas, a prominent lawyer, politician, and poet. In 1908 he returned to the sites of his army service. No one could tell him just where Fort Sedgwick or Fort Cottonwood had been, and no one he talked with knew what had happened there in 1864-65.

The winter that was one of horror for Lucinda Eubank, and one of frustration for Eugene Ware, was one of rejoicing for the plains tribes. They had carried the war to the whites, and they had won. They withdrew to the expanses north of the Platte, to the Powder River and the Black Hills, where not even a white trader had encroached. Their camps were rich with horses, beef, sugar, coffee, and unfamiliar luxuries. The braves could spend long evenings reciting coups and glorying in their victories. For the remaining winter months they would ''put the war in the bag,'' not to take it out until the spring grass was tall enough to feed the ponies. Then they would again show the whites their power.

But some Sioux saw wisdom in making overtures to the whites. In the spring of 1865 the band of Two Face was camped on the North Platte when a trader named Charlie Elliston rode into the village. Elliston had a Sioux wife and was friendly with the tribe. He brought news that the whites were offering ransoms for women and children taken captive in the past year's raids, and he urged Two Face to return Lucinda Eubank to her people.

Lucinda had spent the winter alternately longing for and fearing rescue, afraid she would be killed if the camp were ever attacked. She could scarcely believe her ordeal might be nearly over, but in mid-May Two Face started for Laramie, taking Lucinda and her young son. Her baby strapped to her back, she was put on a log and pulled across the icy waters of the Platte to Bordeaux's trading post. There a white woman found a dress to cover her near-naked, shivering body, and the party proceeded to the fort.

The officer of the fort who listened as Lucinda sobbed out her story was new to Laramie, having been schooled in command in Colorado under Colonel John M. Chivington. He was horrified at her condition—she was 24 but looked nearly 50—and he immediately clamped irons on Two Face and sent Indian police to arrest Black Foot.

Ignoring the fact that Two Face had surrendered his prisoners voluntarily, he asked for and received permission to hang both men. On May 26 the soldiers erected a gallows beside the Laramie River, and Two Face and Black Foot soon swung from artillery chains.

For a week or so Lucinda had the dubious pleasure of watching the crows pick at the rotting bodies of her tormentors. Then she learned an army train would be going east, and she prepared herself and her son to go with them.

110

A Docile People

Spotted Tail had played a major role in the successful winter assault on the Platte trail, but when the tribes rode north he had felt an increasing foreboding. He could not deceive himself that the white man was helpless before the Indian might. He remembered punishment for the Grattan affair had been slow in coming, but deadly when it fell. He remembered the months at Fort Leavenworth that had shown him the depth of the white man's resources. And he realized his country that had seen only a sprinkling of whites just 10 years before was now awash with them. Still, he believed his people could not survive a war with the army, and in spite of the provocations, he stood with Little Thunder for peace.

A. BATTLES

When the bulk of the tribes in the north determined to renew the war in the spring, Spotted Tail and the Southern Brulé detached themselves from the hostiles. They had not gained any lasting good from the fighting. They had, in fact, lost their homeland. They did not want to stay permanently in the north where the game could not support so many people, and they could not return south if they remained at war. When the grass greened in spring, Spotted Tail took 60 lodges of his people to Laramie and sued for peace. With the permission of the soldier chief, the village settled beside the resident Oglalas they called the Laramie Loafers.

Spotted Tail had not found the white soldiers to be an overflowing well of kindness, yet he sensed a new rancor in the troops that now occupied Fort Laramie. The officers he had dealt with before were gone, and the soldiers who had come from the white man's war in the east showed

open disdain for his people. Even so, he was shocked when Two Face and Black Foot were hoisted up and left to strangle. The lesson seemed obvious. It was better to kill captives than to surrender them.

His camp still hummed with hostility over the hangings when the soldiers came with another order. The Indians were to be moved east to Fort Kearny—removed from the zone of battle and from any possible contact with the hostiles. They were to pack up their belongings and be ready to move when Captain W. D. Fouts gave the order.

The Brulé Sioux were outraged. They had come in and agreed to peace, but they had not intended to give up their freedom. Now they were to be treated like prisoners, to be shipped wherever the army decided—even to the territory of the enemy Pawnees, where they might be disarmed and slaughtered.

The chiefs protested. No one listened. In early June a caravan of 1,500 Brulé and Oglala Sioux, and a number of traders' wagons flowed slowly onto the trail east. Escorting the train were 140 cavalrymen under the command of Captain Fouts. With Fouts were his wife and daughters, and Lucinda Eubank and her young son.

As he rode east Spotted Tail relived the events that had led to his journey down this same trail in chains 10 years before. Again he saw Chief Bear crumple into the dirt in front of Grattan. Again he saw himself with Red Leaf and Long Chin, taking their vengeance on the mail wagon. And again he saw the blasted bodies of little children on the Bluewater that had been the white man's answer. As then, he rode under guard down the Platte to captivity. But this time there were no chains on his ankles, in his hand he carried his rifle, and around him rode several hundred Brulé and Oglala braves.

For three days they rode quietly under the insults and threats of Captain Fouts. For three days they endured soldiers who found amusement in throwing babies into the river to see if they could swim. For two nights they suffered their women to be taken into the tents of the soldiers. For three days and two nights they seemed a beaten, docile people, until even Captain Fouts' contempt seemed justified, and the soldiers relaxed what little vigilance they had exercised. They rode as far ahead of the dust-raising crowd as possible, and by Fouts' orders the rear guard marched without ammunition in their weapons.

The third night they pulled into camp at Horse Creek, where all the tribes had met in giant celebration in 1851. Spotted Tail remembered the goodwill and friendship that had warmed that huge camp, when Snake had camped with Sioux, and white with Indian, everyone for peace.

But now the atmosphere was different. The troops and traders' wagons crossed the creek and made camp a mile or two up the east bank, while the Indians stayed on the west side, erecting their lodges near a thicket of willows.

Here, out of reach of the Laramie garrison, Spotted Tail and the chiefs perfected their plan. While the soldiers slept, an Oglala brave named Black Wolf rode to the Platte and planted sticks to mark a crossing.

When reveille sounded before light the next morning, the main force of troops began the march east. The Sioux men secreted their women and children in the willow thicket. Then they waited.

Soon Captain Fouts appeared with a few men. Riding into the middle of camp, he gestured at the lodges still standing and demanded to know why the Sioux weren't moving out.

For answer the Sioux gave him bullets from two rifles, and he fell from his horse, dead. To the Indians' amazement his escort turned and ran without firing a shot.

Immediately the Sioux broke for the river crossing, two miles away. Women and children crowded into the water between the sticks Black Wolf had planted. Warriors guarded the banks. The water was high and fast, but the Indian ponies plunged into it without hesitation. The waterway filled with snorting ponies, tails streaming behind them, and the heads of women, children, and old people who rode or swam beside the horses. On the bank Black Wolf, the crossing leader, shouted instructions and urged them on. He had vowed to endure the tortures of the Sun Dance if Wakon Tonka helped him get all the people over safely.

Spotted Tail and the other chiefs, with several hundred no longer docile warriors, confronted the cavalry. The captain in command after Fouts' death corralled the wagons and rode back with 70 men who now had bullets in their rifles, but a charge of Sioux braves dropped three soldiers and sent the command scurrying back for the wagons.

For an hour or two the Sioux kept the soldiers corralled, chasing them to cover whenever they ventured from the wagons. Then, with their people safely across the water, they too withdrew. A

few rode up and down the north bank, trying to entice the soldiers to follow, but when the challenge failed they headed north after the tribes. Spotted Tail, his hopes to return home in peace destroyed, rode back toward the Powder River and the hostile tribes.

In the circle of wagons the Indians left corralled on Horse Creek, emotions were ugly. Lucinda Eubank had huddled in a wagon with her son, terrified that her new-found safety was to be snatched away. But the Indians had made no real effort to take the train. They had only kept the soldiers bottled up, taunting them in their impotence. When the danger was over, the humiliated troops took out their fury on a Sioux prisoner who had been too lame to escape, pouring bullet after bullet into his body.

Lucinda tried to comfort the hysterical wife of Captain Fouts, but she would not be quieted. She wanted vengeance for her husband. Several of the traders had Sioux wives and families in their wagons, and she screamed for the soldiers to answer the death of their comrades by killing these Indians.

Their blood high and guns hot, some troopers began to move toward the traders' wagons. Then, as tension mounted, an old brave named Green Plum stepped forward with his four grandchildren. ''I am full-blooded Sioux,'' he told Mrs. Fouts. ''If it is your wish to see us killed, now is your chance.''

When Mrs. Fouts looked at the small children, her anger collapsed. She asked the soldiers to spare their lives, and passions cooled. Then the train pulled itself together and marched on east.

Lucinda Eubank traveled on to Julesburg, where she gave testimony on her captivity. In Julesburg she learned that her friend Laura Roper, her daughter Isabelle, and her nephew had been ransomed the past September, after only a month's captivity. They had been taken to Denver, and for awhile they had stayed in the home of a Mollie Sanford. The Sanfords had intended to adopt Isabelle, but the child was so scarred mentally and physically by her experiences that Mollie could not bear to keep her. In February Isabelle had died; the nephew soon after.

With her son, all that was left of her small family, Lucinda traveled on to Missouri to live with relatives and to begin a slow recovery of her health. She lived until 1913, and her son later settled in Pierce, Colorado.

Battle at the Bridge

The weeks following the escape of the Sioux were fairly calm ones for the troops stationed near Laramie along the Platte. After a flurry of raids, the Indians disappeared into the far reaches of the north country, and the trail posts were left in unaccustomed quiet.

n mid-July of 1865, 20-year-old Lieutenant Caspar Collins left his post at Sweetwater Bridge with a detail of men. Their destination was Fort Laramie, where they planned to draw remounts for their company of Ohio Volunteers.

Lieutenant Collins had lived in the vicinity of Laramie ever since he had accompanied his father's 11th Ohio Volunteers west in 1862. Then he had been a cough-ridden, skinny youngster, just along for the ride, hoping the western climate would put some muscle on his frame. Now, as he rode down the familiar trail, Caspar Collins knew the West had done its work. He would never be a big man, but he was lithe and strong, his redhead's complexion hidden beneath a healthy tan, and he sat his mount with ease and assurance.

From the beginning he had embraced the Western life with enthusiasm. Everything, from fish to flower, from trapper to papoose, from prairie dog to Oglala ceremony, had caught his interest and his artist's eye. He loved to sketch, and his letters home were often decorated with his impressions of the unusual sights he was seeing.

Even army life had not dismayed him. He had enlisted in his father's company as soon as he was old enough, and when the majority of the Ohio troops had mustered out with Colonel W. C. Collins in the spring of 1865, Caspar had been glad to stay in the Territories. Now he rode into Laramie having just been promoted to first lieutenant, and his spirits were high.

But as he neared the fort, he noticed the Indian village that had sat close-by since long before he came to Laramie was no longer there. The dogs and ponies were gone, and only barren, hard packed circles marked the long occupation of the many lodges.

Inside the post he found a turmoil of activity and emotion. General Patrick Connor was outfitting an expedition to the Powder River country to find and chastise the recently escaped Sioux. The fort that had been home to Caspar for two years under his father's command was now full of members of the 11th Kansas Volunteers, and these men were not delighted to be at Fort Laramie.

They would not have been delighted to be anywhere but Kansas. They had enlisted to fight in the Civil War. That war was over, and they felt it was unfair they were now expected to fight Indians, too. Sullen and disagreeable, they bordered on mutiny, and the post was rife with dissent.

Caspar wandered around the fort where he had spent so many happy days. He recalled the hunting expeditions, the band concerts, the mint juleps at Colonel Bullock's after theatrical productions, the endless games of poker. But most of all he thought of the Indians who had so often camped nearby. He had been welcome in their lodges; a guest of Red Cloud, a hunting companion of young Crazy Horse, a listener at the campfire of Young Man Afraid of His Horses. He had played with their children and eaten their food, and he had begun to record the legends and customs of their culture.

Now even the Laramie Loafers were gone. He heard that Connor's orders commanded the troops to receive no overtures of peace, and to "kill every male Indian over 12 years of age."

Collins was appalled at the barbarity of the order. He had had some skirmishes with war parties, and he had seen some comrades die, but he could not believe the only way to peace was through extermination.

Collins sent the detail back to Sweetwater with the horses while he remained at Laramie, watching the excitement with growing unease. He was being fitted with a new dress uniform (his promotion was much in his mind) when he made the mistake of letting his path cross General Connor's. Connor, thwarted by late supply trains that delayed his expedition, stalked the fort in a black mood. When he saw that Lieutenant Collins lingered over the unimportant business of a new uniform, he called him in, dressed him down, and ordered him to rejoin his command. Immediately!

Collins obeyed. He rode out of Laramie alone, without waiting for escort, his emotions in a whirl. The rebuke rang in his ears. Never before had he been accused of shirking his duty. And never before had he felt such helpless foreboding about the Indian situation. His father had shown him what respect and understanding could accomplish. But with men like Connor in charge, the Indians could expect not even justice, let alone mercy.

Along the trail Collins caught up with a mail detail, and he accompanied the men on toward Platte Bridge Station, some 100 miles above Fort Laramie. He planned to spend the night at Platte Bridge and continue on to Sweetwater the next morning.

But as the detail neared Platte Bridge on July 25, Indians suddenly whooped down on the beef herd that grazed east of the station. The men

115

raced in to report, and Collins joined a party to relieve the herders. As they rode, the few Indians who had been trying to stampede the herd swelled in number. For a few minutes the fighting was brisk, but when a Cheyenne chief was shot from his horse, the Indians withdrew. The soldiers declined to follow, and Caspar returned with them to the post.

Platte Bridge post was a small station maintained to guard the 1,000-foot span that bridged the Platte here for the trail's last crossing. Like Laramie, it had been garrisoned by Ohio troops, but now the Kansas Volunteers were in charge. The frontier-experienced Ohio troops found themselves outranked and displaced by the newcomers, who knew nothing—and did not care to learn more—about Indian warfare. Hostility was high between the two units, and Collins did not expect a warm welcome to the post. An outsider, he spent the evening in the company of John Friend, a telegraph operator he had known back in Ohio.

Major Martin Anderson, commander of the Kansas troops, saw to it that his men spent the evening running bullets, a duty that did little to improve their dispositions, and then the quarters darkened for the night.

In the early morning hours the post was aroused by the thudding of hooves on the bridge. Lieutenant Henry C. Bretney and 10 men of the 11th Ohio rode in from Sweetwater, on their way to Laramie. Bretney reported to Major Anderson that an army wagon train under command of Sergeant Amos Custard with 24 men was camped to the west and planned to be in about noon the next day. Bretney had seen signs of Indian activity along the trail, and when he learned that 80 to 90 warriors had been involved in the attack on the herd the previous afternoon, he urged that reinforcements be sent to the train under cover of darkness. But Major Anderson took no action on the Ohio officer's suggestion. He returned to bed.

As the sky lightened on July 26, 1865, Lieutenant Collins and the other men could see numerous Indians riding around the hills across the river. They taunted the soldiers and tried to draw them from the fort. Seldom had the Indians seemed so bold and aggressive, and the men began to speculate about their numbers.

Looking the situation over, Major Anderson reconsidered his decision of the night before, and decided to send a relief force to Sergeant Custard's

wagon train. He chose two sergeants and 22 men, ordering Lieutenant Caspar Collins to command the party.

Caspar's eyes widened with amazement when he heard the order. This was not his post, and the Kansas troops were unknown to him. Besides a Kansas captain, there were three Kansas lieutenants who could have been chosen.

Caspar turned to Lieutenant Bretney, who advised him to ignore the order. This was not his responsibility. He was under orders from General Connor to return to his post. The telegraph operator also urged Caspar not to accept the dangerous assignment.

Caspar wavered. It was a hazardous duty, but he had more experience fighting Indians than the Kansas officers, and he thought with some luck he could bring it off successfully. Once he had joined forces with the train, they would be strong enough to fight off any foreseeable attack. He could not bring himself to disobey an order. He would not again be accused of shirking a duty— even one not rightfully his. His decision was made.

He borrowed Lieutenant Bretney's pistols and thrust them into his boottops. As his own horse was travel worn, he was given a large iron-gray mount used by the regimental band leader. It was a powerful horse, but known to be difficult to manage under fire. With the sun glinting on the shiny buttons of his new uniform, Caspar led the column over the bridge, across the bottomland and up onto the bluff. Behind him Lieutenant Bretney moved his 10 men and a unit of the United States Volunteers across the bridge to protect the rear of Lieutenant Collins' small force.

They had scarcely formed a skirmish line when hundreds of Cheyenne warriors charged out of the willows along the river and galloped for Caspar's column. At the same time 1,000 Sioux rode down from behind the hills to the north.

When war cries broke the morning air, Caspar wheeled his men to face the Cheyenne force. Before they had time to act the Sioux broke into the open behind them. Outnumbered by hundreds, Collins ordered retreat.

There was not time. Indians came from every hollow and ravine. They rose from every rock and boulder. The troop got off the one round in their carbines. Then the mass of warriors closed around the blue column in a melee of dust, smoke, shouting men and screaming horses.

Caught in the unexpected nightmare, Caspar

116

fought valiantly to cover the retreat. The Indians, unable to shoot without hitting each other, swung war clubs and spears, trying to drag the soldiers from their horses. The soldiers fired their pistols at point blank range, as they scrambled desperately for the bridge and survival.

Suddenly in the whirling mass Caspar found himself among his old friends, the Oglalas. For an instant Crazy Horse and Caspar stared into each other's eyes. Then the surge of bodies drove Caspar onward. He felt a burning pain in his hip, but the bridge was only a few yards away.

Through the turmoil he heard a wounded man cry for help. Caspar turned back and reached to heave a bleeding private up onto his horse. The excited gray shied away from the extra burden, and Caspar struggled to force him closer to the outstretched hand.

Just then an arrow stabbed into Caspar's forehead. Blinded by blood, Caspar lost his fight to control the horse. The gray bolted into the midst of the Cheyenne warriors. With wild cries of triumph, the braves fell upon the young lieutenant.

The men at the bridge held stubbornly against a force of 500 Sioux and Arapahos who charged from the creek bed. Their fire, plus shots the Cheyennes threw after the retreating soldiers, drove the Indians back and held the bridge. But a group of braves swam the river and cut the telegraph line. The station was now isolated.

Lieutenant Collins and four men were lost, but 20 battered and wounded men had made it back to the post. How long they and 100 others could hold it against 2,000 Indians was problematical. The men at the bridge began to realize the tribes had united for this attack, and they faced the combined strength of several nations.

They watched the Indians mill around across the river and waited grimly. A Cheyenne brave led Caspar's gray mount along the edge of the bluff, as others stripped and mutilated the bodies of their fallen enemies.

Grief-stricken, Lieutenant Bretney charged back and confronted Major Anderson. Five men were dead and Sergeant Custard's train was still out there, unwarned and unreinforced. He accused the Kansas officer of cowardice and demanded to lead a force of 75 men with the howitzer to rescue the obviously periled train.

Anderson refused. He insisted he needed every man to defend the post and the bridge. Enraged, Bretney let go a blast of profanity, and Anderson placed him under arrest.

An attempt to repair the telegraph was beaten back, and then the lookout sang out the dreaded words. "There comes the train!"

Sergeant Custard's train appeared in a saddle in the hills about four miles to the west. Immediately the Indians howled with anticipation and galloped toward it. Major Anderson fired the howitzer in warning, and the wagons pulled up into a rough square.

The next four hours were agony for the men at the post, as within sight and sound the men of the train fought a hopeless battle for life. Gradually the reports of rifles lessened, and in late afternoon a column of smoke curled up from the now quiet train. It was over.

However, Sergeant Custard and his men had exacted a high price. Stunned by their losses, the Indian allies abandoned their plan to overrun the Platte Bridge Station and cut the Oregon Trail. They had come closer than they dreamed. But hindered by inexperience in organized warfare and hampered by their own numbers, they withdrew from the field. They rode back north to the Powder River, where they would tend their wounded, mourn their dead, and ponder the lessons learned at Platte Bridge.

The troops of Platte Bridge Station gathered the remains of their dead for burial, and within a week the Kansas men were marching home, leaving the dusty little station and the echoing war whoops to other men and other days.

Twenty-year-old Caspar Collins left his name— misspelled—on the short-lived army post at the bridge, a stream, a mountain, and the modern city of Casper, Wyoming.

Back in Ohio, Colonel Collins entered the date of Caspar's death in the family Bible. Beside it he wrote these words: "Pure, brave, hospitable, generous, true."

Hearts on the Ground

A. BATTLES

The expedition of the impatient General Connor finally got off
on July 30, too late to be of any help to Caspar Collins; and too late,
too slow, too lacking in skill and knowledge to be of any damage to
the Indians. Weeks of futile marches brought one small victory
over an Arapaho village, but they also brought sickness, starvation,
and death for the soldiers and their horses. Twenty-five hundred men
had marched with Connor, but they stumbled back to Laramie in
September without denting the Indians' prowess.

The force of the winter that followed was to do what all the soldiers
could not.

f the summer had been one of triumph and celebration for the Indians, the winter was one of suffering and endurance. The people of Spotted Tail's village were trapped in the Powder River country, unable to return south to their home. Temperatures fell sharply early in the fall, and they stayed extremely low. Snow followed snow, piling high around the lodges and burying the grasses in bottomless drifts. There was no game, and the little dried buffalo stored in the parfleches did not last long. They had spent the summer making war. Now there was no meat.

Through the endless weeks the Brulé huddled in their lodges. Blankets and ammunition that used to come in the annuity issue were sorely missed, and robes that should have come from the fall hunt were still on the buffalo. Cold and hunger began to sap the strength of the old and the very young. Spotted Tail heard keening in the lodges and saw the hacked off hair and scarred arms of mourning mothers.

In his own lodge, his beloved daughter Mini-aku began to sink under the coughing sickness. She was 17, and having spent much of her life near the forts in friendly camps, she was not accustomed to such hardship. Spotted Tail did what he could. He killed his horses to give her food, and he sent his wives farther and farther for fuel to keep the tepee warm. But every day she grew thinner and her face flushed with fever. When she walked outside she was often bent over with the force of the coughing, and the snow was spotted with red where she passed.

By the time emissaries from the soldier chief at Laramie came plowing through the drifts, the Brulés' "hearts were on the ground." Spotted Tail took the messengers into his lodge, and there he learned the soldiers had again changed their chief at Laramie. The new chief was called Maynadier, a man Spotted Tail had met and liked several years before. Maynadier sent word that he wanted the Sioux to come in and make peace, and he promised the white flag of truce would make them safe at Laramie.

They were words that Spotted Tail wanted to hear, but he did not know if he could believe them. The last time he had gone into Laramie for peace, he had been made a prisoner. But this message was from an officer he trusted. And Mini-aku, who loved the whites and longed to return to life near the fort, urged him to accept the chance of peace

and put away the war forever.

Looking around at the half-frozen, starving people, Spotted Tail could see no real choice. He moved camp to the mouth of the Little Powder, where the chiefs could council, and once again he stood for peace.

Most of the Brulé agreed. Red Cloud and the Oglalas would not go in, but the Brulé women prepared for the march.

Mini-aku, weaker with each passing day, seemed to realize she would not survive the journey. She asked that she be taken in to the fort and buried with Old Chief Smoke, near the white graveyard. Heavy with grief, Spotted Tail promised to carry out her wishes. Even before the village could take the trail, Mini-aku was dead. Spotted Tail sent word to Laramie that he was coming in, and that he wished to bury his daughter at the fort.

It was early March when Spotted Tail's people approached Laramie with Mini-aku's body, wrapped in smoked deerskin, suspended between her favorite white ponies. When they had crossed the Platte, Colonel Maynadier and several officers rode out to meet them. Led by the adjutant bearing a United States flag, the Brulé were escorted into the fort.

Spotted Tail was taken into Colonel Maynadier's headquarters. The Colonel told him that the Great Father would hold another council in the spring, hoping to establish a just and permanent peace. He then expressed his deep sympathy for Spotted Tail's loss, and told him the post was honored that he chose this site for her final resting place. He explained what arrangements had been made for the funeral and expressed the hope that Spotted Tail would be united with his beloved daughter in the land of the Great Spirit.

Spotted Tail could see the Colonel's words were sincere. He looked around at the fine room, at the friendly interest of the other officers, and his eyes filled with tears. He grasped the Colonel's hand and began to speak of the hardships and trials his people had suffered for the past four years.

Which was real, he wondered. The nightmare of betrayal, running, and fighting they had endured, or the bright room in which he sat, warm with friendship? Struggling to control his emotions, he looked out across the sunny parade ground.

"Is this real?" he asked. "I see it is; the beautiful day, the sky blue, without a cloud, the wind calm and still to suit the errand I come on and remind me that you have offered peace.'' He turned back to the Colonel and continued quietly. ''We think we have been much wronged and are entitled to compensation for the damage and distress caused by making so many roads through our country, and driving off and destroying the buffalo and game.'' He paused and his voice sank. ''My heart is very sad and I cannot talk on business.'' But he added a promise. ''I will wait and see the counselors the Great Father will send.''

By sunset the funeral arrangements were ready. A scaffold had been erected at the cemetery, and Mini-aku's body, secure in a pine coffin, was carried up the hill. Spotted Tail, his wives and family, the officers of the fort, and many of the soldiers followed.

They stood in a ring around the scaffold. The women wept quietly while the chaplain read a prayer. Then Mini-aku's family laid in the coffin food and clothing for her journey to the spirit world. The coffin was raised to the platform of the scaffold and covered with a bright red blanket.

Her favorite ponies were killed beneath the platform, and their heads and tails were nailed to the four supporting posts. She would be well-carried on her journey. Then, shadows long on the grass beside them, the people returned to the lodges that rose once again near the fort.

When the spring sun had greened the grass on the hillside beneath Mini-Aku's scaffold, Spotted Tail kept his promise and met with the government's peace commission. Even Red Cloud came down to see what inducements the government had to offer.

But once again the white man's appetite for peace was whetted by desire for a new road. This time he wanted to define and protect the trail to the Montana gold fields that a man named John Bozeman had marked out in 1864. The road cut north from the Oregon Trail above Fort Laramie and proceeded directly through the Sioux's Powder River hunting grounds.

Spotted Tail, given the right to return south in peace, which was all he had long wanted, signed the treaty and took his people home to the valley of the Republican. There he hoped they would be free to hunt the buffalo and count coups on their Pawnee enemies when the spirit moved them.

But the Powder River chiefs were adamant. There would be no road stretching north from the Platte. When the Sioux learned that soldiers had already been sent to build forts along such a road—with the treaty still lying on the table—they responded in fury. They struck their lodges and marched north, warning that any white man who came after them did so at his own peril.

The peace commissioner, refusing to admit failure, wired Washington: ''Satisfactory treaty concluded with Sioux and Cheyennes. Large representation. Most cordial feeling prevails.''

Pleasant Service and Absolute Peace

Many things had left Frances wide-eyed in the weeks since she and her new husband Lt. George Grummond had left Tennessee for George's assigned post with the 18th U.S. Infantry; none of the things left her gasping in delight…And in the strangeness of her surroundings, she reminded herself that she was embarking on a future where none of her past experience would apply.

A. BATTLES

Frances Grummond sat wide-eyed at a filthy table in a ramshackle road ranch which served travelers on the trail up the Platte. A sheltered southern belle who had never so much as made a cup of coffee, Frances watched the slovenly matron of the ranch not only put the coffee to boil, but fry salt pork, mix biscuits, and shoo chickens off the table, all in one effortless motion.

Many things had left Frances wide-eyed in the weeks since she and her new husband Lt. George Grummond had left Tennessee for George's assigned post with the 18th U.S. Infantry; none of the things left her gasping in delight. She had traveled by steamboat, train, and army ambulance, and she had learned that steamboats could be stifling and full of mosquitoes, trains could sit all day behind wrecked engines, and army ambulances could be her carriage by day and her bed by night.

Now she sat in the crowded station while a 14-year-old boy told her matter-of-factly of his seven-year captivity with the Indians, and a brightly costumed member of that race lounged in the doorway. His name was Wild Bill, and he warned Frances that the Indians where she was going might soon take the warpath.

It was not news Frances wanted to hear. And in the strangeness of her surroundings, she reminded herself that she was embarking on a future where none of her past experience would apply.

But with George strong and enthusiastic at her side, and General William Tecumseh Sherman's promise of ''pleasant service and absolute peace'' in her mind, she repressed her fears as they traveled on to Fort Laramie.

The fort, dusty and brown in the September heat, did not particularly interest her, but the chance to move into a real house did. She bustled about her two small rooms, covering the floor with gray army blankets. Then she opened her trunks to find everything buried in dust, and many of her fine dresses shredded by the jiggling of the trays over the long miles.

Faced with mending—and worse yet, cooking—Frances wished for her father's slaves. But as they were unavailable, she did the best she could with the mending and hired a Sioux squaw to do the washing. The cooking problem was solved when the officers gallantly invited the dark-eyed Frances to join their mess.

Frances enjoyed the Sioux children, and she was intrigued by the burial scaffold of Mini-aku, but their days at Laramie were to be short. Knowing they would soon leave the safety of the large post, Frances felt a gnawing fear of the future. Not wanting to burden George, she sometimes closed the windows and door of their quarters and paced the rooms in an agony of anxiety. But she never considered staying behind and when the mail wagon left for Fort Phil Kearny, Frances and George joined it and its eight-man escort. The small party began its 230-mile trudge north to the new post that was building at the edge of the Big Horn Mountains in Red Cloud's country.

Frances, her feet full of cactus thorns and her mind in a panic at the dangers of life on the trail, looked on Fort Phil Kearny as a refuge of comfort, peace, and safety. But her welcome to the post was a severe one: her party had to stand aside at the gate while a wagon with the body of a scalped and naked soldier took precedence for entry.

Still, she was delighted to be there, at last. The fort was on a beautiful site, Little Piney Creek flowing below and the slopes of the Big Horn Mountains rising behind. She met the wife and children of the commanding officer, Colonel Henry Carrington, and the three other officers' wives who lived at the fort. As she watched her tent home being erected, she listened to accounts of the soldiers who had died since Red Cloud and his allies had begun pressing attacks in mid-July. It seemed Wild Bill had told her the truth, and she wondered at the lack of concern shown at Fort Laramie.

When she woke the next morning to find an early snow had sifted into the tent and covered everything, Frances's main problem became how to fix breakfast for her husband. Struggling with the small stove, she managed the coffee and bacon without incident, but she nearly severed her thumb when she tried to slice her hard biscuits. A few days later, sparks from her fire nearly burned down Colonel Carrington's quarters and she found herself moved into a larger tent with safer cooking arrangements (at a safer distance from Colonel Carrington).

After the early snow, the weather settled into the gentle warmth of Indian summer, and Frances began to enjoy life at the fort. She tried to improve her cooking skills, visited with the other wives, and made lemonade for young Jimmy Carrington. She took special pleasure in Jimmy's company, for she was sure now that she would have a child of her own in the spring. Together they sang hymns and watched the 40-piece band which performed at guard-mount every morning and at dress parade every evening.

Between parades the troopers were kept busy cutting wood and hauling it in to the partially completed post. With the nearest source a few miles from the stockade, daily wood trains were a necessity. Indian attacks on the exposed trains became a daily occurrence. A picket stationed on a hill above the fort would signal whenever the wood train was under attack, and reinforcements would ride out to relieve it. Red Cloud seemed content to pick off an occasional man. He made no move against the post itself.

Colonel Carrington was a spit and polish officer, and when he announced that October 31, 1866, would be a day of ceremony for raising the flag pole, the troops of the fort scurried around preparing for a general inspection. Then, with drums playing and cannon saluting, the garrison watched the flag glide up the pole for the first time. Frances, her parasol shading her from the rays of the sun, waved her handkerchief in celebration. But she could not help seeing flashes of light from the hills around, as the watching Indians used mirrors to signal each other.

Early in December Frances was delighted to be able to buy a little black milk cow and a set of crockery for entertaining. Her domestic pleasure at this coup was short-lived, however. George, sent out to relieve the beleaguered wood train, was cut off from his men and nearly killed. Only the speed of his horse saved him, and Frances began to relive his experience in her dreams.

The morning of December 21 dawned cold, but clear. The band played as usual for guard-mounting, and the wood detail moved out for its day's work. With the fort virtually complete and a good stock of firewood already laid in, the wood detail would soon be discontinued. There were signs that the Indians' numbers were increasing, and Frances was grateful the men would no longer have to run the daily gauntlet.

But this time the picket on the hill signaled trouble much sooner than usual. Frances stepped to the door of her cabin in time to see Brevet Lieutenant Colonel William Fetterman, a relative newcomer to the post, ask to take command of the force to relieve the train. Colonel Carrington allowed Fetterman the honor, and then Frances heard her husband's voice requesting command of

the cavalry that would accompany him. She was horrified that he could be so eager to fight Indians after his narrow escape. But she stood quiet while the 80-man force marched out of the gate, after being warned twice by Carrington not to be drawn farther than Lodge Trail Ridge.

Frances stood shivering in the thin winter sun as the muffled thud of hooves faded. Then she pulled her shawl tightly around her and sought the company of the other women. They chatted about the gifts they were making for Christmas, but Frances found herself listening for some sound beyond the voices.

It was nearly noon when the sound came. It was gunfire—from the north—beyond the ridge. Beginning with scattered reports, it swelled in volume for nearly half an hour, and Colonel Carrington sent another force to join Fetterman's command. These men had just cleared the gate when the sound of shooting faltered and died.

Through the long afternoon the women waited. A messenger galloped in and spoke to the Colonel, then galloped away again. Frances sensed his news was bad, but no one approached to tell them what it was.

When the sunset gun signaled the end of the day, Frances started violently, and she felt the child within her move in protest. Food was prepared, but no one touched it except the children. As darkness settled on the fort, the women gave up all pretense of talking and sat in silence.

So it was they heard the crunch of wagon wheels approach the fort, and the squeal of the gate as it was thrown open. Stiffly Frances moved to the door and out into the parade ground. In the glow of the lanterns she could see in the wagon what looked like a pile of white bones, splotched here and there with a darker color. They were naked bodies—countless bloody bodies—over half of Fetterman's command. As Mrs. Carrington put an arm around her and drew her away, she heard a soldier's whisper. None of the command would be coming in alive.

During the night the wind swung to the north, and by dawn snow had begun to fall. Colonel Carrington ignored the protests of his men and set out to recover the rest of the bodies. Eventually the wagons returned with their grisly cargo, and Carrington handed Frances an envelope containing a lock of hair. He had recovered George's body.

Numbly Frances endured the next few days. In the room next to her, soldiers sawed and hammered on coffins, and outside they worked in 15-minute shifts to hack a huge grave in the frozen ground. Finally it was ready and the men were laid to rest.

Through it all, those in the fort—reduced to nearly half-strength—braced themselves for Red Cloud's attack. Carrington had sent a messenger to Laramie for help, but his chances of surviving both the Indians and the blizzard were doubtful.

Snow piled around the walls until the men had to shovel a path to keep it from bridging the stockade. When she slept, Frances dreamed of painted Indians coming over the walls. In the Carrington household where Frances stayed, a Negro servant lost his reason and sat banging his head against the wall.

For two weeks the garrison braced itself for an attack that did not come, and at last relief arrived from Laramie. With it came orders that Carrington was to report to Fort McPherson (formerly Fort Cottonwood) for investigation of the tragedy, by far the worst the army had suffered at the hands of the Indians.

As Frances no longer had a husband in the army, she must also leave Fort Phil Kearny. She asked Colonel Carrington that her husband be disinterred so that she could take him home to Tennessee for burial. She sold her crockery and her furniture to get money for the trip, climbed into an army wagon, and in a raging blizzard the trek south began.

The soldiers had done everything possible to make the wagons comfortable. With double canvas and boarded-up ends, a small stove and a supply of firewood, a buffalo robe and mattresses on the floor, Frances began her journey.

But with snow five to six feet deep and temperatures that dropped to -40°, there was no way to keep warm. Coffee turned to slush in their cups, meat and bread froze so hard they had to use axes to break it, and their kegs of water were useless solid chunks. In the three days it took to reach Fort Reno, the soldiers' feet and fingers turned black with frost, and Frances wondered how long the child she carried could survive the strain. At Reno, many men lost fingers and toes to freezing, and Mrs. Carrington's driver died under the shock of double amputation.

Three more frozen days took them to Deer Creek Station, where only a fireplace stood in blackened ruins. When they reached Bridger's Ferry on the Platte, Frances found her brother William waiting. He had come to take her home.

In seven weeks she was back in Franklin, and on a soft, spring morning she watched her husband's final burial. A short time later she gave birth to a son.

But Frances was not yet finished with army life. Four years later her path again crossed Col. Henry Carrington's. Colonel Carrington had lost his wife, and in 1871 Frances married the man her husband had served at Fort Phil Kearny.

In 1908 the Carringtons returned to the site of the old fort, now a field of irrigated alfalfa. Frances, now round and spectacled, climbed to the monument they had erected where George Grummond and so many others had died. She gathered a handful of wildflowers, leaving some to decorate the monument, and saving some to carry away.

News of Red Cloud's triumph on the snowy slopes of the Big Horns was well-noted in the winter camps on the Smoky Hill and the Republican. If Red Cloud and his allies could close the Powder River road, perhaps there was still hope for the Platte country. Perhaps the Platte could be cleared of the burdens of the white man's way. Perhaps even the iron bars he had flung along the river west of Omaha the past summer could be stopped before their clanking weight manacled the valley forever to the white cities of the East.

Spotted Tail, camped near the old gathering place at Cottonwood Springs in the spring of 1867, saw that the rails had already passed the forks of the Platte. He accepted a ride on the iron horse, and as he felt its surging power through the soles of his moccasins, he knew the tracks spinning out behind him would never be erased by wind or rain or Sioux.

But some had hope, if not belief. Turkey Leg's band of Cheyennes harassed the construction crews while they studied the iron monster for a weakness. Deciding that the iron horse was dependent on the evenness of its tracks, they pried up and spread the rails near Plum Creek. Then they waited to see what would happen when the iron horse came charging down the tracks.

They were not disappointed. There was a glorious crash and the iron monster lay puffing helplessly on its side. Then, they discovered, the men inside were as vulnerable as any warrior who had lost his horse in battle.

Civilization and Bands of Savages

The sudden news on the wire from Plum Creek filled the Omaha depot with a variety of men. One, a small man in a shapeless blue cap, pushed his way through the babble without effort, in spite of his lack of size. He was 26 years old, but he had already lived a lifetime of adventure.

John Rowlands had been raised in a Welsh workhouse under the stigma of illegitimacy, and he had seized the first opportunity that came his way to ship out as a cabin boy on a steamer bound for New Orleans, hoping for better things in the New World.

Better things had come his way for a time. He had been taken in by a Southern businessman, who gave him not only employment, but his name. John, or as he now called himself, Henry Morton Stanley, was soon pressured into joining the Confederate Army, and in short succession he was captured at Shiloh, imprisoned at Camp Douglas, freed to serve the Union, and discharged nearly dead with dysentery. After recovering his heatlh, he joined the Union Navy (probably the only man to serve in the Confederate Army, the Union Army, and the Union Navy) and then deserted to tour the West. He had also managed a side trip to Turkey, where he narrowly escaped execution by bandits. Stanley had not only survived his adventures; through them he had discovered personal talents as a writer, and now he returned west as a newspaper correspondent.

His assignment was to cover Missouri, Kansas, and Nebraska for the *Missouri Democrat*, and he had come to Omaha with the intention of reporting the latest peace conference with the Indians. He had already accompanied an army expedition through Kansas, and now a commission had been established to settle things along the Platte. "We earnestly hope that peace may be secured," Stanley wrote his paper, "although we have grave doubts that anything lasting will come of treaties of peace between a civilized nation and bands of savages."

The story on the wire from Plum Creek made his appellation of savages seem only too apt. Stanley joined the general rush to the depot to meet the four o'clock Special from the west, and now he braced to hold his position in the jostling crowd of men and boys as the Special slowed alongside the depot. Before the drivers had squealed to a stop, he was carried in the excited rush to the baggage car. In another minute the door of the car slid open. The crowd suddenly quieted.

On the floor of the car sat two fresh pine boxes, about 30 inches by 12 inches. And in the boxes were the remains of the engineer and fireman who were crewing the freight train that roared into Turkey Leg's trap at Plum Creek.

The sobered men of the crowd doffed their hats as the boxes were carefully carried to waiting caskets. Whispers of speculation hung in the air. Reports said the men had been burned. What did the bodies look like? How bad could death by Indians be?

With a rasp of nails leaving wood, the first crate was pried open and they had their answer. Involuntarily they drew back at the sight of what was left—a charred portion of trunk that lay like a half-burned log on the cotton inside. Some among them found their curiosity did not require such close examination of the second box. Quickly the remains were transferred to the black velvet interiors of the waiting caskets. Then, with the caskets sealed, tension drained from the crowd, and they gathered in small groups of quiet conversation.

When most of the men trailed off after the wagon that would carry the bodies to the cemetery, Stanley searched the train for anyone who could fill in the details of the attack. He found someone: a telegraph repairman who had been reported killed, but who sat now, pale and weak, with a gaping wound in his neck and a bullet hole in his right arm. Beside his foot in a pail of water sloshed a curled, hairy something. It was his scalp.

Stanley accompanied the gory apparition to a hotel where a doctor tended his wounds. Then Stanley took down his story: how he had been struck down and played dead through the pain of the scalping; how he had seen the scalp dropped close-by; how he had later squirmed to reach it, put it in his pocket, and crawled away to safety. He hoped now that the scalp could be reset on his head, and the doctors Stanley interviewed thought it might be possible.

Another survivor, a brakeman, told Stanley of his run for life down the tracks to a following freight. Stanley added these experiences to his copy and sent the exciting story off to his editor. He could hardly have hoped for more dramatic dispatches from the Platte, but the chances of success for the peace commission now seemed slight. However, Major Frank North and his company of Pawnee Scouts were sent to clear the Platte Valley of hostiles, and the commission determined to meet at least with Spotted Tail and the other friendly chiefs.

Stanley was of two minds about the Indian problem. He sympathized with the suffering of settlers and people like the scalpless telegraph man, and he had seen enough of life in the army to know the often hopeless task that faced soldiers trying to control roving warriors. But he could not stomach the solution that was gaining popularity even in educated circles. Extermination, he thought, was not a policy that became a great nation. Reservations seemed to be the only answer, with the savages kept in strict separation from the white man.

While he waited for deliberations to begin, Stanley took the train on west. He had traveled the Platte before, and he was interested in seeing the civilization that had come with the locomotive. Riding the north bank of the river, he passed a depopulated Fort Kearny, whose usefulness had ceased with the railroad's coming. The engine tiptoed over the bridge that crossed the North Platte and continued up the South Platte, stretching for Julesburg, but giving up its passengers to the stage before the distance was quite completed.

Stanley was impressed with the ease of travel, but he found the train had brought a strange mix of civilization to the New Julesburg that had risen after the raid of 1865. Streets thronged with gamblers, soldiers, teamsters, railroad workers, fancy ladies, and a variety of "ruined men." New stores with the latest fashions, warehouses stacked with goods, and packed saloons lined streets which two months before had separated only four tents and a half-finished hotel.

The population which had lately made the new town of North Platte a crowded jumble of gambling dens now resided in Julesburg, and Stanley was sure murder could be and was accomplished every day for as little as $5.00. Nevertheless he continued his practice of going unarmed. He was an excellent shot, but he thought if he carried guns it would only expose him to unwanted challenges. He was vaguely aware of a moral stiffness in his nature and in his speech that seemed to provoke ridicule rather than comradery from the rough elements of the frontier.

From the glaring clatter of the saloons, the small Welshman moved to the comfort of the Julesburg House. There he was surprised to find a table set with fruit and fine wines, and a company that glittered with gold watch chains and patent leather boots. Thinking he was among great capitalists, he was astonished to learn his tablemates were only clerks, agents, conductors, and other employees of the railroad.

Invited out to see the construction of the Union Pacific, Stanley watched, fascinated, as the railroad crews worked with smooth precision to lay rails on the already-graded road. A horse-drawn car sped to the end of the track, and the rails were seized and slid forward even before the car had stopped. At a run, two crews carried two rails into place over the ties, and in a few seconds the car could move forward over the new rails. The sequence then repeated.

Behind the rail car, four men dropped spikes and straightened ties in place, and the following gang drove home the spikes and packed dirt under the ties. For Stanley's benefit the superintendent urged the men on, and Stanley watched them lay 700 feet of rail in five minutes. With the din of 40 sledges ringing in his ears, he quickly calculated that, if they could keep up the pace, they could lay 16½ miles per day.

But he was there to report a peace conference, and soon it was time to return to North Platte, where the Indians were gathering. At noon on a rainy September day, the chiefs came together to smoke the pipe and hear what the latest paper of the white commissioners was all about.

Stanley thought the chiefs seemed both suspicious and cynical about the new treaty talks. Things got off to an uncomfortable start when Swift Bear remarked that while the whites required many witnesses to a treaty to keep the peace, the Indians needed only the witness of the Great Spirit.

When the white commissioners asked to hear about the Indians' problems, they got quick answer.

Spotted Tail spoke first. His return to his homeland had been bittersweet, for lack of game and ammunition had kept his people hungry. He remarked that since the commission was there — and surely the Great Father had not sent them for nothing — the Indians would listen. But the whites must know that their roads drove away the game and caused all the trouble. He restated his objections to the Powder River and Smoky Hill roads. He reminded them he had been a friend, and he pleaded for recognition of the Brulé efforts to stay peaceable. But they were in desperate need of ammunition. They had to have help. His voice dropped in a final plea. "My friends, help us. Take pity on us."

Man Afraid of His Horses, Pawnee Killer, Turkey Leg, and Big Mouth echoed his objections to the roads. One after another they spoke for peace, but they begged for ammunition to hunt game in the tradition of their fathers. They could not give up the taste of wild meat and begin farming.

Stanley, crouched on the ground with a partition of his valise for a writing desk, strained to hear the words of the interpreter as the canvas of the tent whipped in the wind. He saw that the Indians were humbling themselves in their requests for powder and ball, and that they were ashamed.

But the commissioners had their answer ready. Land would be reserved for the Sioux along the White Earth and Cheyenne Rivers to the north; for the Cheyennes, below the Arkansas River to the south. They were to have houses and cattle and crops like the white man. The roads would not be stopped. The commmission had no powder and lead to give away.

There was silence for awhile, broken only by the sound of grave-faced Indians sucking on the passing pipe. Then Swift Bear rose to speak of the young men he had persuaded to come to the council. It had not been easy to get them to come, and now he felt he had betrayed them. "My friends, take pity on me this day," he said. "I have been friendly. Give these men some ammunition. They don't want much. We won't kill you; we want powder and ball to kill game as we go to our villages."

But the commissioners continued to hesitate. The Cheyenne chief Pawnee Killer, through with begging, stalked to his lodge and emerged in war paint. He leaped on his horse and galloped away from the council. Other Cheyennes rose and followed. Seeing their delegations begin to vanish, the commissioners hurriedly promised ammunition to Spotted Tail's Brulés and to the Oglalas. They set the treaty signing for a later date and adjourned the council.

That night Stanley accompanied the commissioners to a feast hosted by Spotted Tail. There he had a chance to observe the Sioux in peaceful camp and listen to their veneration of the Great Spirit. He watched an old man recite his coups, saw boys wrestling and girls giggling, and began to realize that they were people, too. Observing Spotted Tail's dignified hospitality, appreciating the poetry of their speech, Stanley found his sympathies swinging to the Indians. He began to wonder who was civilized and who was savage. And he "departed with higher appreciation of peaceful Indians" than he had ever had before.

Stanley continued to follow the peace commission, and he watched later when both the Brulé and Oglala Sioux touched the pen to paper. All tribes but Red Cloud's had seemingly agreed to the reservation life, and he expected Red Cloud to follow suit in the spring. By November 25, he was writing his editor that "peace reigns all over the plains."

Convinced there was no more story to report, he traveled back east and gained an assignment from the *New York Herald* to cover an expedition to Abyssinia. This led to further assignments, and in 1869 the *Herald* chose him to go to Africa in search of Dr. David Livingstone, the British missionary.

Making use of knowledge and attitudes gained from observing the American Indians, Stanley not only found Livingstone, he found a continent that absorbed his energies for the rest of his life. He made two more extensive African explorations, toured the world as a lecturer, authored numerous books on Africa, and sat in the English Parliament for five years. In 1899 he was knighted, a pinnacle of success he could not even have envisioned as he labored in the workhouse in Wales, an illegitimate castoff.

But his glory was always tipped with gall. The phrase he had uttered at the meeting with Livingstone—and reported himself, in all innocence— was seized upon by the public and press and soon became an immense joke, burlesqued endlessly in poems, plays, cartoons, and lectures. Stanley could never understand why it was funny, and he died in 1904, a bitter man who considered his greatest achievement cheapened by the laughter that inevitably followed the words, "Dr. Livingstone, I presume."

Little Chief

Stanley was partially correct in anticipating peace over the plains after the councils of 1867. The peace commission concluded its negotiations with the Treaty of 1868, and the Brulé and Oglala Sioux began moving reluctantly up to their reservation in Dakota Territory. Spotted Tail accepted the restrictions he could not fight, but he became a master at passive resistance. The agents who dealt with him in the last dozen years of his life found him a formidable champion of Sioux rights.

The Cheyennes' resistance was far from passive. They failed to retreat to their reservation below the Arkansas and moved instead to the open land along the Republican and its tributaries. In September of 1868, Cheyenne Dog Soldiers fought government scouts on the Arikaree River, and by May of 1869 their occasional raids had grown into a small war. Twenty-six white settlers were dead and two women were Cheyenne prisoners.

It was obvious both peoples could not occupy the land, and there was no question in the army's mind as to who would have to go. Quickly the military organized an expedition to "clear the Republican country of Indians."

A. BATTLES

When Luther North led his company south from Fort McPherson in June of 1869, he took care to keep his motley column well ahead of Major General Eugene Carr's 5th Cavalry, for his command did not present a military appearance. Each man altered the combination of breeches, hat, and jacket to his individual liking, and most showed more brown skin than blue wool.

Moreover, they tolerated the faded army blues only on peaceful marches. When battle seemed imminent, the men quickly dismounted, threw their saddles from their horses, and stripped off the white man's clothing. For these men were not white, but Pawnee, and they fought their enemies

in the ancient way — with war whoop and waving lance, piercing arrow and scalping knife, no quarter given or expected.

The Pawnee Scouts, as the companies of Indians were called, had been recruited by the army in the hard summer of 1864, and by 1869 the army's experiment in using Indians to fight Indians was a proven success. The Pawnees had protected the railroaders, cleared the Platte Valley of hostiles so the 1867 peace conference could be held, and proved useful on several special expeditions.

The leaders of this irregular army were as unsoldierly as their men. Luther North and his older brother Frank had grown up on the frontier near the Pawnee villages. Because they could speak Pawnee, first Frank and later Luther had been enlisted to lead the Scouts. By 1869, 23-year-old Luther had earned command of his own Company A, and as Frank was away gathering more Pawnee recruits when the expedition left Fort McPherson, Lute began the march in sole command of all 100 Scouts.

That Lute could command the 100 Pawnees was not the result of military discipline. He relied on friendship and mutual respect. The North brothers had lived near the Pawnees for eight years and were considered friends and advisors to the tribes. Frank North had been given the name Pawnee Chief, and Lute, six years his junior, was known as Little Chief.

Lute, a slim 140-pounder, fit the name, for though he lacked size he carried himself with an independent manner, and his abilities in riding and marksmanship commanded respect. He loved the frontier life, and he had not hesitated to abandon a course in business college when the chance came to lead a company of Scouts. Classes in bookkeeping were poor competition for the excitement of life with the Scouts.

The Pawnees were in a holiday mood as they scattered to scout the trail toward the Republican. The Sioux and Cheyennes had bloodied their villages often enough, and they embraced the chance to fight their traditional enemies with eager hearts. With army-furnished horses, guns, and ammunition, they no longer had to serve as sitting targets. They could carry the battle to the enemy's lodges.

Lute enjoyed their high spirits and joined with them in celebration. Though he found them childlike in some ways, each week in service with them had increased his regard for their abilities. Twice, he felt, their loyalty and knowledge had saved his life, and he trusted them far beyond any regular soldier.

Lute was not much impressed with the military. The supply train and equipment it took to support the seven companies of cavalry under General Carr hamstrung their movements, and the officers were often distracted by such nonmilitary pursuits as setting greyhounds on antelope. Even the army's scout, Will Cody, traveled with a wagon of canned goods to sell the soldiers. In Lute's experience most of the army's officers were unorganized, unknowledgeable, and incredibly slow to react.

Six days out the command had reached the Republican, and Lute settled his men half a mile below the cavalry. They were eating supper when war whoops started the mule herd to motion. A moment later a herder galloped into camp with an arrow through his body. The other herder was dead at his post. Cheyennes had struck the herd and were driving them off.

Lute and about 20 of his men caught up their horses and started in pursuit. Charging wildly up and down dark ravines in their wake, he managed to recover the mules, and his men killed two of the Cheyennes. He trotted back to camp quite satisfied with the outcome.

But General Carr was not satisfied. He called Lute to his tent the next morning, and, before all the officers, reprimanded Lute for chasing the Indians without an order.

Lute was astounded. He told the bearded general, as politely as possible, that "the only way to fight Indians was to go for them as fast as possible whenever they were found." General Carr replied that he didn't need the advice of a 23-year-old volunteer, and that Lute should obey orders.

Lute replied hotly that any time Indians attacked a camp he was in he intended to go for them, orders or no, and the general responded hotly by putting Lute under arrest.

However, the next morning when the general tried to send out the Pawnees and discovered no one but Lute could speak their language, he quickly cooled down and rescinded the arrest order.

Luckily for them both, Frank North rode into camp soon after with his new company of Scouts, and Lute rather gratefully turned command back to his brother. He could handle Pawnees—and Sioux, Arapahos and Cheyennes—but he wasn't much good at dealing with the military.

They continued to push through the hot, dry grassland of the Republican Valley, with the Scouts ranging many miles into hills on both sides. But they had nothing to show for their efforts except windburned faces and footsore mounts. Occasionally they ran across a trail of a small war party, but the large village of Cheyennes reported to be in the district eluded them.

Then, near sundown on July 9, at the end of a fruitless scout, Lute and six of his men took a look over a last ridge before returning to camp. Moving down the draw on the other side, less than 100 yards away were the Cheyennes, some 600 strong.

The half-dozen Scouts froze where they were, sure that any moment an outrider would jog up their ridge, but none did. The Cheyennes, too, were hot and tired. Their horses were loaded with meat and lodge skins. And they simply plodded down the draw to the river and out of sight.

Lute and his Scouts hurried back to report the whereabouts of the village to the cavalry—only to spend the whole next day sitting in camp while the army waited on a supply train. At last, the following day, the command was ready to move, and leaving the wagon train behind they took the two-day-old trail up the river.

Moving at a slow trot through burning sun and parching wind, the troops split to follow diverging trails. The trails were not difficult to follow, and in one spot they found the unmistakable imprint of a white woman's shoe among the parallel lines of travois poles.

As they picked their way up hillsides of yucca and slid their mounts down sandy draws, Lute reflected on the fact that while an alerted Indian could be impossible to track or surprise, an Indian who felt secure could be incredibly careless. It was obvious the Cheyennes were not aware of the troops' presence.

Just after noon a Scout rode back with the news that the village had been discovered, grouped along a small creek, south of the Platte (near present-day Sterling, Colorado). The Cheyennes were all in camp; the warriors lounging about; the women drying meat. No guards were apparent.

General Carr kept his men behind a ridge of sandhills until his forces were reunited. While they waited, the Pawnees stripped their horses and bodies for action, and Frank gave the Scouts their instructions. Then at a word from General Carr, the bugle sounded the charge and the force broke over the ridge at a gallop.

Down the long valley they thundered, the soldiers' cheers mingling with the Pawnee war cries.

The Pawnees, on fast and unencumbered mounts, quickly pulled away from the cavalry horses. Lute flew along among them, urging his horse to the front of the charge. He could see Frank galloping headlong for the alerted village, 200 yards ahead of them all. Lute could see that a half-dozen warriors had caught up their guns, and he spurred his horse frantically to catch Frank before he hit the village alone.

About a half-mile out they came on the Cheyenne horses, and Lute saw a young herder leap on his horse and try to head the herd toward the village. With the white force at his heels and bullets pinging on the rocks, the boy refused to leave the herd and run for safety. He forced the herd into reach of the warriors, and then turned to fight. He managed to string one arrow before the Pawnees rode him down.

The Pawnees had caught up now, and they rode through the lodges, cutting down the unprepared Cheyenne warriors, while the cavalry circled the village to cut off escape. The quiet village was suddenly a welter of screaming women, crying children, dust and smoke of guns. In the mass confusion some Cheyennes managed to catch horses and flee, while others took cover in nearby ravines to fight.

In the lull after the initial charge, Lute saw a water keg beside a lodge and he stopped with several others to grab a drink. Lute's brother-in-law dismounted to hoist the keg, and as he did a woman crawled out of a lodge and threw her arms around his knees. She was bleeding from a chest wound, and when they looked closer they realized she was white. At first they could make nothing of her hysterical cries, but then they realized she was not speaking English, but German.

As the men tried to comfort and reassure the woman, they took time to pass the water among themselves. Lute, his throat dry with the heat and excitement of battle, raised the keg to his mouth for a drink, and as he did he saw an Indian rise from the grass and fire at him.

He was nearly knocked from his horse as the bullet struck his stomach and exited from his back. Yet, when he pulled open his shirt to check the wound, there was none. He felt his back, and his hand came away without blood. The other men, talking with the woman, seemed to notice nothing. In disbelief that anything could seem so real, Lute decided he must be hallucinating. He finished his drink and said nothing.

Moving on to follow the action, Lute came upon another white woman. This one lay dead, her belly large with child and the mark of a tomahawk in her skull.

He went on and caught up with Frank near the creek just as an Indian raised up from a ravine to fire. The bullet whistled past Frank's head, and quickly Frank jumped off his horse. He handed the reins to Lute and motioned him to ride on. Lute started the horses off at a lope, and when he did the Indian poked up his head to fire again. Frank was ready. His shot struck the Indian square in the forehead and he fell back, dead.

After a moment a Cheyenne woman and child crawled out of the canyon, and Frank sent them to safety with the white woman. Then he and Lute joined the rest to finish off some Cheyenne warriors who still fought from the depths of the canyon, and to chase those escaping through the hills.

By evening the guns were stilled and the men gathered back at the village. They had killed 52 Cheyenne men and two women; captured 17 women and children, rounded up 418 horses.

They found the village rich in quilled shirts and beaded dresses, finely tanned buffalo robes, and Navajo blankets. They also found $640 in gold coins, patchwork quilts, white scalps, and a necklace of fingers. The men gave the money to the surviving white woman, Mrs. Maria Weichel, a German immigrant who had been captured along the Solomon River the preceding May.

Lute wandered through the ruins of the village, watching as soldiers and Pawnees alike celebrated their victory. Bone-tired, he sat down on the bank of the creek, washed the dust from his head and face, and dipped up a cup of water for a drink. After one satisfying draught, he dipped his cup for another. As he raised it to his lips, one of his Scouts spoke up.

"Don't drink that!" he warned. And he gestured to a spot 10 feet up the creek. There the body of a Cheyenne brave lay in the water; blood from his crushed head tinted the water where Lute had been drinking.

Sickened, Lute turned away from the stream and retched until his sides were sore.

The heat of the day was broken near dusk by a thunderstorm, and Lute and Frank crawled under the edge of a ruined lodge for shelter. As hail beat upon the skins that had so recently sheltered Cheyennes, and lightning lit the white-topped puddles, Lute told the others about his strange hallucination of being shot.

One of the men picked up Lute's cartridge belt. The large square buckle plainly showed the imprint of a bullet. And when Lute opened his shirt again he found the buckle's shape repeated in a dark bruise on his stomach.

Later there was a moment of excitement when movement was spotted along the fatal ravine. But the threat turned out to be only a three-year-old Cheyenne child, dumb with terror, who was carried in and placed with the other prisoners.

The first duty the next morning was to bury Suzannah Alderdice, the white captive they had been too late to save. They read a service over her grave and marked it with a wooden headboard.

Then the men spent the day kindling huge fires to burn the skins and poles of 85 lodges, and all the robes, moccasins, shirts, parfleches, dried meat, lances, blankets, shields, and scalps that were not craved by some souvenir hunter.

The smoke hung pall-like over the hills around the small spring. Then the evening breeze swirled it, thinned it, and carried it east, across grasslands that would see Cheyennes no more.

The men called the battlefield Suzannah Springs, in honor of Suzannah Alderdice. But the General wanted something with a more martial ring, and so the trickle of clear water became Summit Springs.

Frank North learned later that the Indian he'd killed in the ravine had been the Cheyenne Chief Tall Bull, leader of the hostiles. When later stories gave credit to Will Cody, Frank couldn't be bothered to argue. "What difference does it make who killed him?" he shrugged. The fact was that Tall Bull's death and the destruction of the village had effectively ended the Cheyennes' resistance.

Lute, still chafing under army discipline, had a few words with General Carr and went home to Columbus. But he did return to army life in 1876 when he and Frank enlisted a last company of Pawnees for the campaign against the Sioux in the Yellowstone country.

Frank North, performing in Will Cody's Wild West Show, suffered injuries that led to his death in 1885.

Luther spent the rest of his life in ranching (a partner with Cody) north of the Platte, and in business in Omaha and Columbus. He lived to see the Pawnees moved from their ancestral lands along the Platte to Indian Territory, where two-thirds of the tribe had perished by 1890. In later years Luther North was recognized as an authority on the Pawnee culture, and he always maintained his sympathy and friendship with the tribes. In 1925 when he wrote of his experiences with the Scouts, he remembered them as "true and loyal soldiers; brave as any body of men I ever saw; and as good trailers as ever lived."

The Dreamer

    With the Cheyennes and Pawnees forced south to the reservations, and the Sioux driven north to the White River agencies, the great watershed of the Platte lay open, waiting for another people—a people who lived not as part of the land, but as its master; a people who would by force of will change the face of the land and bend the river to serve their needs.

The tall, lean, elderly man who stood surveying the land near the mouth of the Cache la Poudre River did not see the stunted brown grasses and the scraggly clumps of prickly pear. He did not see the angry spines of yucca or the dust devils that could swirl east for hundreds of miles without being obstructed by tree or mountain.

Instead, Nathan Meeker saw a dream. He saw ditches of clear water crisscrossing fields of lush, green crops. He saw orchards of fruit trees blossoming. He saw groves of walnuts shading a clean, new city. For Nathan Meeker had chosen this neck of land between the Platte and the Poudre to be the home of his new colony.

Meeker had long been interested in cooperative communities and in agriculture. A writer who was then producing an agricultural column for the *New York Tribune*, he had also spent some years in a colony in Ohio. That colony had eventually failed, and Meeker had gone on to success as a newspaperman, but he still believed in the possibilities of cooperative achievement. When he had visited Colorado Territory in 1869, his interests suddenly melded into a grand vision. He would organize an agricultural colony that would move west, erect a city, and prove the prairie could be successfully farmed by the use of irrigation.

Meeker had hurried back to his comfortable home in a New York suburb and described his dreams to his wife Arvilla. Her long, thin face grew longer still at the thought of leaving New York to pioneer a community in the Colorado Rockies. She remembered too well the labor at the Ohio colony. Their five children were no longer babies, but still—the two younger girls, Mary and Josephine, were nicely settled in school and she hated to drag them off to the wilderness. It would mean separation from their oldest son, Ralph, and a smaller choice of suitors for daughter Rozene—who needed no additional handicaps in finding a husband.

But Nathan's handsome face seemed almost young again as he described his hopes for the colony, and Arvilla could not say no. She would go if the colony became reality.

That question settled, Nathan had approached his employer, *Tribune* Editor Horace Greeley. Greeley knew Colorado and believed in its future, and experimental agriculture was dear to his heart. He gave quick consent, and Meeker spent a full day writing, rewriting, and polishing a "Call" to men interested in joining such a colony.

He asked only for men of temperance who desired an intelligent, educated, thrifty, and moral community. They must have money to invest for joint purchase of land, and they must be willing to work to establish a community that would "exhibit all that is best in modern civilization." The article was run in the *Tribune* on December 14, 1869, with an enthusiastic endorsement from Editor Greeley.

It was as if Meeker had unlocked the door of an imprisoned population. Letters began to pour in, hundreds a day, with pleas to be included. A meeting was scheduled for two days before Christmas, and when Meeker came to work that morning it was to wade through crowds of men who filled the offices and stairs in answer to his call.

Almost frightened at the unexpected popularity of his idea, Meeker found himself engulfed in a whirl of activity. The lyrical description of the colony's location included in his call, which promised pine-studded hills, white mountains, mild climate, and every resource from coal to mineral springs to speckled trout, had borrowed glories from many parts of Colorado and from Meeker's sanguine imagination. There was, as yet, no chosen location.

Thus, in April, Meeker was again in Colorado, one of a committee of three to pick the spot where Utopia would sprout. Faced with the practicality of finding a large enough block of available land with access to water, the group decided on the area of the Cache la Poudre. Urged on by William N. Byers, Colorado Agent for the Denver Pacific Railroad's National Land Company, they purchased some 12,000 acres of the barren flat. And Meeker, secure in his vision of the future, had gone happily back to New York for his family.

When he returned in June of 1870 with Arvilla and his three daughters, he found the 200 colonists who arrived before him in a tizzy. He had hardly stepped off the train when he was engulfed in complaints.

Some 50 settlers had taken a look at the dusty valley and then taken the train back east. There was less land available than the colonists had been led to believe—50,000 acres less. What there was the old settlers told them would not grow crops. The promised groves of pines were actually a few spindly cottonwoods along the river. There was no wood. No coal. No mineral springs to soak away their pains. It was hot. It was dusty. And the women's main occupation was picking prickly pear thorns from their children's feet.

Worse yet, the vaunted system of irrigation was nothing more than a plowed furrow. Instead of four ditches channeling water over 20,000 acres, the colonists struggled to complete one ditch to water their gardens. When the water was finally turned into the ditch, the ground soaked up the water so thoroughly that it was a week before even a trickle made its way to the far end.

Meeker was dismayed at the unidyllic state of his idyllic colony, but he plunged in to try to solve some of the problems. As President of the Executive Committee, he spent much of the summer in meetings considering the myriad complaints. With his long legs stretched out beneath the table, he and the other committee men often sat in meeting well after midnight.

There were disputes over who owned what lots, over where to run the ditches, over the costs of the ditches, over cattle eating crops, over the use of colony property by individuals, over rights to water from the maligned ditch, over how long people could stay in the one substantial building in Greeley—the Hotel de Comfort. (Meeker stayed there a week and then gladly moved to a shanty.)

Nathan Meeker was not temperamentally suited to the role of peacemaker. Opinionated and outspoken, he did not suffer fools gladly. He had no gift for diplomacy, no grace to soothe ruffled feelings. He often offended the person whose good will was most important, and then expressed surprise when their support evaporated.

But he did have unwavering faith that the Union Colony at Greeley (named for his mentor Horace Greeley, rather than for himself) would succeed. And he expended all his physical and financial resources to that end. Partly to prove his commitment, he built his family a huge house, well out from the center of town, an expense he could ill afford.

Arvilla was grateful for the lovely two-story house, the only one for miles around that had two parlors complete with fireplaces. She could furnish it with fine pieces from their New York home, and it gave her comfort that her daughters were not being raised in utter barbarity. Still, Josie, the youngest, was a worry. She was beginning to exhibit a frontier independence of spirit that was not quite proper in a young lady.

By October of 1870, Greeley had grown to some 500 houses, built or under construction, with wide, graded streets, and a population of nearly 1,000. Meeker decided it was time Greeley had a newspaper, and he borrowed $1,000 from Horace Greeley to launch the *Greeley Tribune*. Back in the familiar milieu of type and printer's ink, he felt more at home, and he served the colony nobly with publicity in both the *Greeley* and *New York Tribunes*. But the paper was a losing proposition as far as finances were concerned.

Gradually, however, the colonists began to cope with their unfamiliar surroundings. Unable to find any printed matter that gave them practical information on irrigation systems, they learned by trial and error. It was apparent the ditches were too small and needed to be enlarged. With the colony's resources exhausted, the landowners footed the bill for a deeper ditch. Then they hired experienced men to build a second.

At Greeley's urging, they bought $1,400 worth of trees and planted them, only to see them winter-kill or fall to foraging cattle. Seeking advice from the older settlers, they formed a Farm Club, which met weekly to provide lectures and a forum for exchange of experience.

Meeker did not let them ignore the intellectual pursuits his Utopia required. A school building was in service by fall, with three paid teachers, and colonists donated enough books so that a reading room opened soon after. Thursday and Friday nights were reserved for two lyceums, and packed houses listened to debates of such questions as, "Should the National Capitol Be Removed to the Mississippi Valley?"

Other questions were of surpassing importance, such as whether the colony should allow a billiard parlor, and what to do when a German settler from the rival town of Evans opened up a saloon in the city limits of Greeley.

Temperance had been one of the colony's tenets from the beginning, and when some citizens appeared at church one Sunday morning with liquored breaths, the founders were moved to quick action. The congregation moved *en masse* to confront the unwelcome saloon keeper, and in short order he was not only bought out, but burned out. The billiard parlor suffered similar discouragement.

Editor Meeker was not shy about advising the populace. In the midst of cattle country, he told the stockmen they knew nothing about the cattle business. He encouraged the town members to capture and impound strays found on the streets, which resulted in a "cattle pound" guarded by townies and raided by cowboys. And when this proved inadequate to protect their crops, he decided to fence the whole colony. It cost $12,000 for 50 miles of wire fence, but to Meeker it was worth it to be spared the sight of cows methodically masticating his precious trees.

From the beginning, Meeker had encouraged the participation of women in his colony, allowing them to purchase memberships at $155 along with the men. He urged them to speak at the lyceum, and in one instance in 1871, they were even allowed to vote in an election to choose the local postmaster — 22 years before the state of Colorado granted women suffrage.

As Greeley began to take on substance and flourish, Nathan Meeker himself began to sink. The newspaper still did not meet expenses, and he had expended all his capital. He was better at writing of farming than he was at farming. Better at drawing up plans than at carrying them out with flesh and blood people.

When Horace Greeley died in late 1872, the new editor of the *New York Tribune* refused to buy any more of Meeker's writing, and his only real source of income vanished. The next four years he suffered through grasshopper plagues, defeats in politics, and rejection as a writer. Arvilla could only try to encourage her stooped and graying husband, but Josie, now 18, learned to operate one of those new writing machines and got a job in Denver.

When, in 1877, the lawyers of Greeley's estate gave Meeker one last chance to repay the $1,000 loan before they started court proceedings, Meeker was desperate. He had to have a paying job. He knew of one possibility. If he could land an appointment as an Indian Agent in Colorado, he could earn $1,500 a year — enough to pay off the loan in two years' time if they were careful.

He pulled strings, made calls, wrote letters, and waited. In 1878 he was appointed Agent of the Ute Indians at the White River Agency in western Colorado.

Meeker uprooted Arvilla once more, collected Josie from her job in Denver, and set off to convert the Ute Indians to agriculture. He left Greeley with a happy heart, surveying the fields that were now green, the ditches that did indeed run with clear water, the neat and substantial stores and houses of the colonists, even some trees that were beginning to cast shade. He told his friends that it was seldom a man got "to see his hopes and views so completely realized." He was grateful the colony was beginning to prosper.

He was also grateful, even at 62, to be embarking on a new mission. His face was alight with purpose and his mind was already filled with ideas on how to teach the Utes the joys of farming.

Sixteen months later the colonists of Greeley learned the Utes did not take at all well to farming—at least as Nathan Meeker taught it. Reacting to Meeker's stubborn insistence on plowing up their race track, the Utes struck Nathan down. Six Greeley boys who were helping him farm at White River died with him.

Arvilla and Josie spent three weeks in captivity with the Utes. They were rescued in due time, and matter-of-fact Josie raised eyebrows across the country when she refused to get hysterical about her treatment at the hands of a brave named Persune. "It was what we expected," she said.

The Greeley Board of Trustees passed a resolution to rename Main Street after Nathan Meeker, and citizens began a collection to erect a monument to him. But the collectors failed to gather enough money for a suitable monument, and the name of the street was never changed.

Three years later Josie died of pneumonia in New York. She was carried back to Greeley and placed beside her father in Linn Grove Cemetery. Arvilla joined them in 1905.

By then a town had grown up near the place where the Utes had murdered their stubborn agent. And so Nathan Meeker's name is commemorated by a town on the White River, where his vision failed, rather than on the Platte, where it succeeded.

Succeeding generations, more generous than his contemporaries, have restored Meeker's Greeley home and maintain it as a museum. But perhaps the most meaningful tribute lies in the hundreds of miles of irrigation ditches that lace the valleys of the Platte, carrying wealth and prosperity with their life-giving water.

The Redoubtable Miss I. Bird

The transformation of Greeley from a barren flat to a green oasis was necessarily a slow one, and in September of 1873, when Miss Isabella Bird descended the steps of the train to Greeley's streets, it could not yet be mistaken for Utopia. The short, plump English spinster knew Greeley to be the "most prosperous and rising colony in Colorado." But as she carried her bags through ankle-deep dust and swarming black flies to the canvas cubicle that would be her room for the night, she wondered why anyone would settle where nature was so niggardly and living so coarse.

why would anyone settle where they could see the Rocky Mountains yet not be part of them? Isabella Bird, age 42, minister's daughter, maiden lady author, and late an invalid, had become obsessed with the Rocky Mountains.

Isabella had seen other mountains. Since her early twenties, when doctors first put her aboard an ocean liner in hopes of curing her crippling back pain and recurring depressions, she had seen the Alps, the Apennines, the Appalachians, and the Sierra Nevadas; she had even climbed the harsh volcanic slopes of Mauna Loa in the Sandwich Isles. But as she rode the stuffy coach down from Cheyenne to Greeley and watched range on range of Rockies climb purple in the near distance, she found herself drawn irresistibly to these mountains. She could "look at and feel nothing else."

Flies in her food, bugs in her bed, being obliged to help the landlady cook for 20 men—these were minor inconveniences and not to be fussed about. For Isabella believed it unfair to enlist sympathy for difficulties suffered in the pursuit of pleasure. And just now her pleasure was to journey into the Rocky Mountains. She had heard of a magic glen called Estes Park, and she was set on seeing it, whatever the cost.

Luckily, this diminutive but strangely determined English lady found it easy to enlist the aid of others in her wanderings. Traveling alone, often arriving unknown and unannounced, plain of face and stocky of figure, quiet spoken and self-effacing, she sometimes had to wait patiently for a day or two before her hosts realized this small woman did, indeed, intend to do just what she said. By that time she had made herself "agreeable" to one and all, and they couldn't do enough to assist her toward her goal.

It was nearly three weeks, however, before Isabella was to see the fabled Estes. Three weeks of discouraging advice, false starts, and aborted journeys, while she boarded with settlers around Fort Collins and Longmont.

As a boarder in houses already crowded, Isabella was always careful to do her share, but she thought the settlers' life was one of "hard, unloving, unlovely, unrelieved, unbeautiful, grinding work." And she found their children to be only "debased imitations of men and women," ready to carry adult responsibilities at the age of 10. She thought this loss of childhood one of the cruelest penalties exacted by the harsh land.

With the end of September near and winter hovering over the peaks, Isabella had given up all hope of reaching Estes when she learned two young men were about to make the journey. They agreed to accept her company, providing she could ride a horse well enough not to be a nuisance.

Isabella was not worried about her horsemanship, but she suffered some qualms about mounting her steed under the gaze of the town, for she rode not sidesaddle, but astride. Though her Turkish trousers were modestly covered with an ankle-length skirt, they were still trousers. She called her outfit her Hawaiian riding costume, for it was in relaxed Hawaii she had first dared to test the ease of riding astride and learned that riding need not mean grinding pain in her diseased spine.

Trying to look "insignificant and unnoticeable"—for Isabella did not openly flaunt tradition—she mounted the large, highbred horse that had been rented for her, and joined the two youths who would be her guides. She had decided some months before that men were far preferable to women as traveling companions, but these two were so obviously unenchanted with her company that she felt ill at ease.

However, a few miles up the canyon of the St. Vrain, Isabella forgot her anxieties and lost herself in the glories of the ride. The sunlit peaks before them; the rushing waters of the St. Vrain, now shadowed, now glittering in the sun; the yellow-green of cottonwood along the banks; the great piles of lichened boulders; the gloom of pine slopes brightened by the white and gold of aspen; the charm of flowers scattered through the meadow grasses; each new view claimed her, as they picked their way up the canyon. Each mile gave keener air and greater peace.

At last, after 10 hours of riding, with the canyons deep in shadow, she rode through the opening of a grassy gulch. Squatted there beneath the pines was a tumbledown cabin with smoke issuing from both roof and window. Drying pelts covered the roof and walls, a deer carcass hung from a rafter, antlers lay scattered about, and a large collie barked a warning. Isabella, fresh-faced with the exhilaration of the ride, trotted over to meet the owner. She had found the two young men to be glum escorts, and she longed to talk to someone who might share her feeling for these mountains.

The man who came out to quiet the dog with a kick and a curse gave her pause. He looked to be near her age, but his buckskin suit hung in shreds, a knife stuck in his belt, and a revolver protruded from his pocket. Long curly hair fell in a tangle from his cap, and when he turned toward her, one side of his once handsome face lacked an eye.

Isabella was ready to forego acquaintance when the trapper saw that his caller was a lady. He swallowed the curse, raised his cap, and in a cultured English voice that belied his looks, asked what he could do for her.

The bemused Isabella asked for a drink of water, which the trapper supplied with suitable apologies for his battered cup, and before long the English lady and Mountain Jim Nugent were in deep conversation. She found out he'd lost his eye to a grizzly, and he learned she'd lost her heart to the Rocky Mountains. By the time Isabella rode on toward the ridge that divided Jim's gulch from Estes Park, she was already puzzling over the warm attractions of this incongruous man.

When she topped the ridge and saw Estes Park, all other thoughts went flying. Before her stretched a long, high valley, soft with evening haze, walled with pines and guarded by granite peaks. The last tinge of sunset caught the waters of the Big Thompson, which marked a course in red across the valley floor, and the snows of Longs Peak above echoed the flaming color. For once, Isabella thought, the reality surpassed the dream. She spurred her horse and they raced through the frosty air to a lake and the small group of cabins that made up the ranch where she would stay.

That evening by the fire, Isabella wrote to her sister Henrietta as if she had, at long last, come home. She praised the little cabin, complete with skunk's lair below, her host Griffith Evans and family, the food, the bed, the lack of bugs, and of course, the scenery. Henrietta, home safe in Edinburgh, was Isabella's alter ego, and to her Isabella sent voluminous letters, trying to share her adventures with the housebound Henny. Though neither of the clergyman's daughters enjoyed good health, Henny nursed her ills at home and only Isabella sought relief in wandering.

That she had made the proper choice seemed evident, for in her next letter to Henny, Isabella described her ascent of Longs Peak.

The 14,256 foot peak that closed one end of Estes Park had tantalized Isabella from the beginning. In fact, in spite of her Anglican

upbringing, she had even fantasized that it held special powers, and she was moved to understand how naturally nature worship could develop.

As it was nearly October, she was at first discouraged from making the climb. But one day the weather cleared and Jim Nugent arrived at her door, a willing guide. As soon as they could bake bread, cut steaks, and roll blankets, Jim, Isabella, and the two youths who had ridden up to Estes with her took the trail for Longs Peak.

Isabella, in her bright plaid riding dress, found Mr. Nugent to be better company than the boys. She became so engrossed with the charm of his conversation that she forgot the torn face, the ragged waistcoats, and the flopping furs of his outfit. He had such intelligence, quick wit, and graceful manners that she wondered if the stories she had heard about his dark and desperate side were true. It didn't seem possible that liquor could charge this man with a visciousness feared throughout the settlements of Colorado.

But that was a matter to be pondered at another time. Now the ride took all her attention. Up they went, past the reflected glory of the Lake of the Lilies, through silent pine forests where sharp branches snatched at their clothing, picking their way over the deadfall that littered the forest with giant jackstraws, until the thinning trees grew gnarled and stunted and they had reached the timber line.

There they camped, with the snowy crest of Longs Peak still 3,000 feet above them, a half-moon silvering the small pines, and Jim's dog Ring ordered to Isabella's bed of spruce boughs, to lay at her back and keep her warm. Charged with excitement, she could not sleep, but lay watching the stars wheel slowly above.

Morning came with a lemon sky, and Isabella faced the real part of the climb (up the North Face). As she scrambled over an ice-crusted bed of boulders, her large, borrowed boots proved to be a hindrance. Providentially, they found a pair of small overshoes beneath a rock, left, Isabella supposed, by someone on the Hayden Survey. Enjoying better footing, Isabella followed Jim as he leapt from boulder to boulder.

She was a nearly fearless woman, but she was not a mountaineer. When they passed through the Notch and she stared up the knife-edged ridge that topped a 3,000 foot drop, which she was expected to traverse, her courage nearly failed. She offered to stay behind, knowing her presence only encumbered the men.

But Jim would not hear of it. He roped her to him, and they began what was to Isabella six hours of terror. She slipped and slid, crawled and climbed, stepped in Jim's clasped hands, and stood on Jim's shoulders. Feeling like a bale of goods, she was hoisted up until her arms felt loose in their sockets. Always she was conscious that one slip and she would lie below in a shapeless, bloody heap.

At last, hearts pounding, ears ringing, gasping for breath through painful, parched throats, they stood on the summit.

The physical pain of cold and altitude made their stay short, but Isabella had time to trace the glistening watershed of the Platte's tributaries to its fringes of cottonwoods out on the gray-green plains. She mused how its waters would heat in the tropic sun and be carried by the Gulf Stream to the shoreline of her distant home. In awe she gazed at the glorious vistas. They pulled her eyes to all points of the compass. She felt "uplifted—above love and hate and storms of passion, calm amidst eternal silence."

The sense of calm remained with her during the descent, though she once hung suspended in air until Jim could cut her skirt loose from a rock, whereupon she dropped like a sack of meal into a snow-filled crevasse. Once again she fought across the field of boulders, and then, bruised, aching, and utterly spent, she was lifted onto her horse for the return to camp.

After a few hours of exhausted sleep, she woke to join Jim by the fire, and they talked until the cold, quiet night was ended by another dawn.

Back at Griff Evans' ranch, Isabella paid eight dollars a week to sleep, eat, and ride like a cowhand. She had won the respect of all, and Evans often asked her to lend a hand when they rounded up wild cattle. She reveled in the mountain beauty and in the good health this kind of living brought her. The body that spent most of its time on a couch in Edinburgh now answered her every demand.

Late in October, she tore herself away so that she could see more of the Rockies. Alone except for her mount Birdie, a bay Indian pony, Isabella rode to Denver. There the bustle tired and confused her, and she felt forced to ride sidesaddle, though this now seemed "as if, having the use of two feet, one was compelled to always hop on one." She visited William Byers and ex-Governor Hunt for

letters of introduction, maps, and advice, and then gladly put the city behind her.

Following the course of the South Platte as far as Plum Creek, she trekked through snow and ice to Colorado Springs, Manitou, and up into South Park, the gentle high valley where the South Platte begins its meanderings. She stayed a fearful night in a miners' camp, where, for the first time in all her travels, she felt the code of chivalry might be eroded enough to cause her personal danger. Then she returned to Denver, toured Georgetown, and went back to Estes, having matter-of-factly accomplished a 500-mile ride through wintry mountains alone and unguided.

But her peaceful park could no longer be a refuge. Jim Nugent met her with the disquieting news that he had decided he was in love with her. He poured out all she knew and more of his violent past and his periodic drunken rages.

Isabella reacted with horror. Here was a man "whom any woman might love but no sane woman would marry," as she wrote Henny. "He is so lovable and yet so terrible…" Isabella's common sense told her to run, and she did.

One last morning she watched the red and gold of the winter sunrise on the peaks. And in a shower of frost feathers, she said goodbye to Jim. Then she boarded the coach for Greeley, Cheyenne, the British Isles, and the unthreatening love of Henny.

The next summer Rocky Mountain Jim was shot to death by Isabella's Estes host, Griff Evans. Far away in Edinburgh, Isabella received conflicting stories of who was the villain and who the victim. Though she grieved for the handsome trapper, she had already written finis on that chapter of her life, and she was thankful she had.

Isabella lived until 1904. Never happy or healthy for long at home, she sailed for Japan in 1878 and later traveled India, Malaya, Tibet, China, Korea, Persia, and Morocco. Her letters to Henny from the Rockies were published in 1878 as *A Lady's Life in the Rocky Mountains*, and she was on her way to becoming one of England's most popular travel writers. She also became a photographer, a nurse, and a founder of mission hospitals. In 1892 she became the first woman ever elected a Fellow of the Royal Geographical Society. Demure, ladylike and dignified, she still admitted, on publication of her third book of travels, to "a lurking satisfaction in having vindicated a woman's right to do what she can do well." It became her life conviction.

The Maid From Philadelphia

While Isabella Bird pursued her unusual goals with ladylike dignity, another Greeley visitor in the fall of 1873 took an entirely different approach. She was not much taller than Isabella, and her square-jawed face lacked beauty, but she had never in her lifetime simply faded into a crowd. Her name was Anna E. Dickinson, and it was a name she had made known all across the United States before she reached her twenty-first birthday.

eing known nation-wide was a singular accomplishment for any woman in the 1800s, let alone a teen-aged Quaker maiden who had no wealth, no family backing or social connections, and only limited education. But Anna Dickinson had one thing that made up for all she lacked; she had a genius for oratory. In a time when oratory ranked high as a means of public entertainment and education, Anna's strong, mellow voice, her quick mind, her facility with words, her flair for the dramatic, and her obvious sincerity were well received. She began speaking before small, local groups, and almost before she knew what was happening, she had been propelled to the forefront of public speakers during the Civil War.

An ardent abolitionist and fervent advocate of the war, Anna's fresh young appearance had caught the imagination of the crowds. Calling as she did for support of the war and preservation of the Union, she had earned the sobriquet "Joan of Arc." From the age of 17 she was called to address ever larger and more important audiences. In 1855 she had scrubbed sidewalks to earn the twenty-five cents admission to a lecture by Wendell Phillips. In 1862 she took Phillips' place at the rostrum for a speech in Boston's Music Hall before 5,000 people.

In a time when no woman could vote, and most "decent" women hesitated even to attend public meetings, the 21-year-old Quaker girl was changing the outcome of elections with her speeches. In January of 1864, she stood on a specially built platform in the United States House of Representatives, the first woman ever to be so invited, and addressed her remarks to the members of both houses of Congress, the Supreme Court justices, and President Abraham Lincoln.

It was a heady pinnacle for so young a woman, yet Anna was able to remain at the heights for some time after the war's end. It was Anna, along with Theodore Tilton and Frederick Douglas, who formulated the Fifteenth Amendment in 1866. And it was Anna who ruled as undisputed queen of the lyceum circuit, her friends among the most prestigious families in the country, and her annual income in excess of $20,000.

By the fall of 1873, when Anna journeyed to Greeley, it had all begun to taste of ashes. She was only 30 years old, but she was exhausted. She had had more than a lifetime of excitement and glory, and she lived in dread that the rest of her life would only be a poor echo of her past triumphs.

Crowds and applause were the wellspring of her energy, yet the constant travel the lecture circuit required made her weary and ill. She had earned hundreds of thousands of dollars, but the money had disappeared in support of her aged mother, her spinster sister, and her own lavish habits. Sunk in depression, she lacked the will to put her affairs in order.

Yet she knew she should act to cut expenses and put money aside for the future. The past season had been by far the poorest she ever experienced. Always outspoken, she had antagonized the Republicans, her long-time allies, by supporting Horace Greeley in the presidential campaign of 1872. She had attacked both big business and labor unions. Though a strong advocate of women's rights, she had managed to alienate the Suffragettes. And many of her early admirers were put off by her growing worldliness and free lifestyle.

With interest in the lyceum dropping all over the country, Anna suffered many half-empty houses and cancelled bookings. She had spent a long, cold, dismal winter, weakened by jaundice, bronchitis, and insomnia.

When Nathan Meeker's son, Ralph, invited her to come out West and let the air of the Rockies restore her health, she snatched at the chance. Ralph Meeker was an eager suitor who was well down the list of desirables in Anna's mind, but she needed what he offered now, and Anna did not shrink from using people. She enlisted her brother John as chaperone and insulator, and took the Kansas-Pacific line west.

Anna had spent years in travel on the railroads, but still she was fascinated by the puffing locomotives. She saw them as both helpful and merciless; both beautiful and terrible. She enjoyed the company of railroad men, and thought a good machinist could match anyone in an argument, trained as he was to logical thinking. She often forsook the polite company of the parlour cars for the conversations of railroaders in the caboose.

Even before the peaks of the Rockies broke the western horizon, Anna knew she had done the right thing. For some time she had longed for a real change — "something foreign and remote from all the past" — and as the train puffed across the flats of Kansas, her spirits began to revive. She inveigled the engineer for a ride on the front of the engine and sat ecstatic on the pilot, her skirts billowing around her and her chin thrust squarely into the wind. She thought such a ride would have made even her aged mother young again.

Yet even now Anna's active mind probed the implications of her surroundings. When she passed the dugouts that were homes for the Kansas farmers, she was reminded of the James River during the Civil War, where she had seen men digging frantically in the earth for shelter. Here there were no enemy shells exploding, but the very elements themselves were so inhospitable that the people were forced to seek shelter under-ground. Anna, who bathed in wine and enjoyed all the luxuries life had to offer, wondered what these women saw in their future. She saw the West as a hard place, and thought it must take twice the stuff to succeed here as back East.

But still she loved the freedom and delighted in the sense of space. In the darkness of night, when the engine stopped for water, she climbed again to the vantage of the pilot for the last leg into Denver. With nothing before her or at her side, and the ''great monster choo-chooing behind,'' she watched the sky lighten until the mountain peaks took shades of purple from the rising sun, and the whole range stood out above the dark prairie, each promontory lit with rose in sharp relief against the soft azure of the crevasses. It was a journey of delight, and she reluctantly retreated back to the palace car only when they reached the junction a mile out of town.

The faithful Ralph Meeker met them at the station and took them to breakfast, but Anna did not tarry long in his presence. The newspapers took delight in matching her up with every eligible male, and she did not want to encourage their speculations. What she did want to do was to climb some mountains, and in two days she was off for Pikes Peak.

In her response to the mountains, the outspoken American would have found common ground with the gentle English traveler. She viewed the sunrise from Pikes Peak, and in a few days had conquered both Mt. Elbert and Mt. Lincoln on muleback. As she wrote later, ''One goes to the top of mountains for emotions, not descriptions,'' and she found her usually practical nature quite overcome by the glories she viewed.

Another sunrise experienced on the wind-blasted summit of Grays Peak felt to her like the dawn of creation, with the far plains ''misty blue, cut by the glittering golden line of the Platte.'' It was ''a superhuman revealing,'' and the air, the

exercise, and the exhilaration gave her back her health.

Her enthusiasm carried her up Longs Peak with Dr. Ferdinand Hayden and the men of the United States Geological Survey (the fifth 14,000 foot peak she had conquered). Then it was down into the blackness of a gold mine near Central City. She thought the begrimed miners she met changing shifts looked like alien creatures, and she long remembered the moments she clung to a ladder rung in absolute darkness while she waited for her guide to strike a new light.

Charged with new energy, Anna accepted lecture dates that Ralph Meeker arranged for her in Denver, Golden, and Central City. She drew the

largest crowd yet to grace Governor's Hall in Denver, and when she spoke in the Montana Theater in Central City, every chair was filled and the aisles were crowded with camp stools. Her face sunburned from her outings, her gesturing hand studded with a large diamond, and her voice vibrant with her new-found health, she spoke on one of her favorite subjects, Joan of Arc.

Beginning quietly, Anna sketched the life of the woman to whom she had often been compared. It was a dramatic account of a dramatic life, but Anna was feminist enough that she did not ascribe Joan's powers to spiritual sources. To her mind, there was no reason the French peasant girl could not have accomplished what she did without heavenly assistance, and she held her up as an example of the capabilities of womanhood.

It was a lecture she had given dozens of times, in fine halls, to crowds that dwarfed this group of miners and their ladies, but somehow in this small mountain town it came to life for her again. She paced, gestured, and appealed to the crowd until her plain face was lit with emotion that lent it compelling beauty. Her musical voice rolled easily to the farthest corner, even when she dropped to a near whisper, and though at times she raced through her sentences, every word was enunciated with such clarity that not one was lost.

Her dark eyes challenged the audience to dispute her assertion that Joan's military acumen could put Napoleon to shame. But then, she noted in quiet sarcasm, "The world, in reasonable fashion, demands of a woman that she do twice as much as a man to prove that she can equal him."

The feminist viewpoint did not hold sway with the men of Colorado, but the woman who had lectured San Franciscans on their treatment of the Chinese, and Nevadans for their drinking and gambling, had nothing to fear from the roughnecks of the mine-pocked mountains. They listened in rapt silence for nearly two hours and exploded into cheers and applause when Anna made her final bow.

With their cheers echoing in her ears, Anna prepared to return east. She hated to leave. "Once you have breathed this air, you will always long for it," she wrote. She asked the Meekers to check into property she might buy, and so assure herself of returning to Colorado. She had to firmly detach herself from Ralph, and publicly deny another reported engagement, but she was thankful that she had come, for she could look forward to the winter circuit with new hope and confidence.

Anna's success in Colorado was not to be repeated in the East. The financial panic of 1873 emptied lecture halls and plunged the country into a five-year depression. The lyceum circuit, on which her income depended, never recovered its popularity.

The next years saw Anna struggling valiantly to support herself and her family. She tried writing but made no money. She wrote and performed in plays that failed to gain critical acclaim. She even took to the stage in tights for her own interpretation of *Hamlet*. None of her efforts won back the audience she depended on for both physical and mental sustenance.

As her fame faded and old friends and suitors became disenchanted, she sank into poverty and depression. Unable to accept her fall from favor gracefully, she lashed out in bitter diatribes that revealed a growing paranoia. She began to act irrationally, and the people of her small Pennsylvania town whispered that she had taken to drink. Finally, in 1891, at the instigation of the sister she had always supported, Anna was carried off to an institution for the insane.

There followed six years of legal battles—with sister pitted against sister in public trial. Anna took the stand in her own defense and gave perhaps the most persuasive performance of her life. For a time she was able to recapture the wit and the articulation that had made her famous, long enough to impress a jury to vote in her favor and to have her sanity attested to by the courts.

But it was small comfort. Estranged from her family and forgotten by her public, Anna lived her final years totally dependent on her last friend in a small room above a candy store in the Catskill Mountains. She spent her days sorting and resorting the trunksful of letters, clippings, and awards that were proof of her past glory, only occasionally venturing out for a walk in the gentle slopes of the Catskills.

She could remember other mountains, more rugged, far to the west, that had given her the grandest pleasure she had ever experienced. She could remember stages without end and crowds she had moved at her whim to tears or laughter. She could remember influencing fundamental changes in public opinion and inciting governments to action. But by the time she died in 1932, 68 years after her greatest triumph, there was no one else who remembered what she had been.

Man in a Hurry

The man who led Anna Dickinson to the heights of Longs Peak was quiet where she was outspoken, and objective where she was emotional, but he was no less driven than the Maid of Philadelphia. His name was Ferdinand Vandiveer Hayden, and he, too, had struggled to reach prominence from humble beginnings.

Left virtually on his own at the age of 12, when his parents separated in 1841, Ferdinand had boarded with an uncle until he was 16 and old enough to begin teaching school. Two years of scrimping had given him enough savings to enter Oberlin College, where, a quiet, nervous, dreamy student, he had failed to impress other students with his drive.

But he did make a friendship with a doctor who was interested in geology, and with the doctor's encouragement he entered medical school in Albany. There an understanding professor provided him with board and room in exchange for his work in sorting and cleaning a collection of fossils, and by 1863 he had earned his medical degree.

The problem was he had no desire to be a medical doctor. The geology he had learned from his friend at Oberlin, and the practical experience in paleontology he had gained at Albany convinced him his real interest lay in natural history.

After graduation he eagerly accepted a chance to join a fossil collecting expedition to the White River in Dakota Territory. There, pick in hand, scrambling in excitement from one find to the next amid the grotesque formations of the Badlands, Ferdinand Hayden found his life's calling.

He looked at the immensity of the West—the significance of its topography, the strangeness of its plant life, the variety of its animal populations, the possibilities inherent in its resources—and he knew he wanted to spend the rest of his life in its study. He longed to explore every hidden recess of the intensely interesting country. Considering what there was to be done, he knew even a lifetime would not be enough to accomplish all he wanted. He said he wished only "to add his mite to the sum of human knowledge." But his "mite" was a mountain in anyone else's perspective.

With a new drive and determination, Hayden plunged into his investigations immediately. One way or another he wangled assignments and support from both private and government sources that allowed him to study much of the Platte River drainage. He conducted a geological survey of Nebraska in 1867; followed the Union Pacific across Wyoming in 1868, dipping into North Park in the process; and later explored south along the Rockies. He worked for the State of Nebraska, for the fur companies, for the military, for anyone he could convince of the usefulness of his service.

In the process he learned the organizational arts necessary for successful expeditions into wilderness areas. He learned to stretch his slim resources so that he could cover the greatest possible territory. And because he had to seek out assignments, he learned the delicate art of lobbying government bodies for the authorizations and equipment he needed. When the United States Geological Survey of the Territories was established in 1869, he had gained enough fame as a geologist to be chosen to head the project.

Nothing could have suited him better. At last he had the money and equipment to do the job correctly. Under Hayden's guidance the survey grew to a comprehensive study that touched on all parts of the area it covered.

He added topographers and saw to it that the topographer and geologist worked together so that each could gain from the other's knowledge. He enlisted zoologists, botanists, ethnologists, paleontologists, and ornithologists—both amateur and professional—to add their expertise. And in a stroke of genius, he hired a young Omaha photographer named William H. Jackson to preserve on film the many wonders the members of the survey would come across.

By the time Hayden escorted Anna Dickinson up Longs Peak in 1873, he had spent nearly 15 years in the West. To Anna's eyes he was "tall and slender, with soft brown hair and blue eyes." But to most observers the 44-year-old scientist was small, slightly scruffy in appearance, and always in a hurry.

However, his eager intensity won Anna's friendship as they sat around the campfire in the alpine meadow, and he outlined his current and most ambitious undertaking: he planned to produce an atlas of the Colorado Rockies. Allowing three years for field work and splitting his scientists into several parties, he intended to survey the entire mountain chain, using primary and secondary triangulation, so that the resulting maps would be as accurate as possible.

Hayden always emphasized the practical gains to be had from scientific exploration, and he thought no portion of the continent promised to yield more useful results. The railroads, the mining interests, the military, and the governments of the swelling population could all benefit from accurate knowledge of the chaotic country.

Anna had left the group of young scientists highly impressed with their enthusiastic disregard of bodily comfort—even safety—all for the sake of science. But with at least three years' experience behind them, most of Hayden's men were used to coping with the storms, bears, balky mules, forest fires, and even Indians. And the fact that the Colorado survey would require work parties to scale fifty-two 14,000 foot peaks in order to take their readings was not considered a significant handicap.

Hayden was not overly sociable with his men, but his enthusiasm was infectious. He believed intensely in the importance of their work, and he was willing to work like a Trojan to see it accomplished. He expected no less from his collection of scientists.

The men went east of Denver and established a base line six miles long, with 30-foot-high triangulation pyramids at each end. They split into a half-dozen parties. With a geologist, topographer, assorted naturalists, packers, and a cook to keep each party fed and happy, they fanned out to fulfill their assignments. Photographer Jackson, the supply corps, and Hayden's supervisory party moved where and when they were needed.

Hayden became a familiar figure to the miners and townspeople of the mountains. Short legs stretched to encompass the belly of an army mule, his felt hat gray with dust, his black frock coat flapping, he flew from pass to pass, peak to peak, and camp to camp. He placated hostile ranchers who were dubious about the survey's purpose, and he saw to it that persons who could influence the public mind (like Anna Dickinson and William Byers) were invited to share the exhilaration of discovery.

It was an arduous three seasons. Each peak had to be climbed, and it had to be climbed carrying a 50-pound theodolite to use in observations. While some were easy walks, others were real feats of mountaineering. Often they reached the top to find it shrouded in cloud, and they had to choose between waiting in the freezing air and descending to repeat the climb. They braved lightning strikes on exposed peaks, disturbed grizzlies that charged from cover and army mules that were capable of anything—even attempting suicide by jumping off a ridge to protest too heavy a pack. The altitude taxed their strength, and the frequent rain and snow showers soaked their boots and taxed their tempers. Their woolen trousers were almost never dry.

Hayden had a happy talent for judging men, and he had chosen his scientists well. They remained conscientious in doing their jobs. More than that, they remained enthusiastic for each new peak they could place with accuracy, each new vista that unfolded below them. Jackson struggled up the peaks before and behind the surveyors, lugging his hundred pounds of primitive photographical equipment, recording on fragile glass plates views seen before by few or none.

Hayden, himself, was everywhere. He moved from party to party, supervising, coordinating, and making decisions. His small, wiry frame carried him at a dead run from dawn to dusk, regardless of terrain or weather. The Sioux who had watched him hunting fossils in the Badlands had called him ''Man Who Picks Up Stones Running'' and he had not slowed noticeably since. There was always more to see—and he was always facing a deadline of sunset or season. As the end of each summer approached, he grew more tense, and sometimes he lashed out at his men in fits of temper.

He knew his own failings. Years before, he had noted that his worst fault was trying to do too much. He knew he probably should do less and do it better. But when he got into the field he always saw so much to learn that he lost his restraint. He wanted it all noted, examined, and down on paper.

Hayden's papers were not only for the scientific community. He wanted his work to reach a wide audience. At the end of each season in the field, his key personnel traveled with him to the survey's headquarters on Pennsylvania Avenue in Washington, D.C. There they spent the winter compiling their manuscripts, maps, and photographs.

The Survey's Annual Reports always received wide attention. They had their faults. Like Hayden, they tried to cover too much, too fast. They were sometimes repetitive and poorly organized. They dealt with big issues and ignored finer or opposing points of view. But the maps were unquestionably the finest yet made, and when the *Atlas of Colorado* was published in 1877, it was in a class alone.

There were 10 maps included, and for the first time the people of Colorado and the people of the nation could see where each peak stood in relation to the other, where the passes lay, where there was cropland, forest, pasture, gold, silver, or coal, where the Platte and the Arkansas drew water for the plains. Colorado, declared a state in 1876, had something more to celebrate.

Hayden, himself, was well-pleased. He loved the West and wanted his reports to be of practical value to those who would settle there. As he had written in 1870, ''it is my earnest desire to devote the remainder of the working days of my life to the development of (the West's) scientific and material interest, until I shall see every Territory which is now organized a State of the Union.''

Colorado had made the transition, and for the next three years Hayden turned his attention to Wyoming, Utah, and Idaho. When his Survey was terminated in 1879, Hayden moved to Philadelphia to compile the two volumes of his final report.

The body that had carried him over such vast stretches of the West began to fail, but before he died at 58, he had published 1,306 pages of his own writings, edited 21,142 pages of others' reports, and mapped 417,000 square miles. He had been the first to determine the age of the Rocky Mountains, the first to use topographers and geologists in teams, the first to use photography to illustrate geological features, and the first to see a geological survey as a tool for national development. His survey had been responsible for the establishment of Yellowstone National Park, and for the verification of the ruins of Mesa Verde, which would become a national park at a later date.

On a wider level, his survey had provided detailed scientific information that aided hundreds of common people to choose land, farm, mine, ranch, and develop the potential of the West.

His time had been limited, but he had used it well.

Across the Nebraska Sea

Some of the trains that rocked and rattled their way west along the Platte in the late 1870s stopped at the little, new-wood depots to deposit the settlers who would develop the potential Hayden saw in the Great American Desert. But others were headed farther west. The trains were made up on the Jersey shore with loads of silent, frightened immigrants, who had been shunted from ship to shore, to river boat, to railroad shed, and onto the narrow cars of a train.

A.BATTLES

Since Monday, August 17, 1879, a west-bound train had carried one immigrant past the lights of Philadelphia, across the sweet valley of the Susquehanna, into Pittsburgh, and past Ohio's corn fields. By Wednesday the young Scotsman had been able to buy one real meal and had endured a confused changing of trains in Chicago, where he was packed unceremoniously with citizens and immigrants alike for the leg to Council Bluffs, Iowa.

It had been a tiring, uncomfortable journey, but the gangling, emaciated Scotsman was a writer, and he had enjoyed the stimulation as the vistas of America rolled by his window. Before his steerage crossing, he had thought of America as a place of courage, action, and change; a place where life was lived in the open air, free of social structures. Since his chosen course of action — the decision that had brought him to America — was a direct insult to the standards of his British family and friends, he was relieved to find Americans, indeed, open to the point of rudeness. Shop-keepers served him as a friendly favor, and his upper-class patronizing was neither needed nor wanted.

But when he stood before the Emigrant House in Council Bluffs on Friday morning, he found he had not left all class distinctions behind. The tickets he held for California entitled him only to passage on an emigrant train, and he stood again with a hundred others whose clothing and manners marked them as society's poorest. A grumpy, white-haired railroad official ordered the families to one car, the single men to another, and a group of Chinese to a third. Since he was neither married nor Chinese, Robert Louis Stevenson dragged his valise, his knapsack and his six volume set of Bancroft's *History of the United States* aboard the men's coach.

It was the plainest of accommodations. Nothing but wood met the eye. There was no brocade, no fringe, no cushioned seating. There were only wooden benches, scarcely wide enough to hold two sets of shoulders, a stove that would be needed only for meals in the August heat, and a "convenience" in one end.

If the coach had been full, Stevenson and his fellow travelers would have faced a week's journey with no chance to lie down. Luckily it was only half full, and the reversible seat backs could be set face to face on each pair of seats. For a price the railroad provided a board to span the gap, and with straw-filled cushions to complete the "bed", two emigrants of average height could sleep in relative comfort.

The conductor busied himself in pairing the passengers into bed partners, and Louis was embarrassed when the first man the conductor suggested for his partner declined the honor. He knew he was dirty and disheveled; his long brown hair hung in strings around his angular face, and his soiled clothing sagged between the bony projections of his shoulders.

But he was no dirtier than the others. It was something else that made him different. His long, tapering fingers brushed hair away from huge, intense brown eyes, and his sensitive mouth was only partially disguised by a stylish moustache. Moreover, his face was flushed with fever, and he had the fragile look many had seen before in a body weakened by consumption.

He was, in fact, ill and exhausted. Accustomed to pampering by his landed family, protected by winter seasons in southern France, he risked permanent damage to his precarious health by this arduous journey. When the train finally crossed the Missouri and pulled out of Omaha, and a passenger began serenading the car with "Home Sweet Home," Louis had to fight back tears.

He had abandoned home and family and a budding career as a writer to go to his love, Fanny Van de Grift Osbourne. Fanny was married, a mother, an American, and 10 years his senior, any one of which would have made her unacceptable to Louis' friends and family. But he had loved her from their first meeting in Europe three years before. When he heard she was ill at home in California, and that a divorce from her husband seemed imminent, he had scraped together 30 pounds, begged credit for 150 pounds for works not yet written, and joined the crowd in steerage to begin a 6,000 mile journey. Behind him, his literary friends shook their heads, and his father predicted Louis would be destroyed by this "sinful, mad business."

He was aware they could be right. He risked disinheritance, knowing he had never earned enough writing to support himself. He did not know if Fanny would be free to marry him, if she *would* marry him — a sick, penniless author without prospects — if he would even survive the journey to find out. But he wrote a friend as the train inched across the continent, "No man is any use until he has dared everything; I feel now as if I had, and so might become a man.''

Fortunately for Louis' manly appearance, others in the car found that ''Home Sweet Home'' was raising unwelcome emotions. An elderly man called out for a cheerful tune about the good, new country they were going to, and in an instant the mood had passed. Louis had by now found a seat partner, a young sturdy Pennsylvania Dutchman, and they curled themselves between the seats and tried to sleep, while the wheels clicked over the rails and thunder grumbled overhead.

Louis woke the next morning to a cloudless sky. ''We were at sea,'' he wrote later, ''on the plains of Nebraska.'' After a quick wash—he and two partners had purchased a basin, towel and bar of soap to share—he retired to the top of a coach. It was a cinder-swept and rather precarious perch, but he needed to escape the foul air of the car. And he hoped to see something new.

He enjoyed the wind in his face and the ever-present whir of grasshoppers along the track, but hour after hour brought only empty sky and empty earth, until his head and body seemed to swell in the vacuum. He could look ahead to see rails lined with sunflowers stretching to the horizon. Behind it was the same. The train seemed to move at a snail's pace, and Louis reflected on the weariness of the pioneers, who must have traveled for days with no landmarks to appear and grow and disappear, marking their progress. He thought a man could walk five miles, or 10, or 20, and see nothing different from where he started.

He found an exhilaration in the space and a joy in the great arch of heaven, because he knew his road would eventually bring other sights. But he pondered about the settlers in the tiny dots that grew to cabins and dwindled again to dots as they passed. How could they exist in such a land? How could they endure such monotony?

With a quarter of the universe itself always in view, and the stars of night the only variety, he felt their eyes must cry for relief from distance. The treeless, colorless settlements, each painfully new and each like the last, seemed to him as artificial as a set for a play. With no paths worn, no patina of age, without even litter, he wondered how ''the great child, man (could find) entertainment in so bare a playroom.''

And yet....

And yet there was a fascination about this strange country. As they puffed to a stop at settlements along the tracks, Louis watched the local people who boarded the train to sell milk, eggs, and coffee.

One woman in particular caught his attention. She was a large-boned woman, with an attractive face and kind, dark eyes, and she moved through the aisles with a matriarchal grace. He could see no sign of discontent, no longing for new scenes, only an expression of peace and satisfaction. While the train took on fuel, he climbed out to stretch his legs, and he took the chance to peer into the milk woman's house.

It was one of a dozen new-raised cabins that grouped near the tracks, and the inside was as barren as the outside. It was clean, but to Louis' eyes, certainly not homelike. For him to live there would have been ghastly. Yet it was obvious to him the woman did not need his pity. She was strong and free and happy beside the Platte on the Nebraska plain. He decided the settlers must create their own full existence, with family, cattle, changing seasons, sunflowers, and grasshoppers each taking their part.

Louis could not tarry long in exploration. He had discovered that while the trainmen east of the Missouri had always warned of departure with an ''All Aboard!'', the emigrant conductor extended no such courtesy. The train simply began to move and the passengers were left to scramble on as best they could. Meal stops averaged 20 minutes, and Louis and the rest bolted their food with one eye on the train.

Louis was infuriated at this petty cruelty, and he was even angrier when he learned the conductor refused to answer the simplest question. The conductor's theory was that to answer one would lead to a flood of others, so he answered none. The passengers could only wonder when, where, and how long the next stop would be.

Stops for food were greeted with joy, but other stops were not so welcome. The train spent many half hours sitting on sidings while they waited for more prestigious travelers to pass.

By the time the train had crawled out of the Platte Valley and passed Cheyenne and Laramie, Louis was so sick that he felt a kind of strange detachment. He felt he was doing right, and though he knew no one else would agree, he didn't care. He felt almost as if he were already dead and just riding along to view the final outcome.

Unable to sleep, he sat up through an endless night as the train labored its way across the wastes

of Wyoming desert. And when his fellow passengers awoke, they gave him not comfort, but ridicule. His scarecrow appearance excited various witticisms. With characteristic good humor, Louis tried to smile at their jests.

Perhaps the strain of travel and the anxiety for the unknown future were weighing on them all. It was hardly encouraging that passengers on every train they met from the west called out "Come back, come back!" The trains going east seemed as packed as theirs, and they could only assume that hundreds had failed to find work and home in the West which held all their hopes. Louis thought of all the hungry people on the move across the world, and he was depressed that the place they sought would likely be no better than the places they abandoned. It seemed there was no El Dorado anymore.

Louis himself had to give thought to possible employment. He had sloshed through pelting rain in New York City and visited publisher after publisher, trying to sell some of his writings before he took the train for California. But he had been able to place nothing. The essays, stories, and two small travel books he had managed to publish the previous two years had scarcely made his name known in Britain, let alone overseas. To survive without his family allotment would be a real challenge.

Determined to prove himself as a man, he welcomed the challenge. But when the train finally pulled into Sacramento, after 11 weary days, he staggered off looking like warmed-over death. Somehow he managed to make his way to Monterey and a reunion with Fanny. And Fanny, after an initial hesitation, found the courage to endure the stigma of divorce and cast her lot with the improbable young man who had appeared on her doorstep.

It was nine months before they could be married, and they were the most difficult months of Stevenson's life. He existed on the edge of starvation, driving himself to write, fighting depression and a host of bodily ailments. In December he wrote to a friend in England, "There is something in me worth saying though I can't find what it is just yet; and ere I die, if I do not die too fast, I shall write something worth the boards." So conscious was he of impending death that he composed his epitaph, a poem that would later be titled "Requiem."

The chance that he would have time to find himself as a writer was slim. In March he suffered his first severe hemorrhage, and had it not been for Fanny's devoted nursing, his life would have ended. But he managed to hang on, and in May the pair was married. They retreated to a deserted mining camp in the mountains, where Louis slowly regained his strength and became reconciled with his family.

One year after his first journey up the Platte, Louis and Fanny trained across Nebraska from the west. This time other trains sat on the siding as his roared by, and this time he rode first class, again a moneyed gentleman, secure in the love of his wife, enjoying a new stepson.

But the trip on the emigrant train and the year of suffering had left their mark on both his health and his writing. Though he was never strong again physically, his writing grew in vigor and imagination. He had discovered what he wanted to do was tell stories, and a few months after he returned to Europe he began the first chapter of *Treasure Island.*

He was introduced to the American public in 1883, when *Century Magazine* published *The Silverado Squatters,* the story of his mountain summer in California with Fanny. He never regretted his wild journey of 1879, or his marriage to Fanny. Thirteen years later he wrote, "I think my marriage was the best move I ever made in my life. Not only would I do it again; I cannot conceive the idea of doing otherwise."

Robert Louis Stevenson's experiences along the Platte were published in *Across the Plains* in 1892. He died in 1894, three weeks after his forty-fourth birthday.

Who Could Ask for More?

There was a certain truth to Robert Louis Stevenson's romantic view of the bucolic life along the Platte in 1879. The settlers had chosen to be where they were, and the strong ones appreciated the freedom to build a life for their families. Women did create a full existence from husband, children, stock, crops, seasons, and sunflowers, but it was not quite as uncomplicated and blissful as the young writer imagined.

When Stevenson passed along the Union Pacific tracks on his way east in the fall of 1880, enjoying his new wife and the son he had gained by marriage, he rode within a few miles of the homestead of Luna and James T. Kellie.

Luna and J. T. had staked a claim to land on the south side of the Platte west of Hastings, and at 23, Luna had already devoted four years to the struggle of changing prairie grass to paying farm. She was an energetic and resourceful young woman, but in the fall of 1880 she was burying the second child she and J. T. had lost since coming to Nebraska in 1876, and she was wondering if she could find the strength to endure this newest loss.

Though she had begun life on the prairie afraid to step outside for fear of rattlesnakes and sure every owl hoot was an Indian call, the slender, dark-haired young mother had learned to herd cattle, to put up hay, to defend her chickens — and her child — from rapacious hogs, and to make a home for J. T. and four-year-old Willie in a house with dirt walls, dirt roof, and dirt floor.

She had been able to accept the labor of 18-hour days, the loss of garden to grasshoppers and drought, the tedium of life without newspapers, magazines, or contact with the outside world, because she had the love of J. T., the joy of first-born Willie, and the sincere belief that their efforts were building a secure future for their family.

She was of naturally cheerful nature — one of J. T.'s greatest pleasures was listening to her sing as she worked about the house — and she and J. T. managed to make light of their numerous hardships.

Luna, who was at first repelled by the dirt-brown of soddies she had expected to be green and grassy, could say that moving into their first sod house was a "proud and happy day." They bought a No. 7 stove and enough lumber for a table and bed frame; J. T. built a bureau and a high chair for Willie out of packing crates; they sawed stumps into stools; hung their carpet for a partition; and with some sheets and a quilt around the walls they had "a home and no rent to pay, who could ask for more?"

They laughed about the crooked furrows their headstrong steers cut into the prairie, plowing land they had not intended to break...When a blizzard forced them to share their soddie with 15 cattle for two nights and a day, they "had quite a bit of fun out of it."...When dirty water poured through the sod roof during rains, J.T. made a game of dancing around to find a dry spot to stand....The time that roof finally collapsed in the night, nearly burying them in their beds, they set up housekeeping outside and joked about the neighbors riding horses in their kitchen....The days they had no money to buy kerosene and thus no light, Luna set the table by the door and they ate "romantic" moonlight suppers.

After supper they sat on the doorstep, Luna's head on J. T.'s shoulder and Willie in his lap, and they chuckled over Willie's chatter while they drew pictures in the air of the grand farm their land would someday be. It was all they asked of life, and, sure of success, Luna felt she would not trade places with anyone in the world.

True, they had lived for weeks on potatoes and bread made of shorts and corn meal, unable to buy anything without going in debt, which J. T. refused to do. Luna had dreamed night after night of good wheat bread, but as long as Willie prospered on the heifer's milk, she didn't complain.

There had been a time when their last fifteen cents went for a half bushel of corn, and later Luna shed secret tears because she did not have three cents to send a birthday greeting to her grandmother. Frustrated by the lack of reading material, she once declared she wished she had never learned to read, so she would not miss it so. But she kept such gloomy thoughts from J. T. He, hollow-cheeked and weary, had begun to plow and walk cross-country barefoot, because his boots were nearly used up and they could buy no more.

The death of their second son Jimmie, before his first birthday, had grieved them deeply, but they had clung to their dream that someday Willie would have many brothers and sisters. They thought 12 was a minimum size for a family, and 15 would be better. Children from smaller families, they thought, were too apt to be spoiled and selfish.

In the fall of 1879, Luna had given birth to a daughter, Susie, and they had rejoiced in the blue-eyed girl. Luna found one child could never replace another, but she was grateful to have a baby in her arms again. Someone told them if they could keep her alive for a year, she would be safe. Both Luna and J. T. had silently counted the days, and when Susie was one year and two days old, J. T. had felt bold enough to rouse Luna with the words, "Wake up, Mama. It is September 1, and we have our baby well.''

Less than a month later, Susie, too, lay ready for a small grave beside her brother. She had caught whooping cough from a passing stranger, and for the second time Luna had had to wash and dress a small body for burial. Too numb to cry, she did what she had to do, but she could not bring herself to completely close Susie's blue eyes.

Luna had been repelled when a swarm of strangers had descended for Jimmie's funeral, and she and J. T. decided they would tolerate only family and close friends this time. Luna's father and uncle lived nearby, and they notified Luna's best friend, a tall, dark-skinned woman from Tennessee named Mrs. Strohl.

Mrs. Strohl was considerably older than Luna, and her help and friendship had been of immeasurable value to Luna from their first meeting. Now she came bearing a wash tub full of hot dishes, salads, and coffee to feed the mourners, and after a few songs, scriptures, and prayers at the kitchen table, Susie's coffin was placed in the ground beside Jimmie.

The days that followed were terrible ones for Luna. For the first time she lost faith in her family's future. She did not think she had the courage to have another child and risk losing it. Finally she and J. T. resolved if they did have more, they would not allow themselves to love them so much.

Luna suffered from a constant, stabbing pain in her head, and she decided that cutting off her heavy, dark hair might give her ease. Several times J. T. took up the shears and tried to begin the cutting, but he could not bring himself to do it. At last, one day when the pain seemed unbearable, Luna cut out a chunk herself. Then she walked out to where J. T. was plowing, handed him the scissors, and asked him to finish the job.

He did, but the pain did not go away.

As the weeks dragged on and Luna continued to suffer, J. T. searched his mind for a way to help. He suggested that Luna take Willie and visit her Aunt Hattie for a day. Luna, who often spent months without leaving the homestead, traveled the seven miles to her uncle's farm and the welcoming arms of short, plump, motherly Aunt Hattie. Talk and, finally, tears with the older woman cleansed her spirit, and a new shirt pattern for Willie gave her something to do when she returned home. She began to function again.

Crowded into the 12- by 16-foot shed and lean-to

they had built after the collapse of the soddy, the three Kellies began a long, severe winter. Neither Willie nor Luna had overshoes or heavy clothes, so they were confined to the house most of the time. J. T. tended Luna's prized flock of chickens—much of their cash came from Luna's chickens and garden produce—and Willie spent the days playing with a yellow kitten.

While Luna sat at the sewing machine in the center of the room, making Willie's clothes and sewing J. T.'s dark blue flannel winter shirts, Willie raced around and around the table with the kitten chasing a corn cob on a string. The motion and racket grated on Luna's nerves, but she tried to be grateful that he was getting some exercise.

Other years they had put up freighters who traveled between Hastings and the Republican Valley, and the cash and company the freighters provided were equally welcome. Luna had spent many evenings reading *Tom Sawyer* and *Roughing It* aloud to whatever travelers happened to be sharing their fire. They had also been given a copy of *Harper's Magazine* containing pictures of the wonders discovered by the Hayden Survey along the Yellowstone River, and it inspired excited plans about going to see the area.

But this year the railroad up the Republican was completed, and the freighting wagons no longer creaked past the house. They were left alone by the fire while the wind buffeted the lean-to and snow ticked against the stove pipe.

The snow seemed endless. Day after day it sifted down until the draws were filled to the level of the prairie, and the few characteristics of the countryside disappeared in a monotony of white. On snowless days the wind would work to clean the ridges and sculpt gray edges along the tops of the drifts, but then another storm would move in, drop its load, and erase their world.

Imprisoned in a shroud of white, Luna's soul cried out for color. She waited hungrily for the extra minutes of daylight that meant they had reached bottom and were on the way up.

Some years Luna had begun planting her garden in February, putting out the hardy seeds weeks, even months, before the neighbors. They were scandalized at her temerity and regularly predicted failure, but she had enough good results to continue the practice. This year it was later when she was finally freed to get outside and begin digging in the dirt, and when she did she began to feel better.

It had taken Luna some time to appreciate the beauties of the prairie, but by now she felt at home in the sweep of land and sky. She watched for the subtle changes of color: the pricks of green in the tawny roots of last year's grasses; the spread of yellow green from swale to hilltop; and the gradual deepening of green below a bluer sky. She watched hillside shadows shrink away, as the sun swung north to warm the land.

She had always thought an hour or two in the garden was a good tonic for an overburdened housewife, and while it was harder for her to take interest this year than ever before, the crisp air and exercise did her good. She planted everything in the seed catalog that had a chance of surviving: beets, carrots, onions, sweet corn, watermelons, and so much more—more than they could eat, so they would have enough to sell.

While Luna kept the garden and managed the flock of chickens, J. T. concentrated on the farming and the stock. He was experimenting with types of wheat, and in the fall of 1881 the Kellies had a fine crop. There was enough cash to allow them to add on to their 12 x 16-foot home, and when it was finished with lath and plaster and a double window in the south wall, Luna thought it was truly fine.

A short time later they sent for the Widow Manzer, and on October 30 Luna gave birth to a new baby girl. She was larger than the two they had lost and seemed healthier, but Luna steeled herself to keep their resolution not to love her.

It was difficult with the warm bundle at her side, but she said nothing to J. T. He leaned over the new baby tentatively, trying to remain detached. Then, as a tiny fist closed around his finger, he burst out, "God help us, Mother. We can't help ourselves. She is going to be just as dear as the others."

They named their new daughter Jessie and that winter the secondhand Boston rocker that had comforted Susie was busy once more. Before long J. T. could again listen to Luna singing as she worked.

Luna and J. T. eventually had nine more children, coming close to their ideal family, but their life was never easy economically. Plagued with crop failures and crippling debts, they were forced to trade their homestead for a nearby timber claim, and Luna found herself again in a sod house.

She took comfort in the trees already established, four rows of box elders on the north, two on the south, and a good-sized cottonwood in one corner. She had always thought it pitiful that children on the plains had no shade to play in, and she tried to make their home like the shady oasis her grandfather's farm had seemed to her when she was young. They set out grapevines, raspberries, strawberries, and a wagonload of apple trees, determined to make their home a place their children would remember with joy.

They also worked for the betterment of farmers and of the community. J. T. organized a school for the children, Luna was active in the church, and they both became active in the rural reform movement of the 1890s. Luna was secretary of the Nebraska Farmer's Alliance, edited its newspaper, and wrote several Populist songs.

They eventually moved to a farm near Heartwell, only a few miles from their original homestead. J. T. died in 1918, but Luna survived until 1940, able to see her children and her children's children enjoy a richness of life even beyond the dreams she and J. T. had spun in the evenings on the doorstep of their soddy.

Epilogue

With families like the Kellies settled along the river's length, Platte River history entered another era. The Moonshell days were but a glowing memory to be passed down the generations in tribal legends. The Pawnees and Cheyennes were gone—pushed down to Indian Territory to die off in pitiful numbers. The Sioux were gone—pushed north to reservations, with war chief and peace chief alike capable only of passive resistance to the white man's dictums. Luna Kellie had lived in fear of Indians, but she did not actually see one for 20 years after she came to Nebraska, and that Indian she met in the metropolis of Omaha.

The native plants were uprooted from the land by the plow blade, and the free-flowing sheets of prairie grass became patchwork quilts of corn and wheat, neatly squared into sections by brown strips of road. Small groups of antelope and deer still fed in the evening, but the herds of elk were largely gone. And the masses of bison that had shaken the earth with their passing were so rare that in 1879 Luna Kellie ran to the road to see her first buffalo. She saw a pair of them, yoked in tandem with several oxen, pulling a freight wagon.

The presence of Spanish swords was long forgotten, and the flavor of French influence lived only in an occasional name. Most of the mountain men who mapped the Platte's drainage had gone to the grave. Those who lived were curiosities. The dudes and dandies had turned to other playgrounds; the scientists and soldiers to other fields of conquest.

The works of the artists and writers who had experienced the early days of the Platte remained, as did the settlers. Foreign and natural-born, of every age, status and ethnic background, on farms, ranches, and mining claims, in villages and towns, they worked to build a good life for themselves and their children—some of them conscious, some unconscious, of the fascinating assortment of people who had walked before them along the Platte.

Bibliography

We all walk in others' footsteps. In researching this book, I have received assistance and guidance from many repositories of western history. I am indebted to their staffs, to all the people who realized the importance of "writing it down," and to those who made certain the written record was safely preserved.

The bulk of my research was done in the Western History Department of the Denver Public Library, and I will be ever grateful for its myriad resources.

I also consulted the staffs of the Nebraska State Historical Society, the Colorado State Historical Society, the Museum of New Mexico, the Zimmerman Library at the University of New Mexico, the Historical Department of the Church of Jesus Christ of the Latter-Day Saints, the Scotts Bluff National Monument, the Fort Laramie National Historic Site and the National Archives. My thanks to all.

BIBLIOGRAPHY OF GENERAL READINGS

Billington, Ray Allen, **The Far Western Frontier.** Harper Torch Books, 1956.

Dick, Everett, **Tales of the Frontier.** University of Nebraska Press, 1963.

Fitzpatrick, Lilian, **Nebraska Place Names.** University of Nebraska Press, 1960.

Hillman, Martin, **Bridging a Continent.** Aldus Books (London), 1971.

Mattes, Merrill J., **The Great Platte River Road.** Nebraska State Historical Society, 1969.

Monaghan, Jay, **The Book of the American West.** Bonanza Books, 1963.

BIBLIOGRAPHY BY CHAPTER

THE MOONSHELL

 Roe, Frank Gilbert, **The Indian and the Horse.** University of Oklahoma Press, 1955.

 Sandoz, Mari, **Love Song to the Plains.** Harper and Bros., 1961.

A SILVER CANDLESTICK

 Hotz, Gottfried, **Indian Skin Paintings from the American Southwest.** University of Oklahoma Press, 1970.

 Sheldon, A. E., "New Chapter in Nebraska History," **Nebraska History.** Vol. 6, No. 1, 1923.

 Thomas, Alfred B., **After Coronado.** University of Oklahoma Press, 1955.

 Thomas, Alfred B., "A Chronicle of the Military Apparel in Mexico in the 16-20 Centuries," **Artes de Mexico.** Vol. 15, No. 102, 1968.

 Thomas, Alfred B., "The Massacre of the Villasur Expedition at the Forks of the Platte River," **Nebraska History.** Vol. 7, No. 3, 1924.

THE RIVIÉRE PLATTE
   Folmer, Henri, **Franco-Spanish Rivalry in North America**, 1542-1753. Arthur Clark, 1953.
   Folmer, Henri, "The Mallet Expedition of 1739 Through Nebraska, Kansas and Colorado to Santa Fe," **Colorado Magazine.** Vol. 16, No. 5, 1939.
   Isley, Bliss, **Blazing the Way West.** Scribners, 1939.
   McKee, Russell, **The Last West: A History of the Great Plains of North America.** Thomas Y. Crowell, 1974.

A JOUST WITH THE WILDERNESS
   Lavender, David, **The Fist in the Wilderness.** Doubleday & Co., 1964.
   Rollins, Philip Ashton, **The Discovery of the Oregon Trail; Robert Stuart's Narratives.** Scribner's Sons, 1935.
   Spaulding, Kenneth A., **On the Oregon Trail.** Univ. of Oklahoma Press, 1953.

THE HAUNT OF THE JACKAL
   Benson, Maxine F., **Edwin James: Scientist, Linguist, Humanitarian.** Thesis, University of Colorado, 1968.
   Ewan, Joseph, **Rocky Mountain Naturalists.** University of Denver Press, 1950.
   Fuller, Harlin M. and Hafen, LeRoy R., Editors, **The Journal of Captain John R. Bell.** Vol. 6. Arthur Clark Co., 1957.
   Thwaites, Reuben, "James Account of the Long Expedition," **Early Western Travels.** Vol. 15. Arthur Clark Co., 1905.

BULLETS OF BRASS
   Haven, LeRoy, **Broken Hand.** Old West Publishing Co., 1931.
   Morgan, Dale L., **Jedediah Smith and the Opening of the West.** University of Nebraska Press, 1964.

THE LANDMARK
   Field, Mathew C., **Prairie and Mountain Sketches.** Kate L. Gregg and John McDermott, Editors. University of Oklahoma Press, 1957.
   Mattes, Merrill, Hiram Scott, Fur Trader, NEBRASKA HISTORY Vol. 26, 1943.
   Mattes, Merrill, "Hiram Scott," **The Mountain Men and the Fur Trade,** LeRoy R. Hafen, Editor. Vol. 1, Arthur H. Clark Co., 1971.
   Mattes, Merrill, "Hiram Scott, Fur Trader," in **Mountain Men and the Western Fur Trade.** Glendale, 1965. Vol. 1, pp. 355-366.
   Mattes, Merrill, "Shadow of the Long Rifle," **Pacific Historian.** Vol. 14, 1970.
   Morgan, Dale L., **Jedediah Smith and the Opening of the West.** University of Nebraska Press, 1964.
   Morgan, Dale L., **The West of William Ashley.** Old West Publishing Co., 1964.

JOURNEY TO A FAR COUNTRY
   DeVoto, Bernard, **Across the Wide Missouri.** Bonanza Books, 1947.
   Merritt, John I., III, "Naturalists Across the Rockies," **American West Magazine.** Vol. 14, No. 2, 1977.
   Townsend, John Kirk, "Extracts From a Private Journal," **Waldies Select Circulating Library,** 1836.
   Townsend, John Kirk, **Narrative of a Journey Across the Rocky Mountains to the Columbia River.** 1839.

HIS WILL BE DONE
   Drury, Clifford Merrill, **Marcus Whitman, M.D. Pioneer and Martyr.** 1937.
   Elliott, T.C., **The Coming of the White Women, 1836.** Oregon Hist. Society, 1937.

FROM MOUNTAIN SLOPE TO BIRNAM WOOD
   DeVoto, Bernard, **Across the Wide Missouri.** Bonanza Books, 1947.
   Monaghan, Jay, "The Hunter and the Artist," **American West Magazine,** Vol. 7, No. 6, 1969.
   Porter, May Reed, **Scotsman in Buckskin.** Hastings House Publishers, 1963.

THE SINNERS

Chittendan, Hiram, and Richardson, Alfred, Editors, **Life, Letters, and Travels of Father Pierre-Jean DeSmet, S. J.** 1905.

Dunbar, John, Letter, **Missionary Herald.** Vol. 34, 1838.

Hyde, George C., **The Pawnee Indians.** University of Oklahoma Press, 1951.

A ROBE OF BLACK

Chittendan, Hiram, and Richardson, Alfred, Editors, **Life, Letters, and Travels of Father Pierre-Jean DeSmet, S. J.** 1905.

Terrell, John, **Black Robe.** Doubleday and Co., Inc., 1964.

WAGONS ROLL FROM SAPLING GROVE

Bidwell, John, **A Journey to California.** 1937.

Bidwell, John, **Echoes of the Past About California.** 1928.

Camp, William Martin, **San Francisco Port of Gold.** Doubleday and Co., 1947.

Dawson, Nicholas, **Narrative of Nicholas Cheyenne Dawson.** Grabhorn Press, 1933.

Williams, Joseph, **Narrative of a Tour From the State of Indiana to the Oregon Territory in the Years 1841-2.** 1921.

A STRANGE CREATURE

Nevins, Allan, **Fremont, Pathmaker of the West.** D. Appleton-Century Co., 1939.

Nevins, Allan, Editor, **Narratives of Exploration and Adventure.** Longmans, Green and Co., 1956.

Preuss, Charles, **Exploring With Fremont.** Erwin and Elizabeth K. Gudde, Editors. University of Oklahoma Press, 1958.

CALLING CARDS ON LARAMIE CREEK

Doughty, Howard, **Francis Parkman.** MacMillen Co., 1962.

Parkman, Francis, **The Oregon Trail.** New American Library, 1950.

Wade, Mason, Editor, **The Journals of Francis Parkman.** Vol. 2, Harper & Bros., 1947.

COME YE SAINTS

Clayton, William, **William Clayton's Journal.** The Deseret News, 1921.

Jenson, Andrew, **Latter-Day Saint Biographical Encyclopedia.** Andrew Jensen History Co., 1901.

Stegner, Wallace, **The Gathering of Zion.** McGraw-Hill, 1964.

"The Nauvoo Brass Band," **The Contributor,** Vol. 1, 1880.

SEPARATE FROM ALL THESE FOREVER

Royce, Sarah, **A Frontier Lady.** Yale University Press, 1932.

THE PEOPLE OF THE PRAIRIE GATHER

Hill, Burton S., "The Great Indian Treaty Council of 1851," **On the Platte And North.**

Lowe, Percival G., **Five Years a Dragoon.** University of Oklahoma Press, 1965.

THE DUKE AND THE ARTIST

Butscher, Louis C., "A Brief Biography of Prince Paul Wilhelm of Würtemburg," **New Mexico Historical Review.** Vol. 17, 1942.

Miller, David H., **Baldwin Möllhausen. A Prussian's Image of the American West.** Dissertation. New Mexico, 1970.

THE YELLING SOLDIER

Man Afraid of His Horses. "Narrative of Particulars of Affair of 19th August last by Man Who Is Afraid of His Horses." National Archives.

McCann, Lloyd E., "The Grattan Massacre," **Nebraska History.** Vol. 37, No. 1, 1956.

Nadeau, Remi, **Fort Laramie and the Sioux Indians.** Prentice-Hall, Inc., 1967.

THE AVENGERS

Hyde, George E., **Spotted Tail's Folk.** University of Oklahoma Press, 1961.

Nadeau, Remi, **Fort Laramie and the Sioux Indians.** Prentice-Hall, Inc., 1967.

THE LORD WILL OPEN THE WAY

Hafen, LeRoy and Ann, **Handcarts to Zion.** Arthur H. Clark Co., 1960.

Stegner, Wallace, **The Gathering of Zion.** McGraw-Hill Book Co., 1964.

Stenhouse, T. B. H., "Mr. Chislett's Narrative," **Rocky Mountain Saints.** Appleton and Co., 1873.

Wakefield, Eliza M., **The Handcart Trail.** 1949.

THE NEWSPAPER IN THE ATTIC

Byers, William N., "Early Journalism in Colorado," **Magazine of Western History.** Vol. 9.

Byers, William N., **Encyclopedia of Biography of Colorado.** Century Publishing Co., 1901.

Byers, William N. and Kellom, John H., **Hand Book to the Gold Fields of Nebraska and Kansas.** Facsimile, 1949.

Davidson, Levette J., "Letters of William N. Byers," **The Westerners Brand Book.** 1952.

Hooper, Byron C., Editor, "Byers' 1852 Overland Diary," **Overland News.** Vol. 1, No. 10, 11, 12, 1958.

Perkin, Robert L., **The First Hundred Years.** Doubleday and Co., 1959.

THE PONY RIDER

Burke, John, **Buffalo Bill.** G. P. Putnam's Sons, 1973.

Chapman, Arthur, **The Pony Express.** A. L. Burt Co., 1932.

Cody, William F., **Autobiography of Buffalo Bill.** 1920.

Leonard, Elizabeth Jane, **Buffalo Bill, King of the Old West.** Library Publishers, 1955.

Majors, Alexander, **Seventy Years on the Frontier.** 1893.

Russell, Don, **The Lives and Legends of Buffalo Bill.** University of Oklahoma Press, 1960.

Smith, Waddell F., **The Story of the Pony Express.** Hesperian House, 1960.

Wetmore, Helen Cody, **Last of the Great Scouts.** Grosset and Dunlap, 1899.

KEEPER OF THE WIRE

Ault, Phil, **Wires West.** Dodd, Mead and Co., 1974.

Collister, Oscar, "Life of a Wyoming Pioneer," **Annals of Wyoming.** Vol. 7, 1930.

Hamlin, Herb S. "Evolution and History of the Telegraph," **The Pony Express,** Vol. 10, No. 12, Vol. 11, No. 5, 6, 1944.

Reid, James D., **The Telegraph in America.** Derby Bros., 1879.

Rush, David H. "Singing Wires in the Wilderness," **Westerners Brand Book,** Vol. 15, No. 3, 1958.

REACH OF THE REBELS

Sanford, Albert B., Editor, "Life at Camp Weld and Fort Lyon in 1861-62," **Colorado Magazine.** Vol. 7, No. 4, 1930.

Sanford, Mollie Dorsey, **Mollie. The Journal of Mollie Dorsey Sanford in Nebraska and Colorado Territories.** University of Nebraska Press, 1959.

BLUE COATS COME TO COTTONWOOD

Berthrong, Donald J., **The Southern Cheyennes.** University of Oklahoma Press, 1963.

Hyde, George E., **Spotted Tail's Folk.** University of Oklahoma Press, 1961.

Ware, Eugene F., **The Indian War of 1864.** Crane and Co., 1911.

WINTER OF HORROR

Eubank, Lucinda, "Testimony of Lucinda Ewbanks," U.S. Congress 39th, 2nd Session, Senate Report 156, 1867.

Gilbert, John, "Incidents of the Indian Outbreak of 1864," **Nebraska History Publications.** Vol. 19, 1919.

Hagerty, Leroy W., "Indian Raids Along the Platte and Little Blue Rivers," **Nebraska History.** Vol. 28, 1947.

Kelly, Fanny, **Narrative of My Captivity Among the Sioux Indians.** 1871.

Larimer, Sarah L., **The Capture and Escape.** Claxton, Remsen and Haffelfinger, 1870.

A GLORIOUS INDIAN CAMPAIGN

Ware, Eugene F., **The Indian War of 1864.** Crane and Co., 1911.

A DOCILE PEOPLE

Hyde, George E., **Spotted Tail's Folk.** University of Oklahoma Press, 1961.

Nadeau, Remi, **Fort Laramie and the Sioux Indians.** Prentice-Hall, Inc., 1967.

Sanford, Mollie Dorsey, **Mollie. The Journal of Mollie Dorsey Sanford in Nebraska and Colorado Territories.** University of Nebraska Press, 1959.

Pattison, John J., "With the U.S. Army Along the Oregon Trail 1863-66," **Nebraska History.** Vol. 15, No. 2, 1934.

BATTLE AT THE BRIDGE

Hyde, George, **Life of George Bent.** University of Oklahoma Press, 1968.

Mokler, Alfred James, **History of Natrona County Wyoming, 1888-1922.** R. R. Donnelley and Sons Co., 1923.

Sandoz, Mari, **Crazy Horse.** Hastings House, 1942.

Spring, Agnes Wright, **Caspar Collins.** Columbia University Press, 1927.

Vaughn, Jesse Wendeld., **The Battle of Platte Bridge.** University of Oklahoma Press, 1963.

HEARTS ON THE GROUND

Clough, Wilson O., "Mini-aku, Daughter of Spotted Tail," **Annals of Wyoming.** Vol. 39, No. 2, 1967.

Hyde, George E., **Spotted Tail's Folk.** University of Oklahoma Press, 1961.

Nadeau, Remi, **Fort Laramie and the Sioux Indians.** Prentice-Hall, Inc., 1967.

PLEASANT SERVICE AND ABSOLUTE PEACE

Carrington, Frances C., **Army Life on the Plains.** J. B. Lippincott Co., 1910.

CIVILIZATION AND BANDS OF SAVAGES

Farwell, Byron, **The Man Who Presumed.** Holt, 1957.

Stanley, Dorothy, Editor, **The Autobiography of Henry Morton Stanley.** Houghton Mifflin Co., 1909.

Stanley, Henry M., **My Early Travels and Adventures in America and Asia.** Vol. 1. Scribners, 1895.

LITTLE CHIEF

Berthrong, Donald J., **The Southern Cheyennes.** University of Oklahoma Press, 1963.

Danker, Donald F., Editor, **Man of the Plains: Recollections of Luther North, 1856-1882.** University of Nebraska Press, 1961.

Grinnell, George Bird, **Two Great Scouts and Their Pawnee Battalion.** Arthur H. Clark Co., 1928.

King, James, "Republican River Expedition," **Nebraska History.** Vol. 41, No. 3, 4, 1960.

Reckmeyer, Clarence, "Battle of Summit Springs," **Colorado Magazine.** Vol. 6, No. 6, 1929.

THE DREAMER

Boyd, David, **Greeley and the Union Colony.** 1890.

Sprague, Marshall, **Massacre: The Tragedy at White River.** Little, Brown and Co., 1957.

Willard, James F., **The Union Colony at Greeley, Colorado.** 1918.

THE REDOUBTABLE MISS I. BIRD

Barr, Pat, **A Curious Life for a Lady.** Doubleday and Co., 1970.

Bird, Isabella L., **A Lady's Life in the Rocky Mountains.** University of Oklahoma Press, 1960.

THE MAID FROM PHILADELPHIA

Dickinson, Anna E., **A Ragged Register.** Harper and Bros., 1879.

Giraud, Chester, **Embattled Maiden.** G. P. Putnam's Sons, 1951.

Stanton, Elizabeth Cady, ''Anna Dickinson,'' **Eminent Women of the Age.** S. M. Betts and Co., 1869.

Daily Central City Register: September 6, 7, 11, 13, 17, 1873.

Greeley Tribune: September 17, 24; December 24, 1873.

Rocky Mountain News: August 17, 22, 27; September 2, 6, 16, 1873.

MAN IN A HURRY

Bartlett, Richard A., **Great Surveys of the American West.** University of Oklahoma, 1962.

Bartlett, Richard A., ''The Hayden Survey of Colorado,'' **Colorado Quarterly,** Vol. IV, No. 1, 1955.

Brown, F. Martin, ''Hayden's 1854-55 Missouri River Expedition.'' **Denver Westerners Brand Book,** Vol. 27, No. 3, 1971.

Gardiner, James T., ''The Hayden Survey in Colorado, 1873 and 1874.'' **Colorado Magazine,** Vol. VI, No. 4, 1929.

Ingersoll, Ernest, **Knocking Around the Rockies.** York, Harper and Brothers, 1883.

Howell, J. V., ''Geology Plus Adventure: The Story of the Hayden Survey.'' **Journal of the Washington Academy of Sciences,** Vol. 49, No. 7, 1959.

Sprague, Marshall, **Colorado.** W. W. Norton and Co., Inc., 1976.

ACROSS THE NEBRASKA SEA

Balfour, Graham, **The Life of Robert Louis Stevenson.** Charles Scribner's Sons, 1916.

Colvin, Sidney, Editor, **Biographical Edition of the Works of Robert Louis Stevenson:** Letters, Vol. I and II. Charles Scribner's Sons, 1923.

Mackay Margaret, **The Violent Friend: The Story of Mrs. Robert Louis Stevenson.** Doubleday and Co., Inc., 1968.

Stevenson, Robert Louis, **Across the Plains.** Charles Scribner's Sons, 1905.

WHO COULD ASK FOR MORE

Kellie, Luna E., **Memoirs of Luna Kellie.** Manuscript. Nebraska State Historical Society.

Index

ABOUT THE AUTHOR

NANCY M. PETERSON writes with care and feeling about the Platte River country because she grew up along the North Platte in Scottsbluff, Nebraska, and now lives near the South Platte in the Denver metropolitan area.

Highly interested in the frontier era, she has authored numerous historical articles in regional publications, as well as a column of local history which was the impetus for *People of the Moonshell*.

A diversified writer, she has also published nature essays and light verse in the *Reader's Digest, Good Housekeeping*, and the *Wall Street Journal* and humor pieces in *Families, Catholic Digest*, and magazine supplements of major daily newspapers.

Winner of numerous awards for both prose and poetry, she is past president of both the Denver Woman's Press Club and the Denver Branch of the National League of American Pen Women.

ABOUT THE ILLUSTRATOR

ASA BATTLES' American Indian (Choctaw) ancestry breathes incredible authenticity into the artwork for *People of the Moonshell*. He is a student of the Plains culture: the wildlife, the early residents, the later immigrants. Artist of *Fodor's Guide to Indian America* and *Ritual of the Wind* by Jamake Highwater, Asa has also illustrated several book articles for Houghton Mifflin and J.B. Lippincott publications. His work has been exhibited at shows throughout the western U.S., drawing countless honors and awards. Asa's scratchboard art has become a trademark of his detailed craftsmanship.